L. H. (Liberty Hyde) Bailey

The Horticulturist's Rule-Book

A Compendium of Useful Information for Fruit Growers, Truck....

L. H. (Liberty Hyde) Bailey

The Horticulturist's Rule-Book
A Compendium of Useful Information for Fruit Growers, Truck....

ISBN/EAN: 9783337082833

Printed in Europe, USA, Canada, Australia, Japan

Cover: Foto ©Lupo / pixelio.de

More available books at **www.hansebooks.com**

THE HORTICULTURIST'S RULE-BOOK

A COMPENDIUM OF USEFUL
INFORMATION FOR

*Fruit-Growers, Truck-Gardeners,
Florists, and Others*

BY

L. H. BAILEY

NEW AND REVISED EDITION

New York
THE MACMILLAN COMPANY
LONDON: MACMILLAN & CO., LTD.
1907

All rights reserved

COPYRIGHT, 1895,
BY L. H. BAILEY.

Set up and electrotyped May, 1895. Reprinted February 1896; May, 1897; August, 1898; August, 1899; June, 1901; October, November, 1902; February, 1904; July, 1905; January, 1907.

PREFACE TO THE THIRD EDITION.

The first edition of this manual was published late in 1889, and the second early in 1892, both by the Rural Publishing Company. When the first edition was compiled, the modern or current methods of dealing with insect and fungous pests upon large and commercial plantations were in their first experimental stage. The volume, therefore, recorded the inexact knowledge of the time. It is only within the last two years that the methods of meeting these troubles have come to be generally accepted by horticulturists, and that experimenters have felt that they could give confident advice respecting the many mixtures, appliances, and operations which have been recommended in all quarters. It is time, therefore, that a third and complete edition of this handbook should be issued, to record and advise those practices which have been approved by experiment and experience. The contents of the volume have been gleaned from many sources, and whilst the compiler cannot assume the responsibility of the value of the many recipes and recommendations, he has exercised every care to select only those which he considers to be reliable. At the same time, the book has been thoroughly renovated in all departments, and it has been much extended to meet the needs of the many inquiries which are born of the recent teaching and experimenting in rural affairs. A chapter has been added upon greenhouse work and heating, and another upon the current literature of American horticulture. In its completed form, therefore, it is hoped that the volume will serve to codify and epitomize the best part of the scattered and disconnected horticultural advice and practices of the time.

L. H. BAILEY.

CORNELL UNIVERSITY,
ITHACA, N.Y., March 30, 1895.

PREFACE TO THE FOURTH EDITION.

ALTHOUGH the third edition was given to the public only last May, a fourth edition is now called for by the publishers. I have made various corrections and explanations in the text, and have added paragraphs upon yields of leading seed-crops, the customs regulations, methods of preserving posts in vineyards and other places, some figures of grape packing, a statement of the pollination of grapes, and a scheme for the classification of horticultural industries; and the index has been extended until it now comprises about two thousand entries.

L. H. BAILEY.

January 1, 1896.

CONTENTS.

CHAPTER I.
	PAGE
INSECTICIDES	1

CHAPTER II.
INJURIOUS INSECTS, WITH REMEDIES AND PREVENTIVES . 17

CHAPTER III.
FUNGICIDES, FOR PLANT-DISEASES 46

CHAPTER IV.
PLANT-DISEASES, WITH PREVENTIVES AND REMEDIES 52

CHAPTER V.
INJURIES FROM MICE, RABBITS, SQUIRRELS, AND BIRDS, WITH PREVENTIVES AND REMEDIES 77

CHAPTER VI.
LAWNS, WEEDS AND MOSS 82

CONTENTS.

CHAPTER VII.
Waxes for Grafting and for Wounds . . . 86

CHAPTER VIII.
Cements, Mortars, Paints, and Glues . . . 90

CHAPTER IX.
Seed-Tables 98

CHAPTER X.
Planting-Tables 108

CHAPTER XI.
Maturities, Yields, and Multiplication . . . 123

CHAPTER XII.
Computation Tables 129

CHAPTER XIII.
Greenhouse and Window-Garden Work and Estimates 154

CHAPTER XIV.
Methods of Keeping and Storing Fruits and Vegetables. Market Dates 168

CHAPTER XV.
Collecting and Preserving Specimens for Cabinets or Exhibition. Perfumery. Labels. Wood . 180

CONTENTS.

CHAPTER XVI.
	PAGE
Rules	193

CHAPTER XVII.
Postal and Impost Regulations 215

CHAPTER XVIII.
The Weather 220

CHAPTER XIX.
Literature 229

CHAPTER XX.
Names, Histories, and Classification 241

CHAPTER XXI.
Elements, Symbols, and Analyses 259

CHAPTER XXII.
Glossary 277

INDEX 293

HORTICULTURIST'S RULE-BOOK.

CHAPTER I.

INSECTICIDES.

THE results obtained from the use of any insecticide or fungicide depend upon the operator. *Timeliness, thoroughness,* and *persistence* are the watchwords of success. It is easier to keep an enemy away than to drive him away. The worst foes are often the smallest ones; and the injury is often done before they are detected. Be ready, and begin early.

Insecticides are of three general types, — liquid spray, powder, and fumes or vapor.

Arsenic.—Known to chemists as arsenious acid, or white oxide of arsenic. It is considered an unsafe insecticide, as its color allows it to be mistaken for other substances; but in its various compounds, it forms our best insecticides. From 1 to 2 grains, or less, usually prove fatal to an adult; 30 grains will usually kill a horse, 10 grains a cow; and 1 grain, or less, is usually fatal to a dog. In case of poisoning, while awaiting the arrival of a physician, give emetics, and, after free vomiting, give milk and eggs. Sugar and magnesia in milk is useful.

White arsenic, when applied in solution to foliage, is injurious. The poison can be used with lime, however, if treated as follows: Boil 1 pound of arsenic and 2 pounds of lime in 3 or 4 gallons of water, for half an hour. The sediment, an arsenite of lime, can then be used in about 100 gallons of water, with good results.

Arsenites. — A term popularly used for compounds of arsenic. The leading arsenites used in destroying insects are Paris green and London purple.

ARSENATE OF LEAD. — This compound of arsenic has recently come into use, and it promises to be of much value. It was first suggested by F. C. Moulton, in 1892, and has since been tested in the extermination of the Gipsy-moth in Massachusetts. When used at the rate of 2 pounds in 150 gallons of water, it was effective in destroying the larvæ of the moths, while the foliage of apple trees was uninjured when the poison was used at the rate of 24 pounds in 150 gallons of water. The arsenate of lead may be prepared by dissolving 11 ounces of the acetate of lead in one vessel, and 4 ounces of arsenate of soda in another. When these two solutions are mixed, there is formed a fine white powder, which is sufficient for 150 gallons of water.

LONDON PURPLE. — An arsenite of lime, obtained as a by-product in the manufacture of aniline dyes. The composition is variable. The amount of arsenic varies from 30 to over 50 per cent. The two following analyses show its composition: 1. Arsenic, 43.65 per cent; rose aniline, 12.46; lime, 21.82; insoluble residue, 14.57; iron oxide, 1.16; and water, 2.27. 2. Arsenic, 55.35 per cent; lime, 26.23; sulphuric acid, 0.22; carbonic acid, 0.27; moisture, 5.29. It is a finer powder than Paris green, and therefore remains longer in suspension in water. It is used in the same manner as Paris green, but is sometimes found to be more caustic on foliage. This injury is due to the presence of much soluble arsenic; but it can be averted by the use of lime, as advised under Paris green.

PARIS GREEN. — An aceto-arsenite of copper. When pure, it contains about 58 per cent of arsenic; but the commercial article usually contains less — often as little as 30 per cent, and rarely none. The following may be considered an average analysis: Arsenic, 47.68 per cent; copper oxide, 27.47; sulphuric acid, 7.16; moisture, 1.35; insoluble residue, 2.34. It is applied in either a wet or dry condition; but in any case, it must be much diluted. For making a dry mixture, plaster, flour, air-slaked lime, road dust, or sifted wood ashes may be used. The strength of the mixture required depends upon the plants and insects to which it is to be applied. The strongest dry mixture now recommended is 1 part of poison to 50 of the diluent; but if the mixing is very thoroughly done, 1 part to 100, or even 200, is sufficient.

Paris green is practically insoluble in water. When mixed with water, the mixture must be kept in a constant state of agitation, else the poison will settle, and the liquid from the bottom of the cask will be so strong as to do serious damage, while that from the top will be useless. For potatoes, apple trees, and most species of shade trees, 1 pound of poison to 200 or 250 gallons of water is a good mixture. For the stone fruits, 1 pound to 300, or even 350, gallons of water is a strong enough mixture. Peach trees are very apt to be injured by arsenites; and for them the mixture should be no stronger than 1 pound to 300 gallons. In all cases, the liquid should be applied with force, in a very fine spray. At some seasons of the year, foliage is more liable to injury than at others. The addition of a little lime (twice the bulk of lime as of Paris green) to the mixture, will prevent any caustic injury upon the foliage.

Spraying with Paris green or London purple does not endanger stock pastured in the orchard.

COMBINATIONS OF ARSENITES AND FUNGICIDES. — The arsenites may be used in connection with some fungicides, and both insects and plant diseases in this manner may be combated at the same time. The arsenites may be added to Bordeaux mixture in the same proportion as if the Bordeaux were plain water. The arsenites are also sometimes added to soap and other washes.

The addition of lime to Paris green and London purple mixtures greatly lessens injury to foliage, and, as a consequence, they can be applied several times stronger than ordinarily used, if they are combined with the Bordeaux mixture. The free lime in the mixture combines with the soluble arsenic, which is the material that injures the foliage, and the combination is thus made quite harmless.

London purple and Paris green should rarely be applied with the ammoniacal carbonate of copper, as the ammonia in the latter dissolves the arsenic, making the combination caustic. The addition of sulphate of copper to the arsenites also increases injury.

Bait. — 1. Paris green or London purple, 1 ounce; chopped grass or leaves, 8 ounces; and enough syrup to allow the mass to be worked into balls, which are spread about the garden. For wire-worm beetles, crickets, katydids, etc.

2. Bran, 40 pounds; middlings, 15 pounds; arsenic, 20 pounds; cheap syrup, 2 gallons. Mix in soft water to a paste. For grasshoppers and cut-worms.

Benzine. — Sometimes used to kill weevils and other insects in dry peas, corn, and grain. Less useful than bisulphide of carbon.

Bisulphide of carbon. — A thin liquid which volatilizes at a very low temperature, the vapor being very destructive to animal life. It is exceedingly inflammable, and should never be used near a lamp or fire. It is used for many root-insects. It is poured into a hole, which is immediately closed up, causing the fumes to permeate the soil in all directions. In loose soils it is very destructive to insects. It is also inserted in tight receptacles to kill such insects as pea-weevil and museum pests, where a teaspoonful is sufficient for a receptacle holding 2 or 3 gallons. It may also be used for mites and mealy-bugs on live plants. For this purpose, the plant is covered with a tight receptacle, and 1 fluid dram (60 drops or minims) is sufficient for a space equal to about 6 to 8 cubic feet.

Bisulphide of carbon and kerosene. — 1 part of bisulphide of carbon mixed with from 5 to 20 parts of kerosene will produce vapor sufficient to kill many grain-eating insects.

Burning. — Larvæ which live or feed in webs, like the tent-caterpillar and fall web-worm, may be burned with a torch. The lamp or torch used in campaign parades finds its most efficient use here.

Carbolic acid and soap mixtures. — 1 pint crude carbolic acid; 1 quart soft soap; 2 gallons hot water. Mix thoroughly. This wash is used for borers, and for scale-insects. Apply with a cloth or soft broom. Use only on dormant wood.

Carbolic acid and water. — Add 1 part of acid to from 50 to 100 parts of water. For root-insects.

Carbolic acid emulsion. — 1 pound hard soap or 1 quart soft soap dissolved in 1 gallon boiling water, and add 1 pint of crude carbolic acid, and emulsify by agitation. One part is used in 30 parts of water for cabbage-maggots and other root-insects.

Carbolized plaster. — Stir 1 pint of crude carbolic acid into 50 pounds of land plaster. Or, quicklime may be slaked with the acid. The powder is thrown over the tree when the dew is on, as a remedy for the curculio. It should be applied profusely. This is used by some peach and plum growers for the curculio, with apparent success, but it is of doubtful efficiency.

Carbon bisulphide. — See BISULPHIDE OF CARBON, p. 4.

Cement wash. — 5 tablespoonfuls hydraulic cement to 1 gallon sour milk or buttermilk. Mix, and apply at once to base of peach trees as remedy for borer (N. Carolina Experiment Station).

Coal-tar fumes. — Burn rags coated with coal-tar attached to a pole. Remedy for aphis, but little used.

Copperas (sulphate of iron). — 1 ounce of copperas to a pail of water is sometimes effective in destroying root-insects.

Little used except when forming a saturated solution, to which may be added about 1% of sulphuric acid. This is a standard remedy against grape anthracnose in Europe, in winter.

Corrosive sublimate wash.—Dissolve 1 ounce corrosive sublimate in 1 pint alcohol, stir in 10 gallons soft soap, and add water to make a stiff paint. Apply to base of trees with brush for borers and woolly root-louse. Recommended by N. Carolina Experiment Station.

Fumigation.—Fumigating or "Smoking" or "Smudging" in greenhouses is performed by the slow burning of tobacco stems. Best results are obtained when a sheet-iron vessel made for the purpose is used, having holes in the bottom to supply draft. A quart of live coals is placed in the bottom of the vessel, and about a pailful of tobacco stems is laid on them. The stems should not blaze, but burn with a slow smudge. If they are slightly damp, better results are obtained. Some plants are injured by a very heavy smoke, and in order to avoid this injury, and also to more effectually destroy the insects, it is better to smoke rather lightly and often. It is always well to smoke on two consecutive days, for the insects which persist through the first treatment, being weak, will be killed by the second. If the plants are wet, the smoke is more likely to scorch them. The smudge often injures flowers, as those of roses and chrysanthemums. In order to avoid this injury, the flowers should be covered with paper bags. For aphids (green-fly or plant-lice). See TOBACCO.

Gas (Hydrocyanic), for scale-insects.—3 oz. water, 1 fl. oz. sulphuric acid. 1 oz. 60 per cent cyanide potassium. Gas arising (very poisonous) is sufficient for covered space of 150 cu. ft. For dormant trees. Expose 1 hour.

Glue and arsenites wash.—Common glue 1 pound, soaked a few hours in cold water and then dissolved in ½ gallon of hot water; add 1 ounce Paris green, stir well, and add hot water till the mixture measures 2 gallons. For preventing the attacks of borers. Recommended in various writings, but to be used with great caution, if at all. If applied in the growing season, or more than once, especially upon young trees, it is apt to kill the bark. If the Paris green contains soluble arsenic, much harm may be expected to result.

Hellebore. — See WHITE HELLEBORE.

Hot water. — Submerge affected plants or branches in water at a temperature of about 125°. For aphis. It will also kill rose-bugs at a temperature of 125°-135°.

Kerosene. — In pure state, kerosene has been used as an insecticide upon many plants, with various results. It does not appear to injure the coleus, grape, peach, and pea, but does injure the potato, tomato, and gooseberry and other plants. It is not to be recommended unless in the form of emulsion, however, or much diluted.

Under the name of paraffine oil it is used in England as follows: When plants are infested with lice, wet them at intervals of three or four days for about three weeks with diluted paraffine in the proportion of a wineglassful to watering-can of water.

Kerosene emulsion. — 1. Cook's emulsion. Soft soap 1 quart, or hard soap — preferably whale-oil soap — $\frac{1}{4}$ pound; 2 quarts hot water; 1 pint kerosene. Stir until all are permanently mixed, and then dilute with water to one-half or one-third strength. A good way to make the emulsion permanent is to pump the mixture back into the receptacle several times. Makes a permanent emulsion with either hard or soft water.

2. The Hubbard-Riley, or standard emulsion. Hard soap, $\frac{1}{2}$ pound; boiling soft water, 1 gallon; kerosene, 2 gallons. Churn or pump the ingredients vigorously 15 or 20 minutes. Dilute 10 or more times when using.

Two ounces balsam of fir added to the above appears to increase its efficiency, and it causes it to adhere to foliage better. $\frac{1}{2}$ pint spirits of turpentine is sometimes added.

3. Pyrethro-kerosene emulsion. In the place of pure kerosene in the above emulsions, use a kerosene decoction

of pyrethrum, made by filtering 1 gallon of kerosene through 2½ pounds of pyrethrum. Valuable.

Kerosene and condensed milk emulsion. — Kerosene, 2 gallons, or 64 per cent of the entire mixture; condensed milk, 4 cans of ¾ pint, or 12½ per cent; water, twice the quantity of milk, or 25 per cent.

Kerosene and milk emulsion. — Sour milk, 1 gallon; kerosene oil, 2 gallons; warm to a blood heat and mix thoroughly. Dilute 10 times with water. For scale-insects and plant-lice.

Kerosene and water emulsion. — Goff atomizes kerosene and water as follows: To the Woodason atomizing bellows a small cup is attached directly in front of the fount for holding the liquid to be atomized. From this cup a very slender copper tube is passed through the side of the fount where it enters the larger tube that conducts the liquid from the fount to the mouth of the bellows. It then curves upward, passing through the centre of this tube as far as the mouth of the bellows, where both come to an end at the same point. Kerosene is then placed in the added cup, and water in the fount. On working the bellows the liquids are atomized together. The proportion of kerosene emitted will depend upon the relative diameters of the two tubes, but it may also be regulated by the relative depths of the liquid in their respective founts. A better way would be to use but a single fount and to divide this into two parts, one for kerosene and the other for water. This would permit the mouth of the bellows to be brought nearer to the plant to be atomized.

The value of kerosene applied in this manner is not yet fully determined.

Lead, arsenate of. — See under ARSENITES.

Lime spray. — Slake ½ peck or a peck of lime in a barrel of water, straining the lime as it enters the barrel to prevent its clogging the pump. Apply in a spray until the tree appears as if whitewashed. For rose-chafer.

London purple. — See under ARSENITES.

Lye wash. — 1 pound concentrated lye, or potash 1¼ pounds, to 3 gallons water. On an average, 1 bushel of good wood ashes contains about 4 pounds of potash. For scale-insects.

Common home-made lye is often diluted with water and applied to apple branches with a brush as a remedy for the bark-louse. It is also recommended as a remedy for the cabbage-worm, being sprinkled on the cabbages with a watering-pot. If concentrated lye is used, a pound should be diluted with a barrel of water.

Lye and sulphur wash. — Concentrated lye, 1 pound, or potash, 1¼ pounds; sulphur, 1½ pounds; water, 3 gallons. For scale-insects.

Lye and whale-oil soap wash. — (*a*) Dissolve 1 pound of concentrated lye in one gallon of water; add to this 1½ pounds of sulphur and boil until sulphur is dissolved. (*b*) Dissolve 14 pounds of the best whale-oil soap in 54 gallons of water; add solution *a* to *b* and boil for a short time. For scale; used as a summer wash when the first brood is hatching. Use at 130° Fahrenheit, thoroughly washing the trunks and larger branches and spraying the smaller branches and twigs.

Oil and alkali wash. — 1. 1¼ gallons of whale oil, 25 pounds sal-soda; dissolve the sal-soda in 25 gallons of water and heat it to boiling. When boiling, pour the whale oil in. Apply the wash when cooled to 130° Fahrenheit.

2. 1 pound of concentrated lye (American) of 80 per cent; or ⅘ of a pound of Greenbank powdered caustic soda, of 98 per cent; or 1 pound of solid caustic soda, of 76 per cent; or 1½ pounds of solid caustic soda of 63 per cent. These varying proportions are given because the caustic sodas in the markets are of different strengths and purity. Whichever one is chosen, add to each amount named ½ pound of commercial potash and dissolve in 6 gallons of water.

Both washes are for scale-insects on deciduous trees in winter. (Californian.)

Paraffine oil. — Essentially the same as KEROSENE, which see.

Paris green. — See under ARSENITES.

Persian insect powder. — See PYRETHRUM.

Plaster and kerosene. — 2 quarts of plaster or wood ashes, 1 tablespoonful of kerosene. Mix, and rub with the hands until the oil is well incorporated. Bone-flour may be substituted for the plaster. Repellent; used mostly for flea-beetles and striped squash-beetles.

Plaster and turpentine. — 2 quarts common land plaster, 1 or 2 tablespoonfuls of turpentine, mixed and used as in the preceding.

Potash. — Kainit, 1 ounce to a pint of water, applied in a spray, is recommended for aphis and various leaf-eating larvæ. Muriate of potash, applied in the same strength, is as good, but is more likely to injure the plants. Rarely used.

Potassic fertilizers have been recommended as insecticides against various ground insects.

Promoting growth. — Any course that tends to promote vigor will be helpful in enabling plants to withstand the attacks of plant-lice and other insects.

Pyrethrum. — A very fine and light brown powder made from the flower-heads of species of pyrethrum. It is scarcely injurious to man. Three brands are upon the market:

PERSIAN INSECT-POWDER, made from the heads of *Pyrethrum roseum*, a species also cultivated as an ornamental plant. The plant is native to the Caucasus region.

DALMATIAN INSECT-POWDER, made from *Pyrethrum cinerariæfolium*.

BUHACH, made in California from cultivated plants of *P. cinerariæfolium*.

When fresh and pure, all these brands appear to be equally valuable, but the home-grown product is usually considered most reliable. Pyrethrum soon loses its value when exposed to the air. It is used in various ways:

1. In solution in water, 1 ounce to 3 gallons.
2. Dry, without dilution. In this form it is excellent for

thrips and lice on roses and other bushes. Apply when the bush is wet. Useful for aphis on house plants.

3. Dry, diluted with flour or any light and fine powder. The poison may be used in the proportion of 1 part to from 6 to 30 of the diluent.

4. In fumigation. It may be scattered directly upon coals, or made into small balls by wetting and moulding with the hands and then set upon coals. This is a desirable way of dealing with mosquitoes and flies.

5. In alcohol. (1) Put 1 part of pyrethrum (buhach) and 4 parts alcohol, by weight, in any tight vessel. Shake occasionally, and after 8 days filter. Apply with an atomizer. Excellent for greenhouse pests. For some plants it needs to be diluted a little. (2) Dissolve about 4 ounces of powder in 1 gill of alcohol, and add 12 gallons of water.

6. Decoction. Whole flower-heads are treated to boiling water, and the liquid is covered to prevent evaporation. Boiling the liquid destroys its value.

7. Water extract. Pour 2 quarts hot water through about a half-pound of pyrethrum, held in a coarse bag, and then add cold water enough to make 2 gallons, and it is well to stir in the powder itself. For aphis and cabbage-worms. It will keep but a few days. Or the extract can be made as follows: Make a paste of 2 tablespoonfuls of pyrethrum by adding water. Stir this into 2 gallons of water and apply with a fine nozzle. This is recommended for the rose-chafer.

8. Pyrethro-kerosene emulsion. See under KEROSENE EMULSION.

Good insect-powder can be made from *Pyrethrum roseum*, and probably also from *P. cinerariæfolium*, which are grown in the home garden.

Quassia. — Boil 4 ounces of quassia chips 10 minutes in a gallon of water; strain off the chips and add 4 ounces of soft soap, which should be stirred as it cools. Apply with syringe or brush. Ten or fifteen minutes after it has been applied, give the plant a good syringing with clean water. For plant-lice. Practically out of use in the United States.

Resin and fish-oil soap.—20 pounds of resin, 1 gallon of fish-oil, 8 pounds of caustic soda, and enough water to make 100 gallons. The caustic soda is first dissolved in about 10 gallons of water, after which $\frac{1}{2}$ of the solution is taken out and the resin added to that remaining in the kettle. When all the resin is dissolved, the fish-oil is added to it, and the whole thoroughly stirred, after which the balance of the caustic soda solution is added very slowly and boiled for about an hour, or until it will readily mix with water. Use an iron kettle. For scale-insects on orange and olive. (Californian.)

Resin and petroleum soap.—Water, 100 gallons; resin, $17\frac{1}{2}$ pounds; soda (60 per cent), 7 pounds; fish-oil, 3 pounds; petroleum, 2 pounds. The resin, soda, and fish-oil, with 20 gallons water, are boiled together for four hours, when the kerosene is added and the whole is thoroughly stirred. While hot, place in a barrel and add the remaining 80 gallons water, and emulsify by thoroughly stirring. For scale on citrous trees.

Resin soap.—Ingredients for one barrel of 50 gallons: 10 pounds caustic soda, 98 per cent; 10 pounds potash; 40 pounds tallow; 40 pounds resin. *First.*—Dissolve the potash and soda in 10 gallons of water. When dissolved, place the whole amount in the barrel to be used. *Second.*—Dissolve the tallow and resin together. When dissolved, add the same to the potash and soda in the barrel, and stir well for five minutes or so. Leave standing for about two hours; then fill up with water, stirring well as every bucket of water goes in. Use the following day, 1 pound to the gallon of water. Apply warm. For scale on deciduous trees in summer. (Californian.)

Resin, soda, and tallow soap.—Resin, 2 pounds; caustic soda, 1 pound; tallow, 1 pound. Mix resin and soda, boil about 30 minutes, and then add tallow. For use, add 2 gallons water to a pint. Used in spray for scale.

Rotation of crops is one of the readiest means of overcoming or escaping insect attacks. Even small-fruit plantations can be rotated to advantage. (See Chap. III.)

Salt and lime wash. — 25 pounds of lime (unslaked), 20 pounds of sulphur, 15 pounds of salt, 60 gallons of water. To mix the above, take 10 pounds of lime, 20 pounds of sulphur, and 20 gallons of water. Boil until the sulphur is thoroughly dissolved. Take the remainder — 15 pounds of lime and 15 pounds of salt-slack — and add enough of water to make the whole 60 gallons. Strain, and spray on the trees when milk-warm or somewhat warmer. This can be applied when the foliage is off the tree, and will have no injurious effects whatever on the fruit-buds or the tree itself. For scale on deciduous trees in winter. (Californian.)

Snuff. — Snuff may be used to kill plant-lice upon house-plants, and in other places where fumigation or spraying cannot be employed. Blow it lightly on the plants. See SULPHUR AND SNUFF.

Soap and arsenites. — Soap, 4 pounds, which is dissolved in 1 gallon of hot water; add 4 ounces of London purple or Paris green, mix, and dilute with 50 gallons of hot water. For various leaf-eating insects, but likely to injure tender foliage, when the arsenite contains much soluble arsenic, unless lime is added.

Soap and lime wash. — 5 pounds potash, 5 pounds lard stirred in 5 gallons of boiling water; 1 peck quicklime slaked in 5 gallons of boiling water, and mixed while hot with the potash and lard mixture. Dilute by adding 2 gallons of boiling water for each gallon of the mixture. It will keep indefinitely. Recommended for preventing the attacks of borers, but, like all washes for this purpose, of doubtful utility.

Soap and soda wash. — To soft soap add a strong solution of common washing-soda, until the mixture becomes a thick paint. Used for bark-lice and other scale-insects on the dormant wood.

Soap and tobacco. — Dissolve 8 pounds of the best soft soap in 12 gallons of rain-water, and when cold add 1 gallon of strong tobacco liquor. For plant-lice.

Soap, fish-oil. — Good potash lye, 1 pound; fish-oil, 3 pints; soft water, 3 gallons. Dissolve the lye in the water, and when brought to a boil, add the oil. Boil about two hours. When cold, it can be cut into cakes. For use, put the soap in enough hot water to dissolve or cut it, and then add 6 to 10 gallons water to a pound of soap. For aphis.

Soda and aloes. — Dissolve 2 pounds of washing-soda and 1 ounce of bitter Barbadoes aloes, and when cold add 1 gallon of water. Dip the plants into the solution, and lay them on their sides for a short time, and the insects will drop off. Syringe the plants with clean, tepid water, and return to the house. For plant-lice.

Soda and resin wash. — Sal-soda, 3 pounds, added to 1 pint of hot water; add slowly 4 pounds of resin, and gradually add 2 pints of hot water. Dilute to 5 gallons. For scale-insects; also recommended for curculio.

Soda and whale-oil soap wash. — Dissolve 25 pounds sal-soda in 25 gallons water and heat to boiling, at which time add $1\frac{1}{4}$ gallons whale-oil soap. Used as a winter wash for scale. Apply at a temperature of about 130° Fahrenheit.

Soda wash. — Dissolve $\frac{1}{2}$ pound of common washing-soda in a pail of water. For scale and borers, on dormant wood.

Spraying, a term applied to the application of liquid insecticides or fungicides, by means of a pump or syringe. See the various plants and materials for explicit directions. Spraying must be thoroughly and opportunely done, else it will fail.

Sulphide of soda wash (Hilgard's). — Dissolve 30 pounds of whale-oil soap in 60 gallons of water, by heating the two together thoroughly. Then boil 3 pounds of American concentrated lye with 6 pounds of sulphur and 2 gallons of water. When thoroughly dissolved, it is a dark brown liquid, chemically called sulphide of soda. Mix the two — the soap and the sulphide — well, and allow them to boil half an hour. Then add about 90 gallons of water to the mixture, and it is ready for use. Apply it warm, by means of a spray-pump. Used warm, its effect is better and less material is required than when cold. For scale on deciduous trees in summer. (Californian.)

Sulphur.—Fumes of sulphur are destructive to insects, but should be carefully used or plants will be injured. The sulphur should be evaporated over an oil-stove, until the room is filled with the vapor. The sulphur should never be burned, as burning sulphur kills plants. For greenhouse use.

Sulphur and snuff.—1 pound of flowers of sulphur, 1 pound of Scotch snuff, 1 pound of quicklime, ¼ pound of lampblack, 1 pound of soft soap, with sufficient water to make them into the consistency of paint. Wash every branch, from the ground upwards, with a common paint-brush, before the blossom-buds begin to swell. For plant-lice.

Sulphur and whale-oil soap wash.—Boil 1½ gallons of water, add ⅓ pound of sulphur and boil fifteen minutes. To this add a pound of whale-oil soap and boil for five minutes. Let stand for a week. When wanted for use, mix 1 pound of the compound to a gallon of water, and apply as a spray at a temperature of 130° Fahrenheit. Used for various burrowing larvæ, as the gooseberry fruit-worm and the currant-borer, as a repellent.

Tar is sometimes used to prevent the female and wingless canker-worm from ascending trees. The tar should be placed on cotton, or some material which will prevent it from coming in contact with the bark, and a band of the preparation is then placed around the trunk. Care must be taken to see that the tar does not injure the tree.

Tarred paper may be rolled *loosely* about trees to keep away mice, but it should be removed before warm weather. It is sometimes recommended as a preventive of the attacks of borers, but it very often injures trees, and should be used, if at all, with great caution.

Tobacco. — 1. Stems, placed on the walks and under the benches of greenhouses, for plant-lice. Renew it every month.

    2. Tobacco-water, used with whale-oil soap.
    3. Dust. See SNUFF.
    4. Fumes. Burn dampened tobacco-stems. See FUMIGATION.
    5. Nicotyl. Steep tobacco-stems in water and evaporate the water.
    6. Tea, or common decoction. Boil the stems or dust thoroughly and strain. Then add cold water until the decoction contains 2 gallons of liquid to 1 pound of tobacco.

There are various commercial preparations of tobacco for use in greenhouses.

Whale-oil soap. — 1 pound whale-oil soap to 5 gallons of water. For mealy-bugs and similar insects. It will injure some tender plants.

White arsenic. — See ARSENIC.

White hellebore. — A light brown powder made from the roots of the white hellebore plant (*Veratrum album*), one of the lily family. It is applied both dry and in water. In the dry state, it is usually applied without dilution, although the addition of a little flour will render it more adhesive. In water, 1 ounce of the poison is mixed with 3 gallons; and an ounce of glue, or thin flour paste, is sometimes added to make it adhere. A decoction is made by using boiling water in the same proportions. Hellebore soon loses its strength, and a fresh article should always be demanded. It is much less poisonous than the arsenites, and should be used in place of them upon ripening fruit. Used for various leaf-eating insects, particularly for the currant-worm and rose-slug.

CHAPTER II.

INJURIOUS INSECTS, WITH REMEDIES AND PREVENTIVES.

INSECTS are of two kinds as respects their manner of taking food,—the mandibulate insects, or those which chew or bite their food, as larvæ ("worms") and most beetles; and those which suck their food, as the plant-lice and true bugs. The former class is despatched by poisons, the latter by caustic applications, as kerosene or soap preparations.

Angleworm or **Earthworm.**—The common angleworm often destroys greenhouse plants by its burrowing. It is sometimes annoying in gardens also.
  Remedy.—Lime-water applied to the soil.
Ants.—See LAWNS.
Aphides, Plant-Lice or **Green-Fly,** and **Bark-Lice.**—Minute insects of various kinds, feeding upon the tender parts of many plants, both in doors and out.
  Remedies.—Kerosene emulsion. Kerosene-and-water emulsion. Hot water (about 125°). Coal-tar fumes. Pyrethrum. Fish-oil soap. Tobacco-water. Alcoholic and water extracts of pyrethrum. Hughes' fir-tree oil. In the greenhouse, fumigation with tobacco. Knock them off with the hose. In window gardens, dry pyrethrum or snuff.
Apple. APPLE-BUCCULATRIX (*Bucculatrix pomifoliella*, Clemens).—A minute yellow or green larva feeding upon the upper surface of the leaves, causing the lower surface to

turn brown. The cocoons are white and slender and are laid side by side upon the under sides of twigs, where they are conspicuous in winter.

Remedies. — Burn cocoons in winter or apply strong kerosene emulsion to them. Arsenites for the larvæ in summer.

APPLE-CURCULIO (*Anthonomus quadrigibbus*, Say). — A soft, white grub, about half an inch long, living in the fruit.

Remedies. — Arsenites, as for codlin-moth, are usually recommended. Probably jarring them off the tree, as is done for plum-curculio, is the most effective treatment.

APPLE FLEA-BEETLE (*Graptodera foliacea*, Lec.). — Beetle, one-fifth inch or less long, feeding upon leaves.

Remedy. — Arsenites.

APPLE-MAGGOT or RAILROAD-WORM (*Trypeta pomonella*, Walsh). — Maggot; infests fall apples mostly, occasionally attacks winter fruit. It tunnels apples through and through, causing the fruit to fall to the earth.

Remedies. — Immediately destroy all infested fruit, pomace, and apple-waste from the house. If the orchard is in sod, burn the grass under the trees in fall or spring; if in cultivation, spade or plough up the soil under the trees in spring. Orchards in sandy soil and with a southern exposure are most affected.

BARK-LOUSE (*Mytilaspis pomorum*, Bouché). — Minute insects feeding upon the tender shoots, most active in early spring. Later in the season the insect secretes a scale under which it lives. The old scales become conspicuous on the twigs.

Preventive. — Plant unaffected trees.

Remedies. — Spray with kerosene emulsion, carbolic acid wash, soda wash, or soap-and-soda wash, when shoots start. Wash limbs in winter or before leaves start, with soap-suds or lye water. Scrape off lice.

BLIGHT. — See under PEAR in Chap. IV.

BUD-MOTH (*Tmetocera ocellana*, Fabr.). — A minute insect, the larvæ destroying the flower-buds of apples, pears, plums, etc.

Remedies.—Arsenites applied when the buds begin to open, and again ten days later. Burn infested leaves in June.

CANKER-WORM (*Paleacrita vernata*, Peck).—Larva; "a measuring worm," an inch long, dark and variously striped, feeding upon the leaves.

Preventive.—Bands smeared with tar or printer's ink, or similar devices, placed about the trunk of the tree to prevent the wingless females from climbing. Tedious.

Remedies.—Arsenites, thoroughly applied in spray, are very effective. Jar the worms into straw, and burn the straw.

CODLIN-MOTH (*Carpocapsa pomonella*, Linn.).—Larva (offspring of a small grayish moth), three-fourths inch long, pinkish, feeding in fruit; generally two broods.

Remedies.—Arsenites applied just after the blossoms fall and again ten days or two weeks later. A third application is rarely necessary. The arsenites may be applied with Bordeaux mixture when spraying for the apple-scab. (See Chap. IV.) Swine in the orchard. Cloth band about the trunk of the tree, which is examined at intervals of seven to nine days for larvæ and chrysalids.

FALL WEB-WORM (*Hyphantria cunea*, Drury).—Hairy larva, about an inch long, varying from gray to pale yellow or bluish black, feeding upon the leaves of many trees, in tents or webs.

Remedies.—Destroy by burning the webs, or removing them and crushing the larvæ. Spray with arsenites.

FLAT-HEADED BORER (*Chrysobothris femorata*, Fabr.).— Larva about an inch long, flesh-colored, the second segment ("head") greatly enlarged; boring under the bark and sometimes into the wood. They are readily located in late summer or fall by the dead and sunken patches of bark.

Preventive.—Soap and carbolic acid washes applied early in June and July. Keep trees vigorous.

Remedies.—Dig out the borers in early summer and fall. Encourage woodpeckers.

PEAR TWIG-BEETLE. — See under PEAR.

PLUM-CURCULIO (*Conotrachelus nenuphar*, Herbst.). — Beetle; punctures the fruit and causes it to become distorted.

Remedies. — Arsenites. Often recommended (but of doubtful efficiency) to plant plum trees at intervals throughout the orchard to attract the curculio, and fight the insects on the plums. See under PLUM. Jarring onto sheets is probably the surest procedure.

RAILROAD-WORM. — See APPLE-MAGGOT.

ROOT-LOUSE, "AMERICAN BLIGHT" of England (*Schizoneura lanigera*, Hausm.). — A minute insect which causes swellings upon the roots of the tree, impairing its vitality, or killing it. In another form the insect attacks the young branches. It is then conspicuous from its cottony covering. The treatment for aphis is useful here.

Remedies. — Hot water. Corrosive sublimate wash. Scalding hot water may be poured on the bare roots of trees standing in the soil, or nursery stock may be dipped in water having a temperature of 120° to 150°. Kerosene emulsion or tobacco dug in about the tree. Infested nursery trees should be dipped in kerosene emulsion — root and top — before they are set in the orchard. Mulching about trees is said to bring the lice nearer the surface.

ROSE-BEETLE. — See under ROSE. There is practically no remedy for the rose-beetle on large orchard trees. Ravages can be prevented, to a large extent, by the lime spray and the emulsions. Very heavy applications of Bordeaux mixture sometimes act as a repellent.

ROUND-HEADED BORERS (*Saperda candida*, Fabr., and *S. cretata*, Newm.). — Larva, an inch long when mature, bores into the tree. It remains in the larval state three years.

Preventive. — Soap and carbolic acid, and various other washes applied early in June and July.

Remedies. — Dig out borers in the fall. Force some caustic material, as soda-wash, into the burrows by means of a small syringe. Insert a wire into the holes. The only

INJURIOUS INSECTS. 21

safe procedure is to watch the trees carefully for the chips cast out by the borers, and to examine the trees fall and spring, and dig out the larvæ with a knife.

TENT-CATERPILLARS (*Clisiocampa Americana*, Harris, and *C. sylvatica*, Harris). — Larva, nearly two inches long, spotted and striped with yellow, white, and black; feeding upon the leaves. They congregate in the tents at night and in cool weather, and forage out upon the branches during the day.

Remedies. — Arsenites, as for codlin-moth. Burn out nests with torch. Pick off egg-masses from twigs during winter and spring.

TUSSOCK-MOTH (*Orgyia leucostigma*, Sm. and Abb.). — A handsome caterpillar, an inch long, bright yellow with red markings, very hairy. Eats the leaves.

Remedy. — Arsenites. Collect frothy egg-masses in fall.

TWIG-BORER (*Amphicerus* (*Bostrichus*) *bicaudatus*, Say). — Beetle, three-eighths inch long, cylindrical and dark brown, boring into twigs of apple, pear, and other trees. The beetle enters just above a bud.

Remedies. — Burn the twigs. Catch insects in mating season.

TWIG-PRUNERS (*Elaphidion parallelum*, Newm., and *E. villosum*, Fabr.). — Yellowish white larvæ, about a half inch long, boring into young twigs, causing them to die and break off.

Remedy. — Burn the twigs.

Apricot. PEAR TWIG-BEETLE. — See under PEAR.
PIN-HOLE BORER. — See under PEACH.
PLUM-CURCULIO. — See under PLUM.

Asparagus. ASPARAGUS-BEETLE (*Crioceris Asparagi*, Linn.). — Beetle, less than one-fourth inch in length, yellow, red, and shining black, with conspicuous ornamentation, feeding upon the tender shoots. Larva feeds upon the leaves and tender bark.

Remedies. — Freshly slaked lime dusted on before the dew has disappeared in the morning. Poultry. Draw the hand over the stalks from bottom to top, crushing all the eggs; repeating two or three times during the season will keep them in check. Arsenites, after the marketing season has passed.

Aster. ASTER-WORM. — A small larva boring in the stem of garden asters about the time they begin to flower, causing the heads to droop.

All infested stalks should be burned.

Bean. BEAN-WEEVIL or BEAN-BUG (*Bruchus obtectus*, Say). — Closely resembles the pea-weevil, which see for description and remedies.

Bag-Worm or **Basket-Worm** (*Thyridopteryx ephemeræformis*, Haw.). — Larva working in singular dependent bags, and feeding upon many kinds of trees, both evergreen and deciduous. In winter the bags, empty or containing eggs, are conspicuous, hanging from the branches.

Remedies. — Hand-picking. Arsenites.

Bark-Lice. — See under APHIDES.

Blackberry. CANE-BORER. — See under RASPBERRY.

ROOT GALL-FLY. — See under RASPBERRY.

SNOWY CRICKET. — See under RASPBERRY.

Blister-Beetle (*Lytta* two or three species). — Soft-shelled, long-necked, and slim black or gray spry beetles, feeding upon the leaves of many trees and garden plants.

Remedies. — Arsenites. Jarring.

Cabbage. CABBAGE-WORM, or CABBAGE-BUTTERFLY (*Pieris Rapæ*, Linn.). — Larva an inch long, green with yellow and black markings, feeding upon the heads ; two broods.

Remedies. — Pyrethrum mixed with flour, or in water decoction. Hot water (temperature from 140° to 160°), applied forcibly in a fine spray. Kerosene emulsion. Lye wash. Arsenites: 1 ounce Paris green or London purple to 6 pounds flour, applied while the plant is wet; should not be used after the plant begins to head. Salt water sprinkled into the head. Pyrethrum, dry or in decoction.

FLEA-BEETLE. — See FLEA-BEETLE, under F.

GREEN LETTUCE-WORM. — See under LETTUCE.

HARLEQUIN CABBAGE-BUG (*Murgantia histrionica*, Hahn). — Bug about a half-inch long, gaudily colored with orange dots and stripes over a blue-black ground, feeding upon cabbage ; two to six broods.

Remedies. — Hand-picking. Place blocks about the patch and the bugs will collect under them. In the fall make small piles of the rubbish in the patch and burn them at the approach of winter.

LICE. — Kerosene emulsion. See APHIDES.

MAGGOT (*Phorbia Brassicæ*, Bouché). — A minute white maggot, the larva of a small fly, eating into the crown and roots of young cabbage and cauliflower, radish, and turnip plants.

Remedies. — Carbolic acid emulsion applied the day following the transplanting of the cabbage plants, and repeated once a week for several applications. Remove a little earth from about the plants and spray on the emulsion forcibly. Bisulphide of carbon is generally preferable on cabbages and cauliflowers, however. Use about one teaspoonful to the plant, inserting it in a hole in the soil just underneath, but not in contact with, the root. Press the hole together immediately to prevent the escape of the vapor. All infested plants should be burned.

The "club-root" of cabbage is not due to the maggot, but to a fungus, which see (page 55).

Carnation. TWITTER. — A peculiar curling and tying-up of the leaves and flower-buds on the tips of the stems. Probably due to various species of insects, one of them a plant-louse.

Remedy. — Cut off and burn the affected part.

Carrot. PARSLEY-WORM. — See under PARSLEY.

Cauliflower. CAULIFLOWER or CABBAGE-WORM. — See under CABBAGE.

MAGGOT. — See under CABBAGE.

Celery. GREEN LETTUCE-WORM. — See under LETTUCE.

PARSLEY-WORM. — See under PARSLEY.

Cherry. CANKER-WORM. — See under APPLE.

PLUM-CURCULIO. — See under PLUM.

Rose-Beetle. — See under Rose and Apple.

Slug (*Selandria Cerasi*, Peck). — Larva, one-half inch long, blackish and slimy, feeding upon the leaves; two broods.

Remedies. — Arsenites, for the second brood (which usually appears after the fruit is off), and for the first brood if the trees are not bearing. Hellebore in water. Pyrethrum. Air-slaked lime. Road-dust. Catch mature insects by jarring trees late in the evening or early in the morning.

Chestnut. Weevil (*Balaninus* sp.). — A grub working in chestnuts, making them wormy. The weevil is a curculio-like insect.

Preventives. — Destroy wild trees where the insects breed. Plant the most immune varieties.

Remedy. — Gather and destroy the infested nuts immediately after they fall.

Chrysanthemum. Green Lettuce-Worm. — See under Lettuce.

Chrysanthemum Leaf-Miner (*Oscinis* sp.). — Works upon the leaves of the chrysanthemum.

Remedy. — Hand-picking.

Corn. Bud-Worm. — See Tomato Fruit-Worm.

Cornstalk-Borer (*Helotropha atra*, Get.). — Larva, gray and striped, boring into the stalk.

Remedies. — See Cut-Worm.

Grain-Aphodius (*Aphodius granarius*, Linn.). — Beetle, one-eighth inch long, shining black, feeding on kernels in the ground before they sprout.

Remedy. — Soak kernels in water, then stir them in a mixture of Paris green, one part to twenty parts of flour.

Root Web-Worm (*Crambus* sp.). — Larva feeding in a web on the surface or just below it, on the roots of corn.

Preventive. — Avoid planting corn on sod land where there is any suspicion of the insect having been at work. Fall ploughing.

Weevil or Grain-Beetle (*Silvanus Surinamensis*, Linn.).

INJURIOUS INSECTS. 25

— Reddish-brown beetle about a tenth of an inch long, feeding in stored corn and grain.

Remedy. — Bisulphide of carbon.

The larva of the Angoumois Grain Moth (*Gelechia cereallella,* Oliv.) also devours stored grain. The same remedy applies.

Cranberry. — CRANBERRY-APHIS or LOUSE.

Remedy. — Flooding. See also under APHIDES.

CRANBERRY SAW-FLY (*Pristiphora identidem,* Norton). — Larva, less than one-half inch long, greenish, feeding upon the leaves; two broods.

Remedies. — Flooding. Probably hellebore and arsenites.

FIRE-WORM, CRANBERRY-WORM, or BLACK-HEADED CRANBERRY-WORM (*Rhopobota vacciniana,* Packard). — Small larva, green, black-headed, feeding upon the shoots and young leaves, drawing them together by silken threads; two broods.

Remedies. — Flooding for two or three days when the worms are small. Arsenites. Attract the moths to fires at night.

FRUIT-WORM (*Acrobasis Vaccinni,* Riley). — Small worm working in the fruits, eating out the insides.

Remedy. — Thorough application of arsenites as soon as the berries are set.

WEEVIL (*Anthonomus suturalis,* Lec.). — Beetle, less than one-fourth inch long; cuts off the flower-buds.

Remedy. — Flooding.

YELLOW-HEADED CRANBERRY-WORM (*Teras vacciniivorana,* Packard). — Stout, yellowish-green, small caterpillar, with a yellow head, webbing up the leaves as it works.

Preventive. — Hold the water late on the bog in spring to prevent egg-laying.

Remedy. — Flood the bog 24 to 36 hours when the worms are small.

Cucumber. CUCUMBER or PICKLE-WORM (*Eudioptis nitidalis,* Cram.). — Larva, about an inch long, yellowish white, tinged with green, boring into cucumbers; two broods.

Remedies. — Hand-picking at the first appearance of the caterpillars. Destroy infested fruits.

MELON-WORM. — See under MELON.

SPOTTED CUCUMBER-BEETLE (*Diabrotica 12-punctata*, Oliv.). — Beetle, yellowish and black spotted, about one-fourth inch long, feeding upon the leaves and fruit. Sometimes attacks fruit-trees, and the larva may injure roots of corn.

Remedies. — Same as for STRIPED CUCUMBER-BEETLE, below.

STRIPED CUCUMBER-BEETLE (*Diabrotica vittata*, Fabr.). — Beetle, one-fourth inch long, yellow with black stripes, feeding on leaves. Larva, one-eighth inch long and size of a pin, feeding on roots; two broods.

Preventive. — Cheap boxes covered with thin muslin or screens of mosquito-netting, placed over young plants.

Remedies. — Arsenites in flour. Ashes, lime, plaster or fine road-dust sprinkled on the plants every two or three days when they are wet. Air-slacked lime. Plaster and kerosene. Tobacco powder, applied liberally. Apply remedies when dew is on, and see that it strikes the under side of the leaves.

Currant. BORER (*Sesia tipuliformis*, Linn.). — A whitish larva, boring in the canes of currants, and sometimes of gooseberries. The larva remains in the cane over winter.

Remedy. — In fall and early spring cut and burn all affected canes. These canes are distinguished before cutting by lack of vigor, and by limberness.

CURRANT-WORM, or CURRANT and GOOSEBERRY SAW-FLY (*Nematus ventricosus*, Klug). — Larva, about three-fourths inch long, yellow green, feeding upon the leaves of red and white varieties; two to four broods.

Remedies. — White hellebore, applied early. Arsenites for the early brood. Treatment should begin whilst the larvæ are on the lowermost leaves of the bushes. Before the leaves are fully grown, the holes made by the worms may be seen. The second brood is best destroyed by killing the first brood.

INJURIOUS INSECTS. 27

CURRANT MEASURING or SPAN-WORM (*Eufitchia* [*Abraxis*] *ribearia*, Fitch.). — Larva somewhat over an inch long, with stripes and dotted with yellow or black, feeding upon the leaves.
 Remedies. — Hellebore, applied stronger than for currant-worm. Arsenites, if the bushes are not bearing. Hand-picking.
FOUR-STRIPED PLANT-BUG. — See under F.
GREEN LEAF-HOPPER (*Empoa albopicta*, Forbes). — Small insect working upon the under surface of currant and gooseberry leaves. Also upon the apple.
 Remedies. — Pyrethrum. Kerosene emulsion. Tobacco-dust.
Cut-Worm. — Various species of *Agrotis* and related genera. Soft brown or gray worms, of various kinds, feeding upon the roots, crown, or even the tops of plants.
 Preventives and Remedies. — Encircle the stem of the plant with heavy paper or tin. Arsenites sprinkled upon small bunches of fresh grass or clover, which are scattered at short intervals about the garden towards evening. They will often collect under boards or blocks. Arsenites mixed with shorts, and placed about the plants. Make two or three deep holes by the side of the plant with a pointed stick; the worms will fall in and cannot escape. Dig them out. Plough infested land in fall to give birds a chance to find the worms. Kainit or muriate of potash applied liberally as a fertilizer has been advised.
Cut-Worm, Climbing. — Several species. The worms climb small trees of various kinds at night and eat out the buds.
 Preventive. — Strip of cotton batting tied about the tree by its lower edge and the top then rolled down like a boot-leg. The worms cannot climb over the cotton. Use baits (see page 4).
 Remedies. — Arsenites. Hellebore.
Dahlia. FOUR-STRIPED PLANT-BUG. — See under F.
GREEN LETTUCE-WORM. — See under LETTUCE.

Egg-Plant. POTATO-BEETLE. — See under POTATO.

Elm. CANKER-WORM. — See under APPLE.

ELM LEAF-BEETLE (*Galleruca xanthomelœna*, Schr.). — A small beetle, imported from Europe, which causes great devastation in some of the eastern States by eating the green matter from elm leaves, causing the tree to appear as if scorched.

Remedy. — Arsenites with kerosene emulsion.

WILLOW-WORM. — See under WILLOW.

Endive. GREEN LETTUCE-WORM. — See under LETTUCE.

Flea-Beetle (*Phyllotreta vittata*, Fabr. ; *Haltica striolata*, Harris). — A minute black-spotted beetle, feeding upon many plants, as turnip, cabbage, radish, mustard, potato, strawberry, and stocks. It jumps upon being disturbed. Closely related species attack various plants. Very destructive to plants which are just appearing above the surface.

Remedies. — There are no reliable preventives or remedies. Arsenites, applied dry while the dew is on, are good. Land plaster, lime, ashes, and tobacco-dust, applied in the same manner, are more or less effective. Tobacco decoction used very liberally. Wood ashes applied liberally. Sometimes ashes injure the plants. Kerosene emulsion thrown with great force against the plants. Calomel, mixed with flour or ashes. A heavy application of Bordeaux mixture and soap is one of the best repellents. The same remedies apply to other flea-beetles.

Four-striped Plant-Bug (*Pœcilocapsus lineatus*, Fabr.). — A bright yellow, black-striped bug about one-third of an inch long, puncturing the young leaves and shoots of many plants.

Remedies. — Jarring at any time of day into a dish of dilute kerosene. Kerosene emulsion (2) (diluted five times) when the bugs are young, in their nymphal stage. Cut off and burn the tips of the growing shoots in early spring to destroy the eggs.

Galls. — See ROOT-GALL (page 41).

INJURIOUS INSECTS.

Gipsy-Moth (*Ocneria dispar*, Linn.). — Larva, nearly two inches long when mature, very hairy, nearly black, with a yellow stripe along back and sides. Devours many kinds of foliage. Confined to eastern Massachusetts, where it was introduced from Europe about 1869. It is feared that it will become a serious pest.

Remedy. — Spray with arsenites (particularly arsenate of lead) as soon as the caterpillars hatch in the spring.

Gooseberry. CURRANT-BORER. — See under CURRANT.

CURRANT MEASURING or SPAN-WORM. — See under CURRANT.

FOUR-STRIPED PLANT-BUG. — See under F.

GOOSEBERRY or CURRANT-WORM. — See under CURRANT.

GOOSEBERRY FRUIT-WORM (*Dakruma convolutella*, Hubn.). — Larva, about three-fourths inch long, greenish or yellowish, feeding in the berry, causing it to ripen prematurely.

Preventive. — Spray just before eggs are laid with the sulphur and whale-oil soap wash.

Remedies. — Destroy affected berries. Clean cultivation. Poultry.

GREEN LEAF-HOPPER. — See under CURRANT.

Grape. APPLE-TREE BORER. — See under APPLE.

GRAPE-BERRY WORM (*Eudemis botrana*, Schiff.). — Larva, about one-fourth inch long, feeding in the berry, often securing three or four together in a web; two broods.

Remedy. — Burn the affected berries before the larva escapes.

GRAPE-CURCULIO (*Craponius inæqualis*, Say). — Larva, small, black with a grayish tint. Infests the grape in June and July, causing a little black hole in the skin and a discoloration of the berry immediately around it.

Remedies. — Jarring and removing berries. The beetle may be jarred down on sheets, as with the plum-curculio. Bagging the clusters.

GRAPE-SEED WORM (*Isosoma vitis*, Saunders). — A minute grub, living in the seed of the grape and causing it to become distorted. The injured grapes shrivel.

Remedy. — Burn the affected fruit.

Grape-Slug or Saw-Fly (*Selandria vitis*, Harris). — Larva about one-half inch long, yellowish green with black points, feeding upon the leaves ; two broods.
Remedies. — Arsenites. Hellebore.

Grape-Vine Fidia (*Fidia viticida*, Walsh). — Beetle, resembles the rose-bug, somewhat shorter and broader. It appears during June and July, riddling the leaves. The larva also attacks the roots of grapes, seeming to prefer the Worden.
Remedies. — The beetles can be killed by strong arsenical sprays, and the larvæ on the roots by bisulphide of carbon.

Grape-Vine Flea-Beetle (*Graptodera chalybea*, Illig.). — Beetle, of a blue metallic color, about one-fourth inch long, feeding upon the buds and tender shoots in early spring.
Remedies. — Arsenites. The beetle can be caught by jarring on cold mornings.

Grape-Vine Root-Borer (*Sciapteron polistiformis*, Harris). — Larva, one and one-half inch or less long, working in the roots.
Preventive. — Mounding as for the peach-tree borer.
Remedy. — Dig out the borers. Apply scalding water to the roots.

Grape-Vine Sphinx (*Ampelophaga Myron*, Cramer). — A large larva, two inches long when mature, green with yellow spots and stripes, bearing a horn at the posterior extremity, feeding upon the leaves, and nipping off the young clusters of grapes ; two broods.
Remedies. — Hand-picking. Arsenites, early in the season.

There are other large sphinx caterpillars which feed upon the foliage of the vine and which are readily kept in check by hand-picking and spraying.

Phylloxera (*Phylloxera vastatrix*, Planchon). A minute insect preying upon the roots, and in one form causing galls upon the leaves.
Preventive. — As a rule this insect is not destructive to

American species of vines. Grafting upon resistant stocks is the most reliable method of dealing with the insect yet known. This precaution is taken to a large extent in European countries, as the European vine is particularly subject to attack.

Remedies. — There is no reliable and widely practicable remedy known. Burn affected leaves. Bisulphide of carbon poured in holes in the ground, which are quickly filled, is very effective. Carbolic acid and water used in the same way is also recommended. Flood the vineyard.

ROOT-BORER. — See GRAPE-VINE FIDIA.
ROSE-BEETLE. — See under ROSE.
SNOWY CRICKET. — See under RASPBERRY.
THRIP or LEAF-HOPPER (*Erythroneura vitis*, Harris). — In various stages, one-tenth inch or less long; feeding on leaves, causing them to appear scorched.

Remedies. — Sticky fly-paper secured to a stick and carried over the vines, while another person scares up the insects. Attract to lights at night. Kerosene emulsion. In houses, tobacco-smoke, pyrethrum poured upon coals held under the vines, syringing with tobacco-water or soap-suds. Fumigation in the field should be done before the insects develop wings — late in July or in early August (in the north). Rake ground clean about vines late in fall in order to expose insects to the weather. It has been found in California that thrips can be greatly lessened by feeding off the leaves with sheep, soon after the grapes are picked.

Grasshoppers. — If these pests become serious, they may be kept in check by the following means: Place a tablespoonful of poisonous bait by the side of each tree or vine. The bait is made of 40 pounds bran, 15 pounds middlings, 2 gallons syrup, 20 pounds arsenic; mix with soft water. Costs 25 to 75 cents per acre for orchards. Or Paris green spray may be used where there is no danger of poisoning fruit or grain.

Green-Fly. — See APHIDES.

Hollyhock. Bug (*Orthotylus delicatus*, Uhl.). — A small green bug, attacking the hollyhock with great damage.

Remedies. — Kerosene emulsion. Pyrethro-kerosene emulsion.

House-Plants. — See APHIDES, MEALY-BUG, MITES, and RED SPIDER.

Lawns. ANTS (*Formica* sp.). — Insects burrowing in the ground, forming "ant-hills."

Remedy. — A tablespoonful of bisulphide of carbon poured into holes six inches deep and a foot apart, the holes being immediately filled up.

Leaf-Crumpler (*Phycis indigenella*, Zeller). — Larva, brown, wrinkled, found on leaves of various kinds, which it brings together in masses and attaches them to each other and to the twigs by means of silken threads. The next season young worms appear from the mass and feed on the new crop of leaves.

Remedy. — Gather the masses and burn them. Arsenites before the larvæ cover themselves up.

Lettuce. APHIS or GREEN-FLY. — A plant-louse on forced lettuce.

Preventive. — Tobacco-dust applied on the soil and plants as soon as the aphis makes its appearance, or even before. Renew every two or three weeks if necessary. Fumigating with tobacco is the surest remedy. (See FUMIGATION, Chap. I.)

GREEN LETTUCE-WORM (*Plusia Brassiæ*, Riley). — Larva, somewhat over an inch long, pale green, with stripes of a lighter color, feeding upon leaves of many plants, as cabbage, celery, and endive.

Remedies. — Pyrethrum diluted with not more than three times its bulk of flour. Kerosene emulsion. Hot water.

Lice. — See APHIDES.

May-Beetle or **May-Bug** (*Lachnosterna fusca*, Fröhl.). — A large and familiar brown beetle, feeding upon the leaves of many kinds of trees. The common white grub is the

INJURIOUS INSECTS. 33

larval state. It often does great damage to sod and to strawberries.

Remedies. — For beetle, use arsenites, or jar them early in the morning. For grubs, plough up the lawn so as to expose them to field-birds and poultry, or turn in hogs. Avoid planting strawberries on grubby land. The grubs are often worst upon land which has laid in sod, or which has been heavily treated with stable manure.

Mealy-Bug (*Dactylopius adonidum*, Linn.). — A white scale-like insect attacking greenhouse plants.

Remedies. — Alcoholic decoction of pyrethrum. Whale-oil soap. Carbolic acid and soap. Removing insects with brush on tender plants. Whiskey, applied with a brush. Fish-brine. House-plants, may be washed in soapsuds. The best procedure in greenhouses is to knock them off with the hose. A small hard stream of water upsets their domestic affairs.

Melon. MELON-WORM (*Eudioptis hyalinata*, Linn.). — Larva, some over an inch long, yellowish green and slightly hairy, feeding on melon-leaves, and eating holes into melons, cucumbers, and squashes ; two or more broods.

Remedies. — Hellebore. Arsenites early in the season.

SPOTTED CUCUMBER-BEETLE. — See under CUCUMBER.

STRIPED CUCUMBER-BEETLE. — See under CUCUMBER.

SQUASH-VINE ROOT-BORER. — See under SQUASH.

Mite (*Tetranychus bimaculatus*, Harvey). — Much like red spider in size and shape, but light-colored, with two dark spots behind. Feeds upon the under side of the leaves of many greenhouse plants. The most serious greenhouse pest. Known also as " Verbena Mite."

Remedies. — Kerosene emulsion, or Hughes' fir-tree oil. Kerosene emulsion (2) (1 part to 20 or 25 parts of water) will kill them if it is applied *thoroughly* to the *under side* of the leaves. The application should be repeated two or three times at intervals of a day or two, or until the mite is destroyed. Thereafter, spray once a week. On roses and most greenhouse plants, the emulsion should be washed

D

off the foliage by the hose, an hour or two after the application.

Mushroom. — MUSHROOM-FLY. — The larva bores through the stems of the mushrooms before they are full-grown.

Preventive. — Keep the beds cool so that the fly cannot develop. When the fly is present, growing mushrooms in warm weather is usually abandoned.

Onion. MAGGOT (*Phorbia Ceparum*, Meigen). — Much like the cabbage-maggot, which see.

Remedies. — Carbolic acid emulsion. Bisulphide of carbon.

Orange. KATYDID (*Microcentrum retinervis*, Burm.). — A large green grasshopper-like insect, feeding upon the foliage. It is largely kept in check in some localities by a parasitic chalcid fly.

Remedy. — Collect the eggs, which are conspicuous on the borders of the leaves.

LEAF-NOTCHER (*Artipus Floridanus*, Horn). — Beetle, one-fourth inch long, greenish blue or copper-colored, eating the edges of the leaves.

Remedy. — Jarring.

MITE (*Tetranychus 6-maculatus*, Riley). — On the leaves.

Remedies. — Kerosene emulsion. Sulphur. Practise clean culture.

SCALE. — Many species, preying upon the leaves and shoots.

Remedies. — Kerosene emulsion applied with a brush or in spray, just before the trees bloom, and at intervals of two or three weeks as occasion may require. Lye wash. Lye-and-sulphur wash. Pyrethrum decoction. Resin and fish-oil soap. When young the scale is more easily destroyed. Some species are held in check in California by an Australian lady-bird beetle, which has been introduced for this purpose.

Parsley. PARSLEY-WORM (*Papilio Asterias*, Cramer). — Larva, inch and a half long, light yellow or greenish yellow with lines and spots; feeding upon leaves of parsley, celery, carrot, etc. When the worm is disturbed it ejects two

INJURIOUS INSECTS. 35

yellow horns with an offensive odor, from the anterior end.

Remedies. — Hand-picking. Poultry are said to eat them sometimes. Upon parsnip, arsenites.

Parsnip. PARSLEY-WORM. — See under PARSLEY.

PARSNIP WEB-WORM (*Depressaria heracliana*, De Geer). — Larva, about a half inch long, feeding in the flower-cluster and causing it to become contorted.

Remedies. — Arsenites, applied as soon as the young worms appear, and before the cluster becomes distorted. The worms are easily disturbed, and hand-picking is often advisable. Burn the distorted umbels.

Pea. PEA-WEEVIL or PEA-BUG (*Bruchus Pisi*, Linn.). — A small brown-black beetle, living in peas over winter. The beetle escapes in fall and spring and lays its eggs in young pea-pods, and the grubs live in the growing peas.

Preventive. — It is said that coal ashes or sand saturated with phenyl and sown with the peas will prevent attack.

Remedies. — As soon as the mature peas are picked, and while the grubs are only partly grown, subject the peas to a temperature of 145° for an hour. The seed will not be injured. The ripe peas may also be confined in some tight receptacle, and a little bisulphide of carbon added.

Peach. APHIS (*Aphis Persicæ-niger*, Smith). — A small black or brown plant-louse which attacks the tops and roots of peach trees. When upon the roots it is a very serious enemy, stunting the tree and perhaps killing it. Thrives in sandy lands.

Remedies. — Kerosene emulsion. Tobacco decoction. Tobacco hoed in about the tree will destroy the root-colonies.

APPLE-TREE (ROUND-HEADED) BORER. — See under APPLE.

FLAT-HEADED BORER. — See under APPLE.

FRUIT BARK-BEETLE. — See PIN-HOLE BORER.

KATYDID. — This insect is often troublesome to the peach in the southern States in the early spring, eating the leaves and girdling young stems.

Remedy. — Poisoned baits placed about the tree.

PEACH-LOUSE or APHIS (*Myzus Persicæ*, Sulzer). — A small insect feeding upon the young leaves, causing them to curl and die.

Remedies. — Kerosene emulsion. Soap-and-soda wash. Soap-water. Soap and tobacco.

PEACH-TREE BORER (*Sannina exitiosa*, Say). — A whitish larva, about three-fourths inch long when mature, boring into the crown and upper roots of the peach, causing gum to exude.

Preventive. — Make a mound about the tree in early summer, a foot high, and remove it in September; the moth then lays her eggs about the top of the mound, and the tender larvæ are killed by exposure to the weather. A coat of asbestos roofing applied about the base of the tree is recommended as a preventive. Apply washes as for apple-tree borers. Paint the crown of the tree with ordinary paint, to which Paris green has been added. All preventives are unsatisfactory, however, and the only safety is —

Remedy. — Dig out the borers in late fall and early spring.

PEACH-TWIG MOTH (*Anarsia lineatella*, Zeller). — The larva of a moth, a fourth inch long, boring in the ends of the shoots; it sometimes attacks the apple and strawberry roots.

Remedy. — Burn the infested twigs.

PIN-HOLE BORER (*Scolytus rugulosus*, Ratz). — A black beetle about a tenth of an inch long, boring into the trunk and branches of peach, plum, apricot, and other trees. It is thought to prefer weak or unhealthy trees.

Remedy. — Burn the affected trees or parts. Keep the trees strong and vigorous.

PLUM-CURCULIO. — See under PLUM.

RED-LEGGED FLEA-BEETLE (*Haltica rufipes*, Linn.). — A flea-beetle feeding on the leaves of peach trees, often in great numbers.

Remedies. — The insects fall at once upon being jarred, and sheets saturated with kerosene may be used, upon which to catch them. Spray with Paris green.

INJURIOUS INSECTS. 37

ROOT-GALLS. — See ROOT-GALLS, under R.
ROOT-KNOT. — See ROOT-KNOT, under R.
ROSE-BEETLE. — See under ROSE and APPLE.
Pear. APPLE-TREE BORER. — See under APPLE.
BUD-MOTH. — See under APPLE.
CODLIN-MOTH. — See under APPLE.
FLAT-HEADED BORER. — See under APPLE.
MIDGE (*Diplosis pyrivora*, Riley). — A minute mosquito-like fly; lays eggs in flower-buds when they begin to show white. These hatch into minute grubs which distort and discolor the fruit. New York and eastward. Prefers the Lawrence. Introduced about twelve years ago from France.

Remedies. — Destroy the infested pears. Cultivate and plough in late summer and fall to destroy the pupæ, then in the ground.

PEAR-LEAF BLISTER (*Phytoptus Pyri*, Scheuten). — A minute mite which causes black blisters to appear upon the leaves. The mites collect under the bud-scales in winter.

Remedy. — Burn the twigs in winter or spray with kerosene emulsion.

PEAR-TREE BORER (*Sesia Pyri*, Harris). — A small whitish larva, feeding under the bark of the pear tree.

Remedy. — Same as for round-headed apple-tree borer.

PEAR-TWIG BEETLE (*Xyleborus Pyri*, Peck). — Brownish or black beetle, one-tenth inch long, boring in twigs, producing effect much like pear-blight, and hence often known as "pear-blight beetle." It escapes from a minute perforation at base of bud; probably two broods.

Remedy. — Burn twigs before the beetle escapes.

PSYLLA (*Psylla pyricola*, Forst.). — A curious aphis-like insect infesting the twigs of pear trees when the fruit is setting. They are covered with a sticky material, and in the honey-dew a fungus often develops, giving the twigs a sooty appearance. Often does great damage.

Remedies. — Difficult to combat. Spray with kerosene emulsion just after the leaves have expanded, whilst the nymphs are young. Repeat, if necessary, within a period of two weeks after the nymphs appear, before they are protected by honey dew. During midsummer a forcible spray will destroy a very large proportion of the adults.

Rose-Beetle. — See under Rose and Apple.

Rounded-headed Borer. — See under Apple.

Slug. — See under Cherry.

Twig-Girdler (*Oncideres cingulatus*, Say). — A brownish-gray beetle, about one-half inch long, which girdles twigs in August and September. The female lays eggs above the girdle. The twigs soon fall.

Remedy. — Burn the twigs, either cutting them off or gathering them when they fall.

Twig-Pruner. — See under Apple.

Persimmon. Twig-Girdler. — See under Pear.

Pineapple. Katydid (*Acanthacara similis*). — A large katydid which attacks, among other plants, the leaves of the pineapple.

Remedy. — Arsenites, before the plants are mature.

Plant-Lice. — See Aphides.

Plum. Bud-Moth. — See under Apple.

Canker-Worm. — See under Apple.

Curculio (*Conotrachelus nenuphar*, Herbst.). — Larva, a whitish grub, feeding in the fruit.

Remedies. — Arsenites; apply as soon as the calyx falls and repeat two or three times at intervals of about ten days. Plaster and carbolic acid mixture. Jarring the beetles on sheets very early in the morning, beginning when trees are in flower, and continuing from four to six weeks, is probably the most sure procedure. There are various styles of sheets or receptacles for catching the insects as they fall from the tree. Catching beetles under chips or blocks about base of tree, the insects being taken very early in the morning.

Flat-headed Borer. — See under Apple.

Pear-Twig Beetle. — See under Pear.

Plum-Gouger (*Coccotorus scutellaris*, Lec.). — A small larva, feeding upon the kernel of the plum. The beetle bores a round hole in the plum, instead of making a crescent mark like the curculio.

Remedy.—Same as for curculio.

SCALE (*Lecanium* sp.).—A large circular scale occurring upon plum (and perhaps other) trees in New York.

Remedy.—Thorough spraying with kerosene emulsion (2) (1 part to 5 of water) in the winter. More dilute emulsion in midsummer when the young insects are on the leaves and young shoots.

SLUG.—See under CHERRY.

TWIG-PRUNER.—See under APPLE.

Poplar. COTTONWOOD LEAF-BEETLE (*Lina scripta*, Riley).— A striped beetle feeding on the leaves and shoots of poplars and willows.

Remedy.—Arsenites.

WILLOW-WORM.—See under WILLOW.

Potato. COLORADO POTATO-BEETLE (*Doryphora decemlineata*, Say).—Beetle and larva feed upon the leaves.

Remedies.—Arsenites, either dry or in spray, about a third stronger than for fruits. Handpicking the beetle.

MOLE-CRICKET (*Gryllotolpa borealis*, Burm.).—Mature insect curiously formed, whitish, feeding on tubers in low and mucky ground.

Preventive.—Plant potatoes on upland.

STALK-WEEVIL (*Trichobaris trinotata*, Say).—A grub boring in the stalk of the potato near or just below the ground. Serious at the west and in some places eastward.

Remedy.—Burn all infested vines.

Privet or Prim. PRIVET WEB-WORM (*Margaronia quadristigmalis*, Gn.).—Small larva feeding in webs on the young shoots of the privet, appearing early in the season; two to four broods.

Remedies.—Trim the hedge as soon as the worms appear and burn the trimmings. Attract the moths at night by lights. Probably the arsenites will prove useful.

Quince. ROUND-HEADED BORERS.—See under APPLE.

SLUG.—See under CHERRY.

Radish. MAGGOT (*Anthomyia Raphani* of Harris, but now considered to be identical with the cabbage root-maggot). — Treated the same as the cabbage-maggot, which see.

Raspberry. CANE-BORER (*Oberea bimaculata*, Oliv.). — Beetle, black, small, and slim; making two girdles about an inch apart near the tip of the cane, in June, and laying an egg just above the lower girdle; the larva, attaining the length of nearly an inch, bores down the cane. Also in the blackberry.

Remedy. — As soon as the tip of the cane wilts, cut it off at the lower girdle and burn it.

RASPBERRY ROOT-BORER (*Bembecia marginata*, Harris). — Larva about one inch long, boring in the roots and the lower parts of the cane, remaining in the root over winter.

Remedy. — Dig out the borers.

RASPBERRY SAW-FLY (*Selandria Rubi*, Harris). — Larva about three-fourths inch long, green, feeding upon the leaves.

Remedies. — Hellebore. Arsenites, after fruiting.

ROOT GALL-FLY (*Rhodites radicum*, Sacken). — A small larva which produces galls on the roots of the raspberry, blackberry, and rose, causing the bush to appear sickly, and eventually killing it. The swellings are probably often confounded with the true root-galls, which see under R.

Remedy. — There is no remedy except to destroy the galls; if plants are badly affected they must be dug up and burned.

SNOWY or TREE-CRICKET (*Œcanthus niveus*, Serv.). — Small and whitish cricket-like insect, puncturing canes for two or three inches, and depositing eggs in the punctures.

Remedy. — Burn infested canes in winter or very early spring.

Red Spider (*Tetranychus telarius*, Linn.). — A small red mite infesting many plants, both in the greenhouse and out of doors. It flourishes in dry atmospheres, and on the under sides of the leaves.

INJURIOUS INSECTS. 41

Remedies. — Persistent syringing with water will generally destroy them, if the spray is applied to the under surface. Fumes of sulphur. Sulphide-of-soda wash. Kerosene emulsion as for MITES.

Rhubarb. RHUBARB-CURCULIO (*Lixus concavus*, Say). — A grub three-fourths inch long boring into the crown and roots. It also attacks wild docks.

Remedy. — Burn all infested plants, and keep down the docks.

Root-Gall, Crown-Gall. — A widespread disease, of which the cause is wholly unknown. It occurs upon the peach, apple, pear, raspberry, blackberry, and other plants. The swellings are hard and woody, and appear both at the crown of the plant — where they sometimes attain the size of one's double fists — and on the small roots.

Remedy. — Nothing is surely known in the way of remedy except to destroy badly infested trees. It is recommended to dig away the earth, cut off or pare off the knots, and to paint the wounds with Bordeaux mixture. Nursery trees should be inspected for the galls.

Root-Knot (*Heterodera radicicola*, Müll.). — A disease characterized by the knotting and contortion of the roots of the peach, orange, and many other plants. The knots are mostly rather soft swellings, and on the smaller roots. It is usually most destructive on the peach. It is caused by a nematode, or true worm. Gulf States. Attacks greenhouse plants in the north.

Preventive. — Plant non-infested plants in fresh soil; bud into healthy stocks. Fertilize highly, particularly with potassic fertilizers. Set the trees eight or ten inches deep in high and dry soils. Infested small trees may be remedied, in part at least, by transplanting them into highly manured holes which have been prepared contiguous to them. Does not live in regions where the ground freezes deeply. If it is feared in greenhouses, see that the soil has been thoroughly frozen before it is used. Whitewash the benches. See ROOT-GALL.

Rose. Root Gall-Fly.— See under Raspberry.

Mealy-Bug.— On roses, a gill of kerosene oil to a gallon of water is said to be a good remedy. Syringe the plants in the morning, and two hours later syringe again with clean water. See also under Mealy-Bug.

Rose-Beetle, Rose-Chafer or "Rose-Bug" (*Macrodactylus subspinosus*, Fabr.).— Beetle three-fourths inch long. light brown, feeding upon the leaves, blossoms, and fruit. A very difficult insect to fight. Most abundant upon sandy lands. Often invades fruit plantations, devouring almost everything before it. All methods of dealing with it are unsatisfactory.

Remedies.— Hand-picking. Knocking off on sheet early in morning. Bagging. Pyrethrum. Kerosene emulsion. Pyrethro-kerosene emulsion. Eau céleste. It is said to prefer Clinton grapes, spireas, rose-bushes and magnolias, and it has been suggested that these plants be used as a decoy. Open vials of bisulphide of carbon hung in bushes and vines are recommended by some. Sludge-oil soap, a manufactured material. Spraying with dilute lime whitewash. Hot water, at a temperature of 125° to 130° Fahrenheit. To prevent the insects from breeding, keep the light lands — in which they breed — under thorough cultivation, and especially never seed them down.

Rose Leaf-Hopper (*Typhlocyba Rosæ*, Harris). — Hopper, very small, white, often mistaken for thrips; lives on the leaves of roses. Various stages of growth may be found in the leaves throughout the summer, and even on indoor plants.

Remedies. — Whale-oil soap. Kerosene. Kerosene emulsion. Nicotyl vapor. Dry pyrethrum blown on the bushes when they are wet.

San José Scale (*Aspidiotus perniciosus*, Comst.).— A scale-insect recently introduced into the East from California (supposed to be native to Chile), living upon a variety of fruit-trees. The scale is generally circular, rarely a little elongated or irregular, one-sixteenth inch across (or rarely twice as large on succulent shoots or on the fruit).

Remedies. — Kerosene emulsion, or whale-oil soap (2 lbs. to the gal.), in the winter, for the East. Upon the Pacific coast, resin washes.

Scale-Insects. — Various species of small insects inhabiting the young growth of trees, and sometimes the fruit, in one stage characterized by a stationary scale-like appearance. Kerosene emulsion and resin washes in the winter are the best remedies. Species which migrate onto the young growth in spring can be readily despatched at that time by kerosene emulsion.

Snails. — These animals are often very troublesome in greenhouses, eating many plants voraciously.

Preventives. — Trap them by placing pieces of turnip, cabbage, or potatoes about the house. Scatter bits of camphor-gum about the plants. Strew a line of salt along the edges of the bed. Lime dusted about the plants will keep them away.

Squash. BORER or ROOT-BORER (*Melittia Ceto*, Westw.). — Larva, boring into the root or crown of squashes and other cucurbits. The moth flies only during the day, and lays its eggs in various places upon the plant.

Remedies. — Catch the moths, which are an inch long and blackish-brown with an olive-green lustre, as they settle upon the leaves (near the base on the upper side) at twilight. When the vines begin to run, cover the fourth or remoter joints with earth, in order that they may take root and help support the plant.

Strawberry. CROWN-BORER (*Tyloderma Fragariæ*, Riley). — White grub, one-fifth inch long, boring into the crown of the plant in midsummer. The mature insect is a curculio or weevil.

Remedy. — Burn over the field after the fruit is picked. If this does not destroy the insects, dig up the plants and burn them.

GRUB or MAY-BEETLE. — See under MAY-BEETLE.

Leaf-Roller (*Phoxopteris comptana*, Fröl.).—Larva, less than one-half inch long, feeding on the leaves, and rolling them up in threads of silk; two broods.

Remedies.—In first stage of attack apply hellebore or arsenites if the attack is very early, or if it is after the fruit is off. Burn the leaf-cases.

Root-Borer (*Anarsia lineatella*, Zeller).—Larva, about one-half inch long, whitish, boring into the crown of the plant late in the season and remaining in it over winter.

Remedy.—Burn the plant.

Root-Louse (*Aphis Forbesii*, Weed).—From July to the close of the season the lice appear in great numbers on the crowns and in the roots of the plants.

Remedies.—Rotation in planting. Disinfect plants coming from infested patches by dipping the crowns and roots in kerosene emulsion.

Saw-Fly (*Emphytus maculatus*, Norton).—Larva, nearly three-fourths inch long, greenish, feeding upon the leaves; two broods.

Remedies.—Hellebore. Arsenites for second brood.

Weevil (*Anthonomus signatus*, Say).—Beetle, one-tenth inch long, reddish, feeding on flower-buds, particularly those of the polleniferous varieties.

Preventive.—Covering the plants with newspapers or cloth is said to be the only effective means of checking the pest.

Remedies.—Plaster and crude carbolic acid mixture.

Sumac. Apple-Tree Borer.—See under Apple.

Jumping Sumac-Beetle (*Blepharida Rhois*, Forst.).—Larva, half-inch long, dull-greenish yellow, feeding on leaves; two broods.

Remedy.—Arsenites.

Sweet-Potato. Saw-Fly (*Schizocerus ebenus*, Norton).—Small larva about one-fourth inch long, working upon the leaves. The fly is about the size of a house-fly.

Remedies.—Hellebore and pyrethrum are to be recommended; also arsenites.

INJURIOUS INSECTS. 45

Tomato. FRUIT-WORM (*Heliothis armiger*, Hub.). — Larva, one inch in length, pale green or dark brown, faintly striped, feeding upon the fruit. Also on corn and cotton.
Remedies. — Hand-picking. White hellebore.

TOMATO-RINGER (*Stictocephala festina*, Say). — A leaf-hopper which injures the stem of the young tomato-plant by puncturing it in a ring. Southward.
No remedy is known.

TOMATO-WORM (*Phlegethontius celeus*, Hbn., or *Macrosila quinquemaculata*, Haw.). — A very large green worm feeding upon the stems and leaves of the tomato and husk tomato. Seldom abundant enough to be very serious; kept in check by parasites.
Remedies. — Hand-picking. Hellebore. Arsenites.

Turnip. MAGGOT. — See under CABBAGE.

Verbena. MITE. — See page 33.

White Ants, or **Termites**. — These insects often infest orchard trees in the southern States, particularly in orchards which contain old stumps or rubbish.
Remedy. — The soap-and-arsenites wash brushed over the trunk and branches of the tree.

Willow. WILLOW-WORM (*Vanessa antiopa*, Linn.). — Larva, nearly two inches long, black, feeding upon leaves of willow, elm, and poplar; two broods.
Remedy. — Arsenites.

Wire-Worm (Various species). — Slim and brown larvæ, feeding upon the roots of various plants. They are the larvæ of the click-beetle or snapping-beetle.
Remedy. — Arsenites sprinkled upon baits of fresh clover or other material which is placed about the field under blocks or boards. Sweetened corn-meal dough also makes a good bait. The best treatment is to plough infested land in the fall. A system of short rotations of crops will lessen injury from wire-worms.

CHAPTER III.

FUNGICIDES, FOR PLANT-DISEASES.

THE results obtained from the use of any insecticide or fungicide depend much upon the operator. *Timeliness, thoroughness,* and *persistence* are the watchwords of success. It is easier to keep an enemy away than to drive him away. The worst foes are often the smallest ones, and the injury is often done before they are detected. Be ready, and begin early. Few people spray with sufficient thoroughness.

The two most important fungicides are ammoniacal carbonate of copper and Bordeaux mixture. The former is cheaper and more easily applied. The latter is more adhesive and generally the best. It may be applied even in the rain to advantage, when fair weather does not present itself. In case any disease is not mentioned, or you are in doubt and cannot secure advice, use one or the other of these preparations.

Copper carbonate costs from 40 to 60 cents per pound.

Copper sulphate costs 4 to 6 cents per pound.

Ammoniacal carbonate of copper. — 1. Carbonate copper, 1 ounce; and ammonia ($\frac{1}{2}$ to 1 quart) enough to dissolve it. The best ammonia water to use for dissolving copper carbonate is made by using 1 volume 26° Beaumé, with 7 or 8 volumes of water. It can be kept indefinitely in corked bottles. Dilute with 9 gallons of water when wanted. This is the handiest formula.

FUNGICIDES, FOR PLANT-DISEASES. 47

2. Into a vessel having a capacity of 2 quarts or more, pour 1 quart of ammonia (strength 22° Beaumé), add 3 ounces carbonate of copper. Stir rapidly for a moment and the carbonate of copper will dissolve in the ammonia, forming a clear liquid. The concentrated liquid thus prepared may be kept indefinitely. Dilute to 25 gallons.

3. Carbonate of copper, 5 ounces; ammonia (26°), 3 pints; water, 45 gallons.

It is better to wet the carbonate before dissolving it.

Blue Vitriol.— See SULPHATE OF COPPER.

Bordeaux mixture (copper mixture of Gironde).— 1. Dissolve 6 pounds of sulphate of copper in 4 or more gallons of water. In another vessel slake 4 pounds of quick lime (6 pounds air-slaked) in a small quantity of water. When the latter mixture has cooled, it is poured into the copper solution, care being taken to mix the fluids thoroughly by constant stirring, and water is added to make about 40 gallons of mixture. Stir before applying. Stronger mixtures were at first recommended, but they are not now used. This is the normal mixture.

2. Powdered sulphate of copper, 12 pounds in 15-20 gallons of water; lime, 8 pounds in 10-12 gallons of water. When the materials are thoroughly incorporated with the water, unite the two mixtures.

3. *Patrigeon Method.*— Dissolve 6 pounds copper in water as for (1), and add milk of lime until a drop of ferrocyanide of potassium (yellow prussiate of potash) added to the mixture ceases to give a red-brown color reaction. Used because the minimum amount of lime is added, rendering the mixture more easy of application; but Bordeaux made in this way often injures fruit, particularly in a wet season.

The best way to dissolve the sulphate of copper is to suspend it in a bag of coffee-sacking in the top of a barrel of water. Use the pulverized sulphate.

Bordeaux mixture may be applied in combination with the arsenites. See Chap. I. (page 3).

Bordeaux mixture is the best general fungicide. It is used for downy mildew and black-rot of the grape, blight and rot of the tomato and potato, blights of fruit, and many other diseases.

Sometimes the mixture is not washed off grapes or plums by the rains. In this case, add one quart of strong cider-vinegar to 5 gallons of water, and dip the grapes, allowing them to remain a few minutes, then rinse once or twice. Dip the fruits by placing them in a wire basket.

Carbolic acid (phenic acid). — Soapsuds, 10 gallons; glycerine, 1 pound; carbolic acid, ½ pint. Mix thoroughly to form an emulsion. For orange-leaf scab.

Copper, precipitated carbonate of. — Dissolve 2 pounds of sulphate of copper in hot water, and in another vessel 2½ pounds of sal soda in hot water; when cool, the two are added together with constant stirring. The mixture is then diluted to 25 gallons. For diseases of the grape.

Copper sulphate. — See SULPHATE OF COPPER.

Corrosive sublimate (bichloride of mercury). — Used for potato scab, which see in Chap. IV.

Destroying affected parts. — It is important that all affected parts should be removed and burned, if possible. In the fall all leaves and fruit which have been attacked by fungi should be raked up and burned. Diseased branches should be severed at some distance below the lowest visible point of attack. Fungous diseases often spread rapidly, and prompt action is usually necessary. Practise clean and tidy culture.

Eau céleste. — 1 (*Audoynaud process*). Dissolve 1 pound of sulphate of copper in 2 gallons of hot water. When completely dissolved and the water has cooled, add 1½ pints of commercial ammonia (strength 22° Beaumé). When ready to use, dilute to 25 gallons. For treatment of downy mildew and black-rot of the grape, anthracnose, and blight and rot of the tomato and potato, and many other diseases.

2. Modified eau céleste. Dissolve 1 pound of sulphate of copper in 2 gallons of water. In another vessel dissolve 1

FUNGICIDES, FOR PLANT-DISEASES. 49

pound of carbonate of soda. Mix the two solutions. When chemical reaction has ceased, add 1½ pints of ammonia, then dilute to 25 gallons. For the same purposes as No. 1, and better.

Grison liquid (*Eau Grison*). — Prepared by boiling 3 pounds each of flowers of sulphur and lime in 6 gallons of water until reduced to 2 gallons. When settled, pour off the clear liquid and bottle it. When used, mix 1 pint of clear liquid in 100 parts of water. For European mildew and powdery mildew of vines.

Podeschard's powder. — Dissolve 45 pounds of sulphate of copper in water. When thoroughly dissolved, pour the solution upon 225 pounds of air-slaked lime, which is surrounded by 30 pounds of ashes to keep the liquid from spreading. After 24 hours add 20 pounds of flowers of sulphur. Thoroughly mix the compound, ashes and all. When dry, sift through a sieve with meshes of one-eighth inch. Will keep for months. For downy mildew, mildew and anthracnose.

Potassium sulphide. — See SULPHIDE OF POTASSIUM.

Rotation of crops is one of the most effective and practicable means of heading off fungous diseases. It may be applied to strawberries for the leaf-blight, by fruiting the patch but a single year, and to blackberries and raspberries by destroying the patch after two or three crops have been harvested.

Sulfo-steatite, or Cupric steatite. — An exceedingly fine bluish powder composed of steatite, or talc, and about 10 per cent of sulphate of copper. Considered the most adherent of all fungicide powders. Is often injurious to foliage and should be applied with care. For mildews.

Sulphate of copper (Blue Vitriol). — 1. Dissolve 1 pound of pure sulphate of copper in 15 gallons of water. For downy mildew and black-rot of grape and apple-scab in winter, or in spring before the buds swell. Use 25 gallons water for peaches. Should be applied only to dormant wood.

2. Dissolve 5 to 8 pounds in 10 gallons of water. For

E

soaking grains previous to sowing, to destroy spores of smuts. The Germans use a ½-per cent solution, and soak the grains for about 16 hours.

3. A saturated solution with 1 per cent sulphuric acid added is sometimes used in place of a similar one of iron sulphate for grape anthracnose in winter.

Sulphatine powder, the Esteve process.—Mix 2 pounds of anhydrous sulphate of copper with 20 pounds of flowers of sulphur and 2 pounds of air-slaked lime. For mildew, downy mildew, and black-rot of grape, tomato, and potato-blight and rot.

Sulphate of iron.—1. Simple solution in water of 4 to 8 pounds to the gallon. To be used only as a wash before the buds swell. A saturated solution to which about 1 per cent of sulphuric acid is added is successfully used in Europe, for anthracnose of the vine, etc., in winter.

2. For a spray, dissolve about 1 pound to the gallon.

Sulphide, or sulphuret, of potassium (liver of sulphur).—Simple solution in water of ¼ to 1 ounce to the gallon. For mildew in greenhouses, mildew on roses, erinose of vine, orange leaf-scab, celery leaf-blight, pear and apple-scab and various rots.

Sulphide-of-soda wash (*Hilgard's*).—Dissolve 30 pounds of whale-oil soap in 60 gallons of water by heating the two together thoroughly. Then boil 3 pounds of American concentrated lye with 6 pounds of sulphur and 2 gallons of water. When thoroughly dissolved, it is a dark-brown liquid, chemically called sulphide of soda. Mix the two — the soap and the sulphur — well, and allow them to boil for half an hour, then add 90 gallons of water to the mixture, and it is ready for use. Apply it warm by means of a spray-pump. Used warm, its effect is better, and less material is required than when cold. For scab diseases.

Sulphur.—In its dry and pulverized state, sulphur, known as flowers of sulphur, is often a valuable fungicide, particularly for surface mildew. In the greenhouse it may also be used in fumes. Evaporate it over a steady heat, as an oil-stove, until the house is filled with the vapor. It should never be heated to the burning point, as burning sulphur quickly destroys most plants. To prevent burning, place the sulphur and pan in a pan of sand, and set the whole upon the oil-stove. It may also be used in water, in the proportion of an ounce of sulphur to 5 gallons of water.

Sulphur and lime. — A mixture of sulphur and lime in equal parts by weight. For dusting on surface mildews.

Sulphuric acid. — Used in connection with sulphate of iron or of copper, which see.

CHAPTER IV.

PLANT-DISEASES, WITH PREVENTIVES AND REMEDIES.

As a general rule, all fungi which attack the leaves and cause them to become spotted, as the various leaf-blights and mildews, are readily kept in check by the thorough applications of fungicides. Fungi which destroy the deeper tissues, as black-knot of plums and red-rust of the quince, can also be kept off if the plant is always covered with a fungicide. For the germ or bacterial diseases, like pear-blight and others, there are no specific preventives or remedies, and the horticulturist must resort to timely pruning, rotation of crops, or various methods of strategy.

The Bordeaux mixture is now considered to be the best fungicide, but as it is essentially a whitewash (colored with blue vitriol) it discolors fruits and foliage. On ornamental plants, therefore, ammoniacal carbonate of copper or modified eau céleste is preferable. Upon fruits which are nearly full grown, the Bordeaux mixture may also be displaced by the other fungicides, if it is necessary to spray at that period.

Almond. LEAF-BLIGHT or ALMOND DISEASE (*Cercospora circumcissa*, Sacc.). — Attacks the foliage, making perforations and causing the leaves to fall. Serious in parts of California.

PLANT-DISEASES. 53

Remedies. — Spray with ammoniacal carbonate of copper, or modified eau céleste (ammonia is added before sal-soda).

Apple. BLIGHT. — The same disease as pear-blight, which see.

BROWN-ROT. — See under CHERRY.

POWDERY-MILDEW (*Podosphæra Oxycantha*, DeBary). — Attacks nursery stocks, covering leaves with a grayish and powdery meal-like mildew.

Remedies. — Bordeaux mixture, or ammoniacal carbonate of copper, applied four or five times.

RIPE-ROT or BITTER-ROT (*Glœosporium fructigenum*, Berk.). — A rot which attacks ripe apples and grapes. It attacks the fruit before it is picked, usually, although it may not become apparent until it is stored. Many of the culls in packed fruit are due to this fungus.

Remedies. — Spray the fruit late in the season (beginning early in August) with ammoniacal carbonate of copper, or potassium sulphide ($\frac{1}{2}$ ounce to gallon of water).

RUST (*Species of Rœstelia*). — Bright yellow rust appearing on the young leaves and fruit, causing the whole tree to become enfeebled. It is now known that one stage of this fungus is the "cedar-apple" which grows on red cedars and junipers, where it is known as *Gymnosporangium*. Several species have been described. Also attacks quince.

Preventive. — Destroy the cedars or keep them free from the "apples." Destroy hawthorns and escaped apples, which are liable to be infested. Some varieties of apples appear to be more susceptible to injury than others.

Remedy. — Spray early with Bordeaux mixture, as for apple-scab.

SCAB (*Fusicladium dendriticum*, Fckl.). — Olive green, brown or blackish sooty and scab-like spots on the leaves and fruit, arresting growth and causing the parts to become distorted, and often causing the very young fruit to fall. Very common. When bad, the foliage looks brown and dry.

Remedies. — Spray with sulphate of copper while the trees

are dormant, if apple-scab is feared. Thereafter spray with Bordeaux mixture. The first application of this should be made as soon as the leaves appear and before the blossoms open, and the second as soon as the blossoms fall. Two or three subsequent sprayings may be necessary at intervals of two or three weeks. Ammoniacal carbonate of copper, applied as above, has also given good results.

Apricot. LEAF-RUST. — See under PLUM.

Aster. LEAF-RUST (*Coleosporium Sonchi-arvensis*, Lév.). — Orange-colored spots or pimples on the leaves (chiefly underneath) of China Asters, causing the foliage to shrivel and die.

Remedy. — Spray with Bordeaux mixture or ammoniacal carbonate of copper.

Balm of Gilead. LEAF-RUST. — See under POPLAR.

Bean. ANTHRACNOSE, or POD-RUST (*Colletotrichum Lindemuthianum*, Briosi and Cav.). — Reddish-brown scab-like spots appearing upon bean-pods, particularly upon the yellow-podded string-beans. It is said to attack the watermelon, cucumber, and other cucurbits. The fungus sometimes lies dormant in bean seeds and destroys the plantlets.

Preventive. — Plant in dry and airy places, on light soil, and avoid rotations with melons, cucumbers, etc.

Remedies. — Copper sprays, especially Bordeaux mixture. Sulphur and water.

Bean, Lima. BLIGHT (*Phytophthora Phaseoli*, Thaxter). — Attacks the pods in August and September, covering them with a white, felted coating. It also attacks the young shoots and leaves.

Remedy. — Bordeaux mixture.

Beet. LEAF-SPOT (*Cercospora beticola*, Sacc.). — The trouble begins as light or ash-gray spots upon the leaves. Eventually the leaf becomes much cracked and torn. Common in the eastern States.

Remedies. — Bordeaux mixture. Burn diseased leaves.

ROOT-ROT (*Phyllosticta* sp.). — A coal-black dry rot of

beets in storage. The fungus probably also lives upon the leaves, making large circular spots.

Preventives. — Rotation of crops. Be careful to remove all spotted leaves when storing the roots.

Remedy. — For the fungus on the leaves spray with Bordeaux mixture.

RUST (*Uromyces Betæ*, Pers.). — Powdery reddish-brown spots on the leaves of beets in California, often doing much injury.

Remedies. — Bordeaux mixture. Burn the infested leaves.

SCAB (*Oospora scabies*, Thax.). — The fungus which causes scabby patches; also attacks potatoes.

Preventive. — Do not grow beets where potatoes have grown the preceding year or two.

Blackberry. CANE-RUST or ANTHRACNOSE. — See under RASPBERRY.

RED or ORANGE-RUST. — See under RASPBERRY.

Buttonwood. LEAF-SCORCHING. — See under PLANE-TREE.

Cabbage. CLUB-ROOT or CLUB-FOOT (*Plasmidiophora Brassicæ*, Woronin). — A contorted swelling of the root of the cabbage in the field, preventing the plant from heading and causing it to assume a sickly appearance. It also attacks the cauliflower, turnip, and allied plants, and radish, shepherd's-purse, and the common hedge mustard.

Remedies. — Burn the roots as soon as the disease appears. Alternate crops. Keep down the weeds upon which the disease breeds. It is thought that stable-manures aggravate the disease. Lime put upon the land, 75 bushels to the acre, is thought to be a partial remedy.

Carnation. ANTHRACNOSE (*Volutella* sp.). — Attacks cuttings, and also stems near the joints, making dirty brown depressed areas, marked with minute black pimples.

Preventives. — Be careful to select only perfectly healthy stock in propagation, — advice which also applies to other carnation diseases. Keep the fungus off healthy stock by spraying with Bordeaux mixture.

FAIRY-RING SPOT (*Heterosporium echinulatum*, Cooke). — Produces circular light-colored spots upon the leaves. The fungus grows centrifugally, usually giving rise to successive rings of light and dark color.

Preventives. — Care in selecting stock. Bordeaux mixture.

RUST (*Uromyces caryophyllinus*, Schr.). — Produces gray blisters upon the leaves, the spots finally rupturing and showing the rusty discoloration of the spores.

Preventives. — Careful picking and burning of the infected parts is one of the surest preventives of further attacks. Spray with Bordeaux mixture.

SPOT or BLIGHT (*Septoria Dianthi*, Desm.). — Attacks the leaves in large brown or purplish spots, which have a whitish centre, or occasionally the whole leaf becomes discolored and wilts. Sometimes attacks the flower-stems and the flowers do not open.

Preventives. — If the disease is feared, be careful not to apply water to the leaves. Ammoniacal carbonate of copper or Bordeaux mixture. Burn all infested leaves.

Celery. CELERY LEAF-BLIGHT, RUST or SUN-SCALD (*Cercospora Apii*, Fries). — Appears in hot and dry places and seasons, about midsummer. Small yellowish spots appear upon the leaves; later the leaves turn yellow, then brown, and die.

Preventives. — Plant in a moist and cool place, and shade the plants if necessary. Destroy all diseased leaves in autumn.

Remedy. — Spray with Bordeaux mixture early in the season, and with ammoniacal carbonate of copper later on if continued treatment is necessary.

Cherry. BROWN-ROT (*Monilia fructigena*, Pers.). — Attacks flowers, leaves, and fruit. The flowers die and decay, the leaves become discolored with brownish patches, and the fruit rots on the tree. Attacks also peaches, plums, and apples.

Remedies. — Burn all infested fruit and leaves in the

fall. Before buds expand in spring spray with sulphate of iron or copper. When the flowers are falling, spray again with Bordeaux mixture, and thereafter with ammoniacal carbonate of copper or modified eau céleste, and repeat the operation at intervals of a week or two until the fruit begins to color. See under PEACH.

LEAF-RUST. See under PLUM.

POWDERY-MILDEW. See under APPLE.

Chrysanthemum. LEAF-SPOT (*Septoria* sp.). — First appears as dark brown spots which increase in size until the leaf dies. Also causes cuttings to damp off.

Remedy. — Pick and burn all diseased leaves, and then spray the plant with Bordeaux mixture or ammoniacal carbonate of copper.

Corn. ROT or BURRILL DISEASE. — Due to bacteria (*Bacillus Cloacæ*). The plants are dwarfed, and unusually slender. The roots become mucilaginous and decay, as do the leaf-sheaths and the ears.

No remedies or preventives are known, except rotation. Once thought to cause a disease of cattle, but this is now disproved.

SMUT (*Ustilago Maydis*, DC.). — Attacks the ears and stalks of corn, producing familiar black abnormal growths.

Preventive. — Plant seed from clean fields.

Remedies. — Cut out smut and burn it. It is held by some that the plant is infected from diseased seed, and that soaking the seed in sulphate of copper or ammoniacal carbonate of copper is a preventive; experiments upon this point have thus far been unsatisfactory, however.

Cottonwood. LEAF-RUST. — See under POPLAR.

Cranberry. GALL-FUNGUS or RED-RUST (*Synchytrium Vaccinii*, Thomas). — Minute red galls or pimples upon the leaves, flowers, and stems, causing the parts to become misshapen and dwarfed.

Remedies. — Burn the infested plants and also wild plants about the bog, which are infested. Withholding the water from the bog in winter and spring may subdue it.

SCALD. — Attacking the fruit early in the season, at first producing a scalded appearance, and later decay.

Remedies. — Sanding or earthing the bog an inch deep, and keeping water off in summer, are partial remedies.

Cucumber. BLIGHT. — A bacterial trouble, causing the entire vine, or a branch of it, to droop and die. No remedy is known.

MILDEW (*Erysiphe Cichoracearum*, DC.). — A white mold-like mildew which appears in spots upon the upper surface of the leaves of cucumbers, especially under glass.

Remedies. — Evaporated sulphur. Spray with ammoniacal carbonate of copper.

POWDERY MILDEW. — See under MUSKMELON.

Currant. ANTHRACNOSE (*Glœosporium Ribis*, M. & D.). — Small, dark brown or blackish spots chiefly on the upper surface of the leaves, but within the tissues. The cuticle over the spots is pushed up, giving the spots a whitish blister-like appearance. The leaves finally turn yellow, and they fall in July and August.

Preventive. — Thorough application of Bordeaux mixture.

RUST or LEAF-SPOT (*Septoria Ribis*, Desm.). — Appears about midsummer, on leaves of white, red, and black currants, as whitish spots with black centres. It causes the leaves to fall. Another spot disease is caused by *Cercospora angulata*, Wint.

Remedies. — Destroy infested leaves. Spraying with Bordeaux mixture and carbonate of copper, as for grape-rot.

Damping-off. — A term applied to the decay of young seedlings and cuttings at or near the surface of the ground. The trouble is undoubtedly due to a great variety of causes, but it is thought to be oftenest the work of fungi, particularly *Artotrogus DeBaryanus*. *Phytophthora Cactorum* (or *Pythium omnivorum*) causes a similar disease of small seedling trees. It is probably sometimes due to some fungus which exists in the seed, and in such cases — if they could be determined — soaking the seed in carbonate of copper is to be recommended (see BEAN). Other diseases, much like damping-off in general external characters, seem to be due to bacteria. A confined atmosphere, compact and wet soil, favor damping-off.

Preventives and *Remedies.* — Ventilate the cutting or seed-beds, do not let the plants crowd, and do not keep very wet, and keep the soil equally moist throughout its depth, and the surface dry. When the trouble appears among valuable plants, the healthy ones should be transplanted into fresh soil. Dusting the soil with sulphur, and sifting upon it and the plants very hot clean sand are to be recommended.

Dropsy. — See ŒDEMA.

Gooseberry. MILDEW (*Sphærotheca Mors-uvæ*, B. & C.). — A downy mildew attacking the fruits and young growth of English varieties of gooseberry (varieties of *Ribes Grossularia*).

Remedies. — Potassium sulphide (liver of sulphur), ½ ounce to a gallon of water is a sure remedy, if applied as soon as the leaves begin to unfold, and at intervals of two or three weeks thereafter. Bordeaux mixture is equally good.

Grape. ANTHRACNOSE or SCAB (*Sphaceloma Ampelinum*, De Bary). — The fungus attacks the leaves, where it forms definite brown spots, and also the young shoots and the fruits, where it forms pits or scabs. Generally distributed east of the Mississippi. Probably introduced from Europe.

Remedies. — It is difficult to combat. Before growth starts, cut out and burn affected canes and then spray plants and trellises with a saturated solution of sulphate of iron. After the leaves open, use Bordeaux mixture to prevent new attacks.

BLACK-ROT (*Læstadia Bidwellii*, V. & R.; *Phoma uvicola*, B. & C.). — Attacks nearly full-grown berries. The fruit becomes black, hard, dry, and shrivelled, and is covered with minute pimples. Occurs east of the Rocky Mountains, especially southwards. Of American origin.

Preventive. — A board placed over the trellis, as mentioned under the downy mildew, is some protection; but the spray is sure.

Remedies. — Burn infested fruits in autumn. If an attack is feared, spray with a plain solution of sulphate of iron or copper before the buds swell. Thereafter use Bordeaux mixture or ammoniacal carbonate of copper, at intervals of 10 to 15 days, continuing for five or six applications if necessary. The first spraying is made just before the blossoms open. Perhaps the best method is to use Bordeaux mixture for the first applications, and ammoniacal carbonate of copper for the last one or two, as this removes the danger of discoloring the grapes by the Bordeaux mixture. Very good results are obtained by the continuous use of the carbonate of copper, and it is applied more easily than the Bordeaux mixture.

The cost of spraying grapes six times during the season, including the cost of the chemicals, is estimated at two cents per vine for ammoniacal carbonate of copper and three cents for Bordeaux mixture. These figures assume that the best appliances are used, and that the plantation is a half acre or more in extent, and that the copper carbonate costs not to exceed 40 cents per pound and the copper sulphate not to exceed 6 cents per pound.

NOTE. — The following are synonyms for black-rot: *Sphæria Bidwellii, Physalospora Bidwellii, Phoma uvicola, Phoma uvicola* var. *Labruscæ, Sphæropsis uvarum, Phoma uvarum, Nemaspora ampelicida, Phyllosticta Labruscæ* (the "leaf-spot" form), *Phyllosticta viticola, Phoma ustulatum, Phyllosticta ampelopsidis, Sacidium viticolum, Septoria viticola, Ascochyta Ellisii.*

CALIFORNIA VINE-DISEASE. — An obscure disease, probably of fungous or bacterial origin, causing the leaves to assume red or yellow markings and discolored edges; the canes make a short growth and become discolored and shed their leaves early, and the berries shrivel and dry up or sometimes fall. The leaves usually curl more or less. Remedies are unknown.

PLANT–DISEASES.

DOWNY MILDEW, BROWN-ROT, GRAY-ROT (*Peronospora viticola*, De Bary). — Appears in small frost-like patches on the under surface of the leaves, and causes yellowish discoloration on the upper surface. It also produces the brown-rot and the gray-rot of the fruit. The young berries remain small and firm, usually not wrinkled, being at first gray in color, while the older ones become brown. The disease is worst on thin and smooth-leaved varieties, as the Delaware and others. It extends generally throughout N. America. Of American origin.

Preventive. — A wide board nailed flatwise on the top of the trellis so as to protect the vines somewhat, as with a roof, is a considerable protection, as it tends to keep the vines dry. Vines trained against a building rarely suffer.

Remedies. — The same as for black-rot, which see.

POWDERY MILDEW (*Uncinula spiralis*, B. & C.). — Appears early in the season as delicate dust-like patches or covering on the leaves, mostly on the upper surface, and on shoots and fruits. Berries attacked by it become checked in growth, and may remain small and die, or they sometimes grow and crack before death ensues. It attacks grapes in vineries which are not properly ventilated and managed. Occurs generally throughout the Union, but is less destructive than the downy mildew. American origin.

Remedies. — Dry sulphur applied to the vines, two or three times — once when the shoots just begin to push, again when in blossom, and usually again shortly before the grapes begin to turn. Apply in warm and bright weather, after the dew is off. In vineries, the sulphur may be scattered on the hot pipes. Any of the sprays of copper compounds are specifics, and are to be recommended for use in vineyards suffering from the disease, in preference to sulphur.

RATTLES. — A shelling of the grapes from the cluster when they are nearly ripe. Particularly serious in western New York. It is supposed to be due largely to lack of available potash in the soil. Other uncongenial conditions of soil and climate may aggravate it.

RIPE-ROT (*Glœosporium fructigenum*, Berk.).—See under APPLE. The treatment for black-rot is efficacious for this.

Hollyhock. RUST (*Puccinia Malvacearum*, Mont.).—Appears upon leaves of hollyhocks and a few related plants in small, light brown patches. Introduced from Europe, and becoming common in this country.

Remedies.—To destroy the plants is the only general method yet employed to prevent the spread of the disease, but spraying early with Bordeaux mixture is to be advised.

Lettuce. MILDEW (*Peronospora gangliformis*, De Bary).— A delicate mildew, attacking lettuce-leaves and causing yellow or brown spots, and finally killing the leaf.

Preventives. (According to Maynard.) — Grow at a low temperature (35° to 40° at night, 50° to 70° during day); give abundance of plant-food; give abundance of water, but apply it in morning and bright days only; avoid sudden extreme changes of temperature.

Remedy.—Fumes of sulphur.

ROT (*Botrytis vulgaris*, Fries.).—Forced lettuce often rots down, particularly the heading varieties. The fungus which causes the rot lives in manure and decaying matter. If manure is used, mix it well with the soil, keep the soil stirred on top and avoid keeping it too wet. Spreads most rapidly in a moist, confined atmosphere.

Maple. LEAF-SPOT (*Phyllosticta acericola*, C. & E.).—Attacks the leaves of red, silver, and striped maples in spring, causing them to become spotted and unsightly, and lessening the vigor of the tree.

Remedies.— Rake and burn the leaves in autumn. When the leaves are two-thirds grown spray with Bordeaux mixture, and repeat every three or four weeks as long as necessary.

Moss or **Lichens** on trees is readily removed by spraying with Bordeaux mixture, or strong alkaline washes. (See Chap. VI.)

PLANT-DISEASES. 63

Muskmelon. POWDERY MILDEW (*Plasmopara Cubensis*, B. & C.). — Attacks the leaves of the melon, cucumber, watermelon, and pumpkin. It causes large, angular discolorations upon the upper surface of the leaf, and violet, frost-like patches beneath. Badly affected leaves become ragged.

Remedy. — Bordeaux mixture.

Other leaf-diseases are frequent upon the muskmelon.

Nursery Stock. — Various leaf fungi attack young trees in nursery rows, causing the foliage to blight and sometimes to fall.

Preventives. — Good tillage and well-drained soil. Strong stock.

Remedy. — Spray with Bordeaux mixture.

Œdema or **Dropsy** is a disorder of various plants under glass, as tomatoes, violets, geraniums, which have insufficient sunlight, stimulating temperature and soil, and too much moisture. It has also been observed on twigs of the apple. It is usually indicated by elevated corky or spongy points or masses, much resembling fungous injury. The leaves curl. The only remedy is to improve the conditions under which the plant grows.

Onion. RUST (*Peronospora Schleideniana*, Unger). — The leaves turn yellow about the time the onions begin to bottom, or a little later, and wilt and die.

Remedies. — Grow on land not infected, and destroy all affected onions. Spray early with copper fungicides.

SMUT (*Urocystis Cepulæ*, Frost). — Attacks the first leaf or leaves of seedling onions, producing dark, irregular spots, and killing or weakening the plants.

Remedy. — The sulphur and lime mixture drilled into the ground with the seed, about an ounce of the mixture to 50 feet of drill.

Orange. ORANGE-LEAF SCAB (*Cladosporium*). — The leaves become yellow and distorted.

Remedies. — Spray with copper fungicides, or carbolic acid and glycerine mixture.

Pansy. RUST (*Peronospora Violæ*, De Bary). — Blackish or brown spots upon the leaves.

Remedies. — Bordeaux mixture or ammoniacal carbonate of copper.

Pea. MILDEW (*Erysiphe Martii*, Lév.). — A whitish fungus overspreading the foliage of peas, particularly the late crops.

Remedies. — Try Bordeaux mixture or ammoniacal carbonate of copper.

Peach. BLACK-SPOT (*Cladosporium carpophilum*, Thm.). — Sooty-black scab-like patches upon the fruit, causing it to crack deeply. Some varieties, as Hill's Chili, are very liable to attack.

Remedies. — Probably spraying with dilute Bordeaux mixture, or ammoniacal carbonate of copper, would be useful.

BROWN-ROT. — See under CHERRY.

CURL, LEAF-CURL or "FRENCHING" (*Exoascus deformans*, Fuckl.; written also *Ascomyces deformans* and *Taphrina deformans*). — The leaves become blistered and crumpled early in the season and fall off.

Remedies. — Good culture, to enable the tree to put forth new leaves, is to be recommended. Spray in spring, before the buds open, with sulphate of copper or iron, and follow with two or three applications of Bordeaux mixture.

LEAF-RUST. — See under PLUM.

POWDERY MILDEW. — See under APPLE. Spray with weak Bordeaux mixture. Attacks both foliage and fruit of the peach.

ROOT-GALL and ROOT-KNOT. — See entries under R, Chap. II.

ROSETTE. — An obscure southern disease of peach trees and some kinds of plums, characterized by bunchy growths containing very many rolled and yellowish leaves which fall prematurely. The tree dies the first or second year. There is no premature fruit, as in yellows. It is often accompanied by gummosis of the roots. The disease is communicable by budding, and it may enter through the roots. All affected trees should be exterminated. Known in South Carolina, Georgia, Kansas, and Arkansas.

ROT and BLIGHT (*Monilia fructigena*, Pers.). — This is the

familiar quick rotting of peaches when nearly ripe or after they are picked, and the same fungus causes the blighting of young shoots. It also destroys the flowers, and its injury may then be mistaken for effects of frost. It also attacks plums, cherries, apricots, and to a smaller extent apples and pears. The rotted fruits sometimes dry up and hang on the tree all winter. In such cases, the fruit spur is apt to be killed by the fungus. Partial to some varieties.

Preventives. — Burn or bury all affected fruits as soon as they appear. In wet weather, when peaches are rotting badly on the tree, systematic attempts should be made to pick and destroy the injured fruits. Burning or ploughing under the leaves in the fall is to be recommended. Before the leaves appear, spray with some copper compound, as sulphate of copper or Bordeaux mixture, and spray thereafter several times. It is said that harvested fruit can be preserved for a short time against the fungus by dipping it in a solution of potassium sulphide (liver of sulphur).

YELLOWS. — A fatal disease of peaches ; also attacks nectarine, almond, apricot, and Japanese plum. Cause unknown. The first symptom in bearing trees is usually the premature ripening of the fruit. This fruit contains definite small red spots which extend towards the pit. The second stage is usually the appearance of "tips," or short, late, second growths upon the ends of healthy twigs, and which are marked by small, horizontal, usually yellowish, leaves. The next stage is indicated by very slender shoots, which branch the first year and which start in tufts from the old limbs, bearing narrow and small yellowish leaves. Later the entire foliage becomes smaller and yellow. In three to six years the tree dies. The disease spreads from tree to tree. It attacks trees of any age. Known at present only in regions east of the Mississippi. Peculiar to America, so far as known.

Preventive. — Pull up and burn all trees as soon as the disease appears. Trees may be reset in the places from which the yellows trees were taken. Laws aiming to

F

suppress the disease should be enacted in all peach-growing States.

Pear. BLIGHT (*Micrococcus amylovorus*, Burrill). — A very serious bacterial disease. The microbes work in the young wood, causing it to die. The bark becomes brown and sunken over the diseased parts. The death of the shoots causes the leaves to die. The disease is readily distinguished from the leaf-blight in the fact that the leaves are equally brown and discolored over their entire surface, and they become dry and hang on the tree. The disease enters through growing points, probably largely through the blossoms, and it proceeds rather slowly down the twig. If short twigs or spurs along the trunk or large branches are attacked, the disease frequently spreads in the large branch, showing as a sunken patch, and it may girdle the branch and thereby cut off food supply to the points beyond. Generally distributed east of the 100th meridian. Known only in America. Attacks the apple and quince.

Preventives. — Some varieties, like Duchess, Lawrence, and Kieffer, are partially immune. See that useless spurs or sprouts do not grow upon the trunk or large branches.

Remedy. — As soon as the disease is discovered, cut off the affected parts a foot below the point of lowest visible attack, and burn them. A tree which has been seriously mutilated may be top-grafted the following year.

LEAF-BLIGHT and CRACKING OF THE FRUIT (*Entomosporium maculatum*, Lév.; *Morthiera Mespili* is the same). — Attacks nursery-stocks of pears, beginning as small and circular brown spots on the leaves; soon the entire leaf turns brown and falls. Also causes the cracking of the fruit, being particularly serious upon some varieties, such as Flemish Beauty, Seckel, and Virgalieu (White Doyenne).

Remedies. — Bordeaux mixture, eau céleste (2), or ammoniacal carbonate of copper, applied four or five times. Begin when the leaves are half-grown, and follow at intervals of from two to four weeks. The Bordeaux is now most commonly used, and is a specific when properly applied.

Root-Rot (*Polyporus versicolor*, Fries). — Attacks the roots, the white and felt-like threads of the fungus at length becoming very abundant and conspicuous. The trees produce a short and thick growth, the new wood being reddish, the leaves becoming yellowish or bronzed, and there is an unusual tendency to form fruit-buds. The tree may die quickly or may live for several years. The roots rot away and the tree tips over. The disease is worst on poor and dry soils and in grassy orchards.

Remedies. — Give good culture. Remove the earth from the crown and apply a dressing of lime.

Rust. — See under Apple.

Scab (*Fusicladium pyrinum*, Fuckl.). — Brown or blackish scab-like spots on the leaves and fruit, arresting the growth and causing the parts to become distorted.

Remedy. — Spray several times during May, June, and July with Bordeaux mixture, the same as for apple-scab.

Plane-Tree. Leaf-Scorching (*Glœosporium nervisequum*, Sacc.). — Attacks the leaves in spring, causing them to appear as if scorched. They finally fall off. Attacks both the native and oriental planes.

Remedies. — Burn all leaves when they fall. Spray with copper compounds.

Plum. Brown-Rot. — See under Cherry.

Leaf-Blight or Shot-Hole Fungus (*Cylindrosporium Padi* or *Septoria cerasina*, Peck). — Appears as spots upon the leaves in July, and these spots assume definite outlines, and often fall out, leaving holes like shot-holes. The leaves fall early, preventing the fruit from maturing. The disease is sometimes designated simply "Falling of the leaves." Very serious. Some varieties are very liable to attack.

Remedies. — Bordeaux mixture, modified eau céleste, or ammoniacal carbonate of copper applied several times during the season, beginning as soon as the leaves appear.

Leaf-Rust (*Puccinia Pruni-spinosæ*, Pers.). — Small, round, powdery spots of yellowish brown on the under surface of the leaves, and reddish spots on the upper surface directly above them.

Remedies.—Spray trees early in the season with Bordeaux mixture, ammoniacal carbonate of copper, eau céleste (2), or other fungicides.

PLUM-KNOT or PLUM-WART (*Plowrightia* [*Sphæria*] *morbosa,* Sacc.).—A black and irregular swelling, from one to five or six inches long, appearing on the small limbs of plum and cherry. The point of attack is generally in the crotch of young shoots or at the junction of the annual growths. Peculiar to America. A very serious disease.

Remedies.—Burn all affected parts in the fall. If the knot is found upon a large limb or trunk, cut it out and wash the wound with sulphate of copper. Wash the parts as soon as the swelling begins to appear, with linseed oil, turpentine, or kerosene, using the two latter with caution. A paint of red oxide of iron in linseed oil has been recommended. Spraying with Bordeaux mixture in early spring and during the summer will prevent attacks. There should be laws in every State aimed at the destruction of the knot.

PLUM-POCKETS or BLADDERS (*Exoascus Pruni,* Fuckl.).— Causes the fruit to become inflated and hollow. These "bladders" begin to appear soon after the flowers fall, and continue to grow for several months, when they fall. They are at first globular, but finally become oblong, often reaching two inches in length. Similar fungi attack the fruit of the Chickasaw and American plums, and various species of plum and cherry.

Remedies.—Destroy the "bladders" before they mature, together with small portions of the wood on which they are borne. Spray before buds expand with strong sulphate of copper or iron, and follow with copper fungicides.

POWDERY MILDEW.—See under APPLE.

ROT or BLIGHT.—See under PEACH.

Poplar. LEAF-RUST (*Melampsora populina,* Lév.).—An orange rust attacking, during summer, the leaves of various species of poplar, including the cottonwood, balm of Gilead, etc.

Remedies. — Rake and burn the leaves. Spray with copper compounds.

Potato. EARLY BLIGHT. (Probably caused by *Macrosporium Solani*, E. & M.). — A blight of the foliage, appearing rather early in the season, generally before August. The leaves become yellowish and sickly and are marked with small fungous patches. Progresses slowly. Does not attack the tubers. Associated with flea-beetle attacks.

Remedy. — Bordeaux mixture.

POTATO-ROT or BLIGHT, LATE BLIGHT (*Phytophthora infestans*, De Bary). — The spores first germinate upon the tops or vines, causing the foliage to become marked with very large blotches, which generally cover a third or more of the leaflet. Progresses rapidly. The disease soon spreads to the tubers, causing discolored and diseased potatoes. It is a "dry rot." The fungus may remain in the tubers during winter.

Preventives. — Plant on light or loamy, well-drained soil. Plant only sound and disinfected tubers. Hill deep.

Remedy. — Spray the tops with Bordeaux mixture, or other fungicide, upon the first indication of the blight, and make three or more applications at intervals of ten days or two weeks.

The tubers should be stored in a cool and dry place. Dusting them in the cellar with dry air-slaked lime is to be recommended. Subjecting the tubers to a temperature of 105° to 110° for a few days will destroy the fungus and will not injure the tubers for planting.

There is another kind of potato blight and rot widely distributed over the country, and probably due to a germ or bacterium. The leaves curl, the plant droops and finally dies, and the tubers contract a putrid rot. Very serious. No remedy is known. Practise rotation.

SCAB (*Oospora scabies*, Thax.). — Well-known scabby and pitted roughness of potato tubers. The same fungus is supposed to attack beets. Lime or ashes added to soil in which scabby potatoes have been grown, increases the disease, probably by modifying the acidity of the soil.

Preventives. — Do not plant upon land which has grown scabby potatoes. Plant clean seed. Cook scabby potatoes or beets before feeding them to stock to prevent dissemination of the fungus in the manure. Dig suspected tubers as soon as they are ripe, to check the deepening of the scabs. If scabby seed is planted, soak it in corrosive sublimate (1½ hours in 2 ounces sublimate to 16 gallons water), or Bordeaux mixture. Corrosive sublimate is probably the better remedy. Spraying the open furrows, before covering the tubers, is also useful.

Pumpkin. POWDERY MILDEW. — See under MUSKMELON.

Quince. BLACK-ROT (*Sphæropsis Malorum*, Peck). — A trouble which usually appears at the blossom end of young quinces, causing the fruit to perish with a black, dry rot. Also attacks the apple and pear.

Remedy. — Spray with Bordeaux mixture.

BLIGHT. — See under PEAR.

LEAF-BLIGHT and FRUIT-SPOT (*Entomosporium maculatum*, Lév.). — Leaves become spotted and then turn yellow and fall. The fruits also become spotted with sunken brownish or black scab-like patches. This disease often causes considerable damage. It is the same as the leaf-blight of the pear, which see.

RUST. — See under APPLE.

Raspberry. CANE-RUST or ANTHRACNOSE (*Glœosporium necator*, E. & E.). — The spots or patches of fungus appear on both the canes and leaves. The disease attacks the base of the canes first and spreads upwards. It makes sunken patches on the canes and causes the fruit to dry up.

Preventives. — Give plants an abundance of light and air by broad planting and high training. In pruning out the young shoots, select those which are the most diseased and burn them. Frequent rotation — not fruiting the plantation after the disease appears — is a most satisfactory procedure.

Remedies. — Spray before the buds swell with sulphate of iron, and follow later with Bordeaux mixture or ammoniacal carbonate of copper. Spraying has never been very successful with this disease, but frequent applications ought to keep the fungus off. Burn all canes that are past recovery.

Red or Orange-Rust (*Cœoma luminatum*, Link). — Attacks the under surface of the leaves of black and sometimes red raspberries, and of blackberries, in patches of whitish yellow, but the fungus finally covers the whole under surface with an orange-red coating. One form of the fungus is a leaf-rust generally known as *Puccinia Peckiana.*

Preventives. — Plant such varieties as are least susceptible to attack. Among blackberries, Kittatinny is particularly susceptible. Rotation.

Remedy. — Burn the plants, roots and branch, as soon as the disease appears.

Rose. Leaf-Blight or Black-Spot (*Actinonema Rosæ*, Fries). — Attacks the full-grown leaves, first appearing as small black spots, but later covering nearly or quite the whole surface with blotches. The spots have frayed edges. Common in outdoor and house culture.

Remedies. — In the house, fumes of sulphur or copper sprays. Outdoors, burn the affected leaves and spray with Bordeaux mixture or ammoniacal carbonate of copper. Spray before the leaves unfold.

Leaf-Spot (*Cercospora rosæcola*, Pass.). — Black or reddish black spots on the leaves, shading into red at the definite edges. Later the centre of the spot becomes light brown or gray. Attacks plants growing outdoors.

Remedies. — Burn diseased parts. Spray with copper fungicides.

Mildew (*Sphærotheca pannosa*, Lév.). — Whitish mildew attacking roses. It is brought on, according to Maynard, by exposure to drafts of extremely cold air when the plants are growing rapidly, by high temperature running the same day and night, by watering just before night, by too little water, by extreme dryness, by poor drainage, by deficiency in plant-food.

Remedies.—Fumes of sulphur. Copper fungicides.

RUST (*Phragmidium mucronatum*, Winter).—Appears in small and scattered bright yellow spots or pustules on the leaves, which at length become distorted, and upon the young growth.

Remedy.—Spray with Bordeaux mixture or other fungicides.

Spinage.—Several fungi attack the spinage, of which the following are the worst:

ANTHRACNOSE (*Colletotrichum Spinaceæ*, Ell. & Hals.).— Producing brown and gray blotches upon the leaves;

LEAF-BLIGHT (*Phyllosticta Chenopodii*, Sacc.).—Forming many minute pimples on the leaf, usually upon its under surface;

MILDEW (*Peronospora effusa*, Rabenh.).—Producing violet-gray patches upon the under side of the leaves and yellow spots above;

WHITE SMUT (*Entyloma Ellisii*, Hals.).—Covering the whole leaf with a white coat.

Remedies.—No definite remedies are yet known for these diseases. Spraying with copper fungicides will undoubtedly check them, but this procedure is generally impracticable upon spinage. Burning all affected plants, and rotation, are to be advised.

Squash. POWDERY MILDEW.—See under MUSKMELON.

Strawberry. LEAF-BLIGHT, RUST or SUN-BURN (*Sphærella Fragariæ*, Sacc., including *Ramularia*).—Small purple or red spots appearing on the leaves. They eventually become larger and browner, making the leaf appear blotched. Most serious after the fruit is picked, lessening the crop of the following year.

Remedies.—Spray with Bordeaux mixture or ammoniacal carbonate of copper at intervals of two weeks, beginning as soon as the fruit is picked. Destroy all affected leaves. The leaves are easily destroyed without injury to the plants by quickly burning off a thin layer of straw which is spread over the patch after the fruit is off. Where the disease is feared, the best treatment, in general, is to fruit the plantation but once.

MILDEW (*Sphærotheca Castagnei*, Lév.). — A whitish cobweb-like mildew spreading over the fruit and leaves and causing the latter to curl as if wilted.

Remedies. — If the disease is discovered early enough, some liquid fungicide, as ammoniacal carbonate of copper or Bordeaux mixture, should be employed. Sulphur scattered upon the foliage and upon the soil about the plants is said to check the disease.

Sweet-Potato. BLACK-ROT (*Ceratocystis fimbriata*, Ell. & Hals.). — A dry-rot of the tuber, and a black rust upon the stems. Upon the tuber it appears in large scab-like patches, and is usually evident at digging time. It may appear upon the young plants in the hotbed and persist upon them throughout the season.

Remedies. — Rotation of crops. Spray the young plants, if attack is feared, with copper fungicides.

DRY-ROT (*Phoma Batatæ*, Ell. & Hals.). — The upper end of the tuber becomes dry and wrinkled and bears a multitude of pimples, and its flesh becomes dry and powdery.

Preventive. — Destroy all affected tubers.

LEAF-BLIGHT (*Phyllosticta bataticola*, E. & M.). — Produces white, dead patches upon the leaves.

Remedy. — Spray with some of the copper fungicides.

SCURF (*Monilochætes infuscans*, Ell. & Hals.). — The whole surface of the potato becomes scurfy, and it causes the tuber to shrink.

Preventive. — Use only healthy potatoes for seed.

SOFT-ROT (*Rhizopus nigricans*, Ehr.). — The tubers rot with a soft and putrid decay. It is most destructive after the potatoes are stored.

Preventives. — Store in a well-ventilated, artificially

warmed room, at a temperature of about 70°. Store only sound and perfect tubers, and remove at once any which are attacked.

SOIL-ROT (*Acrocystis Batatas*, Ell. & Hals.). — The tubers are attacked when young, and the diseased portion ceases to grow, causing the potato to become constricted or variously contorted.

Preventive. — Rotation. It is probable that the sweet-potato cannot be grown again safely on infested soil for a number of years, without treatment.

Remedy. — When the furrows are open and ready for planting, before the manure is added, spray the soil with Bordeaux mixture.

STEM-ROT, BLACK-SHANK. — An obscure disease attacking the young shoots near the ground and the tops of the young tubers, causing the tubers to rot away above, and to send up sprouts below the injured portion.

Preventives. — Rotation. Heat the soil used for seed-bed.

WHITE-MOLD or LEAF-MOLD (*Cystopus Ipomœæ-panduranæ*, Farl.). — The leaves become pale and brown patches appear, and small whitish patches occur on the under surface. It thrives upon the wild potato-vine or man-of-the-earth (*Ipomœa pandurata*).

Preventive. — Destroy the wild potato-vine upon which the fungus grows.

Remedy. — Some copper fungicide applied in a spray.

WHITE-ROT. — This disease causes portions of the tuber to become white and chalk-like, and sometimes the whole tuber assumes a chalk-like consistency.

Preventives. — Use only healthy stock, and probably a rotation of crops will be useful.

Tomato. BLIGHT (*Cladosporium fulvum*, Cooke). — Soft brown irregular spots appear on the under surface of the leaves, and the upper surface becomes spotted with yellow. The leaves finally shrivel. Most serious in greenhouses.

Preventive. — In houses, keep the temperature as even as possible. In particular, avoid sudden changes. In mild attacks the disease can be kept in check by picking off and burning the injured leaves.

Remedies. — Bordeaux mixture or ammoniacal carbonate of copper sprayed on the plants every week or ten days.

FIELD-BLIGHT or SOUTHERN BLIGHT. — Attacks plants in the field, causing the leaves to become dull or slightly yellowish and curled, as if suffering from drought. The ends of the leaves, or the individual leaflets, often die and droop. Apparently common North and South. Probably bacterial. It is thought to attack the potato also; if it does, potatoes and tomatoes should not follow each other upon the same land. No remedy is known.

ROOT-KNOT. — A nematode disease in forcing-houses (see under R, Chap. II.), causing the plants to curl their leaves and become weak. Remove the crop and freeze the soil.

ROT (*Macrosporium Tomato*, Cooke). — The rotting of the nearly grown or ripe fruit.

Preventives. — The small cherry and plum tomatoes are not attacked, and the old-fashioned angular sorts are comparatively free. Training the vines so as to give the fruit plenty of light and air is useful. Heavy applications of fresh stable manure appear to augment the injury. Burn all infested vines and fruits in the autumn. The trouble is usually worst rather early in the picking season during hot and moist weather. In the cooler weather of fall it is rarely serious. Therefore, aim to prolong the bearing season by early planting and good tillage.

Remedy. — Spraying with Bordeaux mixture seems to be useful.

The bacterial potato-blight or rot also attacks tomatoes. See under POTATO.

WINTER-BLIGHT. — Probably a bacterial disease. Attacks tomato plants grown under glass, causing the leaves to curl and to become marked with translucent dots or spots. No remedy is known. Destroy diseased plants, and do not use the same soil again.

Verbena. RUST (*Erysiphe Cichoracearum*, DC.). — A whitish rust, or mildew, which appears on the leaves, eventually destroying the plants.

Preventives. — Start with perfectly healthy and vigorous stock, and give good culture. In the house, endeavor to avoid drafts, but give plenty of air on bright days.

Remedies. — Sulphide of potassium sprayed upon the plants every few days. Bordeaux mixture.

Violet. VIOLET DISEASE or RUST (*Cercospora Violæ*, Sacc., and perhaps also *Peronospora Violæ*, De Bary). — Appears on the leaves as small rounded light or brown spots, causing the leaf finally to wither and die.

Preventives. — It is supposed that any neglect or improper handling renders the plants more liable to the disease. Burn all infested plants, and do not use the same soil again for violets. Sprays of copper compounds applied during summer and fall.

Watermelon. ANTHRACNOSE or POD-RUST. — See under BEAN.

BLIGHT, WILT, or WATERMELON DISEASE (*Fusarium niveum*, Smith). — Vines wilt suddenly and soon die, without apparent cause. The fungus occurs in the vessels of the stem. Serious in the South.

Preventives. — Rotation. Burn all diseased vines. Do not throw the old vines on compost piles, for a common source of infection is the manure spread upon the and.

POWDERY MILDEW. — See under MUSKMELON.

CHAPTER V.

INJURIES FROM MICE, RABBITS, SQUIRRELS, AND BIRDS, WITH PREVENTIVES AND REMEDIES.

IF the plantation is free of litter, and the adjacent fields contain no harbors of brush, mice and rabbits are rarely annoying to orchards. In hard winters, with deep snow, these animals are more destructive than in open winters. Rabbits often browse off the young growth of nursery stock and small trees. Sheep and hogs rarely girdle trees if they are given sufficient food and water, the latter being especially important.

To **prevent mice from girdling trees in winter.** — In heeling-in young trees in the fall, do not use straw or litter, in which mice can make their nests. In orchards, see that tall grass, corn-husks, or other dry material does not gather about the trees in fall. If danger from mice is apprehended, tramp the first snow firmly about the trees, in order to compact the grass and litter so that mice cannot find shelter.

Where the paper-birch grows, it will be found a good plan to place sections of birch-bark from limbs or small trunks about the base of the tree. These sections roll up tightly about the tree, and yet expand so readily with the growth of the tree that they may be allowed to remain, although it is advisable to remove them each spring, so that they will not become a harboring-place for insects. Tie thin strips of wood, as laths or shingles, about the tree. Common window-screen placed about the tree is effective and safe. Tarred paper is sometimes advised to keep away mice and borers, but it is very apt to kill the bark, especially on young trees, if tied on, or if left on in warm weather.

Washes to protect trees from mice. — Wash the trees with some persistent substance in which is placed Paris green. Maynard finds the following substances useful for holding the poison: Portland cement of the consistency of common paint; Portland cement 10 parts and gas-tar 1 part; Portland cement 10 parts and asphaltum 1 part; Portland cement 10 parts and Morrill's tree-ink 1 part.

Lime-wash, to which is added a little sulphur, tobacco-decoction, and soapsuds.

Carbonate of baryta for rats and mice. — Sugar and oatmeal or wheat flour, of each 6 ounces; carbonate of baryta, $\frac{1}{4}$ pound; oil of anise-seed, enough to give the mixture a pretty strong odor.

Tartar emetic for rats and mice. — Tartar emetic, 1 part; oatmeal or flour, 4 parts; beef or mutton suet enough to make all into a paste.

Camphor for rats and mice. — Mix a few pieces of camphor with vegetable seeds, to repel vermin.

French paste for rats and mice. — Oatmeal or wheat flour, 3 pounds; powdered indigo, $\frac{1}{2}$ ounce; finely powdered white arsenic, 4 ounces; oil of anise-seed, $\frac{1}{2}$ drachm. Mix, and add of melted beef suet or mutton tallow $2\frac{1}{2}$ pounds, and work the whole up into a paste.

Commercial forms of phosphorus are popular as exterminators of vermin.

Wash for keeping rabbits, sheep, and mice away from trees. — Some writers recommend fresh lime, slaked with soft water (old soapsuds are best); make the wash the thickness of fence or house wash. When 1 peck of lime is used, add, when hot, $\frac{1}{2}$ gallon crude carbolic acid, $\frac{1}{2}$ gallon gas-tar, and 4 pounds of sulphur. Stir well. For summer wash leave gas-tar out and add in place of it 1 gallon

INJURIES FROM MICE, ETC. 79

of soft soap. To keep rabbits and sheep from girdling, wash late in fall, or about the time of frost, as high as one can reach.

Blood for rabbits. — Blood smeared upon trees, as high up as rabbits can reach, will generally keep them away.

To drive rabbits from orchards. — Dip rags in melted sulphur and then secure them to sticks which are stuck promiscuously through the orchard.

It should be an imperative rule with all orchardists not to allow brush heaps or piles of poles and rails to remain upon their premises if rabbits are troublesome in the neighborhood, for it is in such places that the animals live.

Wash to protect trees from rabbits. — Fresh cow-dung, 1 peck; quicklime, $\frac{1}{2}$ peck; flowers of sulphur, $\frac{1}{2}$ pound; lampblack, $\frac{1}{4}$ pound. Mix the whole into a thick paint with urine and soapsuds.

California rabbit-wash. — Commercial aloes, 1 pound to 4 gallons of water, both sprinkled on leaves and painted on the bark gives a bitter taste, which repels rabbits.

California rabbit-poisons. —

1. Pieces of watermelon, canteloupe, or other vegetables of which they are fond, may be poisoned with strychnine and then scattered around the orchard.

2. To 100 pounds of wheat take 9 gallons of water and 1 pound of phosphorus, 1 pound of sugar, and 1 ounce oil of rhodium. Heat the water to boiling-point and let it stand all night. Next morning stir in flour sufficient to make a sort of paste. Scatter it about the place.

3. Another preparation is $\frac{1}{2}$ teaspoonful of powdered strychnine, 2 teaspoonfuls of fine salt, and 4 of granulated sugar. Put all in a tin box and shake well. Pour in small heaps on a board. It hardens into a solid mass. Rabbits lick it for the salt, and the sugar disguises the poison.

Sulphur for rabbits. — Equal proportions of sulphur, soot, and lime, made into a thick paint with cow-manure Smear upon the trees.

Cow-manure for rabbits. — A mixture of lime, water, and

cow-manure, made strong, forms an excellent anti-rabbit composition.

Asafœtida for rabbits. — A teaspoonful of tincture of asafœtida in ½ pailful of liquid clay, mud, or muck of any kind. Apply with a brush to the stem and branches of young trees. Two or three applications during winter.

California ground-squirrel remedies. — Take 5 quarts of clean wheat; scald with water; drain. Take ⅔ cup of white sugar, dissolve with sufficient water to make a syrup; add 1 ounce powdered strychnine, stir thoroughly until a thin paste is formed. Pour this on the damp wheat. Stir thoroughly for at least 15 minutes. Add 1 pint powdered sugar, stir; add 5 to 10 drops of rhodium and 5 to 10 drops of oil of anise-seed. Place a few grains in each squirrel-hole, putting it as far in as possible.

Bisulphide of carbon is also largely used. A small quantity is poured into the burrow, and the hole is immediately closed securely with dirt.

Tying newspapers about trees in such manner as to allow the upper part of the paper to project loosely a few inches, frightens the squirrels away.

To remedy the injury done by mice, rabbits, and squirrels. —

1. Pare and clean the wound, and cover it thickly with fresh cow-dung, or soft clay, and bind it up thoroughly with a cloth. Grafting-wax bound on is also good. Complete girdling, when done late in spring — when settled weather is approaching — can be remedied in this manner.

2. Insert long scions over the wound, by paring them thin on both ends and placing one end under the bark on the upper edge of the wound and the other under the bark on the lower edge. Wax thoroughly the points of union, and tie a cloth band tightly about the trees over both extremities of the scions.

Bird-poisons. —

1. Place a shallow box on the end of a pole and put it 4 or 5 feet from the ground to keep the poison out of the way

of domestic fowls. In the box sprinkle corn-meal and a very little strychnine, which mixture the birds eat. It will not hurt dogs or cats to eat the dead bird, for the reason that there is not enough poison absorbed by the bird. (Californian.)

2. Put the strychnine in pieces of apples and stick them on the ends of limbs of the trees. (Californian.)

Poison for English sparrows. — Dissolve arsenate of soda in warm water at the rate of 1 ounce to 1 pint ; pour this upon as much wheat as it will cover (in a vessel which can be closed so as to prevent evaporation), and allow it to soak for at least 24 hours. . Dry the wheat so prepared, and it is ready for use. It should be distributed in winter in places where the sparrows congregate.

To protect fruits from birds. — One of the best devices is mosquito-bar spread over the bushes or trees. For bush-fruits and small trees the expense is not great. There is a commercial netting made for the purpose.

Have a taxidermist mount several hawks and place them in natural positions in the trees or vines.

In large plantations of cherries or other fruits subject to the depredations of birds, the injury is generally proportionately less than in small areas. Some cherry-growers plant early sweet varieties to feed the birds, which, getting their fill, give less attention to the main crop.

To protect newly planted seeds. — Coat the seeds with red lead by moistening the seeds slightly and stirring in red lead until all the seeds are thoroughly coated. Let the seeds dry for two or three hours before sowing.

To protect planted corn from crows. — Dip the kernels in coal-tar and then dust them with plaster.

G

CHAPTER VI.

LAWNS. — WEEDS AND MOSS.

1. **How to make lawns.** — A lawn which is to be permanent should be thoroughly and carefully made. See that the land is well drained. Plow it or trench it deeply. Rake the surface fine and smooth, removing lumps and stones. Use freely of chemical fertilizer — rich in nitrogen — or clean stable manure. Sow the seed very early in the spring, so that the grass becomes established before dry weather; or else sow just before the fall rains are expected. If the land is in readiness, the seed may be sown on a late spring snow. The best lawn grass is June grass (known also as Kentucky blue grass). Sow 3 or 4 bushels to the acre in order to secure a close, soft turf. Two or three quarts of timothy seed may be used when seeding, as this grass makes a better cover the first year, and it is gradually crowded out by the June grass. If one likes white clover in a lawn, it may be added at the rate of a couple quarts to the acre. Weeds will come up the first year; keep them closely mown, and the June grass will crowd them out in a year or two. Reseed and repair all poor spots in the lawn from year to year, as recommended in Section 3. Give a top dressing every spring. Well-made lawns, which are well cared for, rarely need watering.

2. **Weeds in general.** — Weeds rarely trouble the good cultivator, particularly in vegetable gardening. Intensive methods of cultivation allow no weeds to appear. It is economy, both in labor and returns from the crop, to prevent weeds from appearing, rather than to hoe or pull them out after

they are partly grown and have done some damage. Frequent light stirrings of the soil with cultivator, harrow, or rake are the cheapest mode of weed destruction. Rotation of crops and continuous cropping of the land are amongst the best preventives and exterminators of weeds. The better the system of husbandry the fewer the weeds.

In the struggle with weeds it is well to consider the longevity of the various species. Annual weeds, those which naturally die after the season's growth, require no special treatment. Biennial species, those which die at the end of the second year, may be held in check by preventing them from seeding, as by mowing them when coming into flower. Examples of this class are the mullein, wild carrot, and field or bull thistle. Perennial species, those which live indefinitely, often require particular treatment. Some of the worst perennial species are Canada thistle, white or ox-eye daisy, toad-flax, live-forever, docks, and various grasses. Very frequent, persistent, and thorough cultivation will destroy any of these. Cultivation should be repeated even before the weeds recover sufficiently to take root again. Seeding down and mowing the weeds with the hay will destroy most weeds. In dry and sandy soils three or four thorough plowings during the season will destroy Canada thistles and other pests, particularly in dry years, but on richer and retentive soils greater thoroughness must be practised.

3. **Weeds in lawns.** — Weeds usually come up thickly in newly sown lawns. They are to be prevented by the use of commercial fertilizers or very clean manure and clean grass-seed. Clean June-grass, or blue-grass, seed is usually best. Grass-seed should be sown very thickly — 3 to 4 bushels to the acre — and annual weeds cannot persist long. Frequent mowings during summer will keep these weeds down, and most species will not survive the winter. In old lawns most perennial weeds can be kept down by frequent mowings, with a good lawn-mower. Grass can stand more cutting than weeds. If mowing cannot be practised often

enough for this purpose, the weeds may be cut off below the surface with a long knife or spud, and the crowns are then readily pulled out. Or a little sulphuric acid — oil of vitriol — may be poured upon the crown of each plant.

It will usually be found that weedy lawns are those in which the sod is poor and thin. The fundamental remedy, therefore, is to secure a strong sod. This is done by raking or harrowing over the lawn in late spring when it is somewhat soft, and sowing a liberal dressing of chemical fertilizer and grass-seed. Roll the land down level. All poor spots in lawns should be repaired in this manner every year. The use of stable manure on lawns should be discouraged, both because it is offensive and it generally abounds in weed seeds.

Weeds on walks. — Walks should be so made that weeds cannot grow in them. This can be done by making a deep stone foundation and filling between the stones with cinders, coal ashes, or other similar material. But when weeds become established they can be destroyed by the following methods:

SALT. — Hot brine (1 pound of salt to 1 gallon of water), boiled in a kettle on wheels and dipped out into watering-pots. Brine is better than dry salt, because it leaves very little color upon the walk.

LIME AND SULPHUR. — 10 gallons of water, 20 pounds of quicklime, and 2 pounds of sulphur are boiled in an iron vessel. After settling, the clear part is dipped off and used when needed. Care must be taken, as it will destroy edgings.

OIL OF VITRIOL. — 1 part oil of vitriol (sulphuric acid) to 30 parts of water. Apply with a watering-pot. Choose a clear evening after a hot day. Keep clear of the edgings. The pot should be well painted, or a wooden pail should be used.

ARSENITE OF SODA. — Place 1 pound of powdered arsenic in 3 gallons of cold water, boil and keep stirring; then add 7 gallons of cold water and 2 pounds of crushed soda; stir well while boiling. Apply in dry weather.

CARBOLIC ACID. — 1 ounce of carbolic acid to 1 gallon of water, sprinkled from a watering-pot. Also destroys ants.

COAL-TAR COATING. — Mix coal-tar with gravel to the consistency of mortar; spread over the path 1 to 2 inches thick; cover this with gravel, then roll and add another thin coating of gravel to finish.

5. **Moss on walks and lawns.** — In damp and shady places, and also in sterile places, moss may appear on walks and lawns. If the conditions cannot be improved, the following treatments may be tried:

1 pound oil of vitriol (sulphuric acid) to 10 quarts of water. Wet the surface thoroughly, being careful not to sprinkle edgings or good sod.

In early spring, while the ground is soft, work it backwards and forwards, with a long-toothed rake, in order to bring the moss to the surface. Clear away the moss and leave the ground untouched for a fortnight. Early in March repeat the operation, and about the middle of that month apply a dressing of rich compost, which may consist of any old rubbish well decomposed, adding $\frac{1}{6}$ of fresh lime. Mix with compost a few days before using. Cover the ground with the compost at the rate of 200 barrow-loads per acre, passing it through a $\frac{3}{4}$-inch sieve, to save the trouble of rolling. Rake it evenly over the surface, and when dry seed down. An English method.

Endeavor to improve the sod, as recommended in Section 3, and thereby drive out the moss. In shady places, where grass will not grow, plant some shade-loving plant, as periwinkle (*Vinca minor*), lily-of-the-valley, or moneywort (*Lysimachia nummularia*), or species of carex.

6. **Moss or lichen on trees.** — Moss on fruit-trees is usual.y an indication of lack of vigor. Cultivate and prune. Wash the trees with soap or lye washes. Scrape off the bark, exercising care not to expose the "quick," or the tender inner bark. A good scraper is made of a small and much-worn hoe with the handle cut to about two feet long.

The moss is readily destroyed by Bordeaux mixture.

CHAPTER VII.

WAXES FOR GRAFTING AND FOR WOUNDS.

1. **Common resin and beeswax waxes.**
    1. RELIABLE WAX.—Resin, 4 parts by weight; beeswax, 2 parts; tallow, 1 part. Melt together and pour into a pail of cold water. Then grease the hands and pull the wax until it is nearly white. One of the best waxes, either for indoor or outdoor use.
    2. Resin, 4 pounds; beeswax, 1 pound; tallow, 1 pound.
    3. Resin, 6 pounds; beeswax, 2 pounds; linseed oil, 1 pint.
    4. 6 pounds resin, 1 pound beeswax, and 1 pint linseed oil; apply hot with a brush, one-eighth of an inch thick over all the joints.
    5. FOR WARM WEATHER. — 4 pounds of resin, 1 pound of beeswax, and from half to a pint of raw linseed oil; melt all together gradually, and turn into water and pull. The linseed oil should be entirely free from cotton-seed oil.
    6. Resin, 6 parts; beeswax, 1 part; tallow, 1 part. To be used warm, in the house.
    7. Resin, 4 or 5 parts; beeswax, 1½ to 2 parts; linseed oil, 1 to 1½ parts. For outdoor work.
2. **Alcoholic waxes.**
    8. LEFORT'S LIQUID GRAFTING-WAX, or ALCOHOLIC PLASTIC. — Best white resin, 1 pound; beef tallow, 1 ounce; remove from the fire and add 8 ounces of alcohol. Keep in closed bottles or cans.
    9. ALCOHOLIC PLASTIC WITH BEESWAX.—Melt 6 parts white resin with 1 part beeswax; remove from stove and partially cool by stirring, then add gradually—with con-

tinued stirring—enough alcohol to make the mixture, when cool, of the consistency of porridge. In the temperature of the grafting-room it will remain sufficiently plastic to permit applying to the cut surfaces with the finger.

10. ALCOHOLIC PLASTIC WITH TURPENTINE. — Best white resin, 1 pound; beef tallow, 1 ounce; turpentine, 1 teaspoonful; add enough alcohol (13 to 15 fluid ounces of 95 per cent alcohol) to make the wax of the consistency of honey. Or, less alcohol may be added if the wax is to be used with the fingers.

3. **French and pitch waxes.**

11. COMMON FRENCH. — Pitch, $\frac{1}{2}$ pound; beeswax, $\frac{1}{2}$ pound; cow-dung, 1 pound. Boil together, melt, and apply with a brush.

12. COMMON FRENCH BANDAGE WAX. — Equal parts of beeswax, turpentine, and resin. While warm spread on strips of coarse cotton or strong paper.

13. GRAFTING CLAY. — $\frac{1}{3}$ cow-dung, free from straw, and $\frac{2}{3}$ clay, or clayey loam, with a little hair, like that used in plaster, to prevent its cracking. Beat and temper it for two or three days until it is thoroughly incorporated. When used it should be of such a consistency as to be easily put on and shaped with the hands.

14. 2 pounds 12 ounces of resin and 1 pound 11 ounces of Burgundy pitch. At the same time, melt 9 ounces of tallow; pour the latter into the former, while both are hot, and stir the mixture thoroughly. Then add 18 ounces of red ochre, dropping it in gradually and stirring the mixture at the same time.

15. Black pitch, 28 parts; Burgundy pitch, 28 parts; beeswax, 16 parts; grease, 14 parts; yellow ochre, 14 parts.

16. Black pitch, 28 pounds; Burgundy pitch, 28 pounds; yellow wax, 16 pounds; suet or tallow, 14 pounds; sifted ashes, 14 pounds. When used, warm sufficiently to make it liquid.

17. Melt together $1\frac{1}{4}$ pounds of clear resin and $\frac{3}{4}$ pound of white pitch. At the same time melt $\frac{1}{4}$ pound of

tallow. Pour the melted tallow into the first mixture, and stir vigorously. Then, before the stuff cools, add, slowly stirring meantime, ½ pound of Venetian red. This may be used warm or cold.

4. **Waxed string and bandage.**

18. WAXED STRING FOR ROOT-GRAFTING. — Into a kettle of melted wax place balls of No. 18 knitting-cotton. Turn the balls frequently, and in five minutes they will be thoroughly saturated, when they are dried and put away for future use.

This material is strong enough, and at the same time breaks so easily as not to injure the hands. Any of the resin and beeswax waxes may be used. When the string is used it should be warm enough to stick without tying.

19. WAXED CLOTH. — Old calico or thin muslin is rolled on a stick and placed in melted wax. When saturated it is allowed to cool by being unrolled on a bench. It is then cut in strips to suit.

5. **Waxes for wounds.**

20. Any of the more adhesive grafting-waxes are excellent for dressing wounds, although most of them cleave off after the first year. Stiff and ochreous paints are also good. Tar is useful.

21. COAL-TAR. — Apply a coating of coal-tar to the wound, which has first been pared and smoothed. If the wound contains a hole, plug it with seasoned wood.

22. HOSKINS' WAX. — Boil pine-tar slowly for three or four hours ; add ½ pound of beeswax to a quart of the tar. Have ready some dry and finely sifted clay, and when the mixture of tar and wax is partly cold, stir into the above-named quantity about 12 ounces of the clay ; continue the stirring until the mixture is so stiff and so nearly cool that the clay will not settle. This is soft enough in mild weather to be easily applied with a knife or spatula.

23. SCHÆFELL'S HEALING-PAINT. — Boil linseed oil (free from cotton-seed oil) one hour, with an ounce of litharge to each pint of oil ; then stir in sifted wood ashes until the

WAXES FOR GRAFTING AND FOR WOUNDS. 89

paint is of the proper consistency. Pare the bark until smooth, as the fuzzy edge left by the saw will cause it to die back. Paint the wound over in dry weather, and if the wound is very large cover with a gunny-sack.

24. TAR FOR BLEEDING IN VINES. — Add to tar about 3 or 4 times its weight of powdered slate or some similar substance.

25. HOT IRON FOR BLEEDING IN VINES. — Apply a hot iron to the bare surface until it is charred, and then rub into the charred surface a paste made of newly burnt lime and grease.

26. COLLODION FOR BLEEDING IN VINES. — In some extreme cases 2 or 3 coats will be needed, in which case allow the collodion to form a film before applying another coat. Pharmaceutical collodion is better than photographic.

CHAPTER VIII.

CEMENTS, MORTARS, PAINTS, AND GLUES.

1. Cement and mortar.

CEMENTS FOR IRON. —

1. Sal ammoniac, 2 ounces; sulphur, 1 ounce; clean iron-borings or filings reduced to powder, 12 pounds; water enough to form a thin paste.

2. Sal ammoniac, 2 ounces; iron-filings, 8 pounds; sufficient water.

3. 1 or 2 parts of sal ammoniac to 100 of iron-filings. When the work is required to set quickly, increase the sal ammoniac slightly and add a small amount of sulphur.

4. Iron-filings, 4 pounds; pipe-clay, 2 pounds; powdered potsherds, 11 pounds; make into a paste with moderately strong brine.

5. Equal parts of red and white lead, mixed into a paste with boiled linseed oil. Used for making metallic joints of all kinds.

6. To 4 or 5 parts of clay, thoroughly dried and pulverized, add 2 parts of iron-filings, free from oxide, 1 part of peroxide of manganese, $\frac{1}{2}$ of sea salt, and $\frac{1}{2}$ of borax; mix well, and reduce to a thick paste with water. Use immediately. Expose to warmth, gradually increasing almost to white heat.

7. Sifted coal ashes, 2 parts, and common salt, 1 part. Add water enough to make a paste and apply at once. This is also good for stoves and boilers, as it stands heat.

BOILER CEMENTS. —

8. Chalk, 60 parts; lime and salt, of each, 20 parts;

CEMENTS, MORTARS, PAINTS, AND GLUES.

sharp sand, 10 parts; blue or red clay and clean iron-filings, of each, 5 parts. Grind together and calcine or heat.

9. Powdered clay, 6 pounds; iron-filings, 1 pound. Make into a paste with linseed oil.

10. Powdered litharge, 2 parts; silver sand and slaked lime, of each, 1 part; boiled oil enough to form a paste.

These cements are used for stopping leaks and cracks in boilers, iron pipes, stoves, etc. They should be applied as soon as made.

TAR CEMENT.—

11. Coal-tar, 1 part; powdered slate (slate flour), 3 or 4 parts; mix by stirring until thoroughly incorporated. Very useful for mending watering-pots, barrels, leaky sash, etc. It remains somewhat elastic. It does not adhere to greasy surfaces. It will keep for a long time before using.

COPPER CEMENT.—

12. Beef blood thickened with sufficient finely powdered quicklime to make it into a paste is used to secure the edges and rivets of copper boilers, kettles, etc. Use immediately.

FIREPROOF OR STONE CEMENT.—

13. Fine river sand, 20 parts; litharge, 2 parts; quicklime, 1 part; linseed oil enough to form a thick paste. Used for walls and broken stonework.

EARTHENWARE CEMENT.—

14. Grated cheese, 2 parts; powdered quicklime, 1 part; fresh white of egg enough to form a paste. Use as soon as possible.

For fine earthenware, liquid glue may be used.

CEMENT FOR GLASS.—

15. Methylated spirit (wood alcohol) to render liquid a half dozen pieces of gum-mastic the size of a large pea; in another bottle dissolve the same quantity of isinglass, which has been soaked in water and allowed to get surface dry, in 2 ounces of methylated spirit; when the first is dissolved add 2 pieces of gum-galbanum or gum-ammoniac; apply gentle heat and stir; add the solution of isinglass,

heat again and stir. Keep in a tightly stoppered bottle, and when used set in boiling water.

SEALING CEMENTS. —

16. Beeswax, 1 pound; resin, 5 pounds. Stir in sufficient red ochre and Brunswick green, or lampblack, to give the desired color.

17. Black pitch, 6 pounds; ivory-black and whiting, of each, 1 pound. Less attractive than the former.

These are used for sealing up bottles, barrels, etc.

MORTAR FOR HEAVY RUBBLE-WORK OR BRICKWORK. —

18. 1 part of slaked lime, 2 parts of sand, and $\frac{1}{3}$ part of blacksmith's ashes; for brickwork, 1 part of lime, 1 of sand, and 1 of blacksmith's ashes.

2. Approximate Estimates of Mason-Work. —

$3\frac{1}{2}$ barrels of lime are required to cover 100 square yards plastering, two coats.

2 barrels of lime will cover 100 square yards plastering, one coat.

$1\frac{1}{2}$ bushels of hair are needed for 100 square yards plastering.

$1\frac{1}{4}$ yards good sand are required for 100 square yards plastering.

$\frac{1}{3}$ barrel of plaster (stucco) will hard-finish 100 square yards plastering.

1 barrel of best lime will lay 1000 bricks.

2 barrels of lime will lay one cord rubble-stone.

$\frac{1}{2}$ barrel of lime will lay 1 perch rubble-stone. (Estimating $\frac{1}{4}$ cord to perch.)

To every barrel of lime estimate about $\frac{5}{8}$ cubic yard of good sand for plastering and brickwork.

3. Concrete, etc., for floors, borders, and walks.

GROUT FLOOR. —

1. To secure a good grout or cement floor, make a good foundation of small stones or brickbats and cover 3 or 4 inches thick with a thin mortar, made of 2 parts sharp sand and 1 part water-lime.

2. Fresh powdered lime, 2 parts; Portland cement, 1

part; gravel, broken stone, or brick, 6 parts. Mix with water to a liquid consistency, and let it be thrown forcibly, or dropped into its position. It should be well beaten or rammed to render it solid. A "skim" of thin, rich mortar may be placed on top as a finish.

3. Equal parts of gravel, well screened, and clean river or pit sand. With 5 parts of sand and gravel mix 1 part of Portland cement. Mix with water and apply 1 inch thick.

FOR GARDEN BORDERS. —

4. 9 parts gravel and 1 part unslaked lime; slake the lime and cover it with gravel, then add water sufficient to make a very thin mortar. Apply 3 inches deep, allow it to stiffen a little, then roll. Finish with an inch thick of 1 part lime and 3 parts gravel. Apply soft.

FOR WALKS. —

5. Walks should always have a well-made foundation of stones or brickbats to give hardness and insure drainage. The top of the walk may be made of gravel, sifted coal ashes, cinders from foundries, furnaces, etc. If gravel is used, care should be exercised to avoid the round or washed gravel, particularly that lying in the beds of streams, for it will not pack. 1 part of clean clay to 4 or 5 of gravel makes a good walk. Or the following may be used (6-11):

6. 1 part mineral pitch, 1 part resin, 7 parts chalk, and 2 parts coarse sand. Boil together, and lay it while in a hot state, adding a little gravel.

7. Boil for a short time 18 parts of mineral pitch and 18 parts of resin in an iron kettle; then add 60 parts of coarse sand; mix well, and lay on the path to the thickness of 1 inch; then sift a little fine gravel over it and beat it down before the cement sets.

8. Put down a coat of tar and sift some road sand or coal ashes over it very thickly. When this is dry, repeat the operation until you have four coats of tar and as many of coal ashes or road sand.

9. 2 parts of thoroughly dried sand, 1 part cinders,

thoroughly dried. Mix together; then spread the sand and cinders on the ground and make a hole in the centre, into which pour boiling-hot tar and mix into a stiff paste; then spread on the walk, beat, and roll.

10. 2 parts lime rubbish and 1 part coal ashes, both very dry and finely sifted; in the middle of the heap make a hole; into this pour boiling-hot coal-tar; mix to a stiff mortar and spread on the ground 2 or 3 inches thick. The ground should be dry and beaten well. Cover with coarse sand; when cold, roll well.

11. Artificial stone walks of great durability may be made as follows: Upon a well-drained foundation (preferably one of stone, which cannot heave with frost), place 4 inches of a well-mixed mortar made of 3 parts Portland cement and 1 part water-lime, with 2 or 3 times the quantity of sand as of Portland. Before this is set, put on a finishing layer of 1 inch of 1 part Portland, 1 part water-lime, and 1 part sharp sand.

4. **Paints and protective compounds.**

HOME-MADE WASHES FOR FENCES AND OUT-BUILDINGS may be made by various combinations of lime and grease. The following are good formulas:

1. Slake fresh quicklime in water, and thin it to a paste or paint with skim-milk. The addition of 2 or 3 handfuls of salt to a pail of the wash is beneficial.

2. 2 quarts skim-milk, 8 ounces of fresh slaked lime, 6 ounces of boiled linseed oil, and 2 ounces of white pitch, dissolved in the oil by a gentle heat. The lime must be slaked in cold water and dried in the air until it falls into a fine powder; then mix with $\frac{1}{4}$ part of the milk, adding the mixed oil and pitch by degrees; add the remainder of the milk. Lastly, add 3 pounds of the best whiting and mix the whole thoroughly.

3. Slake $\frac{1}{2}$ bushel of lime in boiling water, keeping it covered; strain and add brine made by dissolving 1 peck of salt in warm water, and 3 pounds rice flour, then boil to a paste; add $\frac{1}{2}$ pound whiting and 1 pound of glue dis-

CEMENTS, MORTARS, PAINTS, AND GLUES. 95

solved in warm water. Mix and let stand for a few days before using.

FIRE-PROOF PAINT. —

4. In a covered vessel slake the best quicklime, then add a mixture of skim-milk and water, and mix to the consistency of cream; then add 20 pounds of alum, 15 pounds of potash and 1 bushel of salt to every 100 gallons of the liquid. If white paint is desired, add to the above 6 pounds of plaster of Paris.

FOR DAMP WALLS. —

5. ¾ pounds of hard soap to 1 gallon of water. Lay over the bricks steadily and carefully with a flat brush, so as not to form a froth or lather on the surface. After 24 hours mix ½ pound of alum with 4 gallons of water; let it stand 24 hours, and then apply it in the same manner over the coating of soap. Apply in dry weather.

6. 1½ pounds resin, 1 pound tallow, 1 quart linseed oil. Melt together and apply hot, two coats.

WATER-PROOFING PAINTS. — FOR LEATHER. —

7. ½ pound of shellac, broken into small pieces in a quart bottle; cover with methylated spirit (wood alcohol), cork it tight, put it in a warm place, and shake well several times a day; then add a piece of camphor as large as a hen's egg; shake again and add 1 ounce of lampblack. Apply with a small paint-brush.

8. Put into an earthen jar ¼ pound of beeswax, ½ pint of neat's-foot oil, 3 or 4 tablespoonfuls of lampblack, and a piece of camphor as large as a hen's egg. Melt over a slow fire. Have both grease and leather warm and apply with a brush.

9. 1 pint of linseed oil, ½ pound mutton suet, 6 ounces of clean beeswax, and 4 ounces of resin; melt and mix well. Use while warm with a brush on new boots or shoes.

FOR CLOTH FOR PITS AND FRAMES. —

10. Old pale linseed oil, 3 pints; sugar of lead (acetate of lead), 1 ounce; white resin, 4 ounces. Grind the acetate with a little of the oil, then add the rest and the resin.

Use an iron kettle over a gentle fire. Apply with a brush, hot.

FOR PAPER. —

11. Dissolve 1¾ pounds of white soap in 1 quart of water; in another quart of water dissolve 1½ ounces of gum arabic and 5 ounces of glue. Mix the two liquids, warm them and soak the paper in it and pass through rollers, or simply hang it up to dry.

TO PREVENT METALS FROM RUSTING. —

12. Melt together 3 parts of lard and 1 part of powdered resin. A very thin coating applied with a brush will keep stoves and grates from rusting during summer, even in damp situations. A little black lead can be mixed with the lard. Does well on nearly all metals.

TO PREVENT RUSTING OF NAILS, HINGES, ETC. —

13. 1 pint of linseed oil, 2 ounces black lead ; mix together. Heat nails red-hot and dip them in.

AMOUNT OF PAINT REQUIRED FOR A GIVEN SURFACE. — It is impossible to give a rule that will apply in all cases, as the amount varies with the kind and thickness of the paint, the kind of wood or other material to which it is applied, the age of the surface, etc. The following is an approximate rule : Divide the number of square feet of surface by 200. The result will be the number of gallons of liquid paint required to give two coats; or divide by 18, and the result will be the number of pounds of pure ground white lead required to give three coats.

5. Glues.

LIQUID GLUE. —

1. Dissolve 2 pounds of best pale glue in 1 quart of water in a covered vessel, placed in a hot-water bath; when cold, add to it 7 ounces of commercial nitric acid. When cold put in bottles.

2. Finest pale orange shellac, broken small, 4 ounces ; methylated spirit, 3 ounces ; put in a warm place in a closely corked bottle until dissolved. Should have the consistency of molasses. Or, borax, 1 ounce ; water, ¾ pint ; shellac as

CEMENTS, MORTARS, PAINTS, AND GLUES.

before; boil in a closely covered kettle until dissolved; then evaporate until nearly as thick as molasses.

FLOWER GUM. —

3. Very fine white shellac mixed with methylated spirit in a stone jar; shake well for $\frac{1}{2}$ an hour and place by a fire, and shake it frequently the first day. Keep in a cool place. Leave the camel's-hair brush in the gum. Never fill the brush too full and gum the petals close to the tube.

GUM FOR LABELS AND SPECIMENS. —

4. 2 parts of gum arabic, 1 part of brown sugar; dissolve in water to the consistency of cream.

5. 5 parts of best glue soaked in 18 to 20 parts of water for a day, and to the liquid add 9 parts of rock candy and 3 parts of gum arabic.

6. Good flour and glue, to which add linseed oil, varnish, and turpentine, $\frac{1}{2}$ ounce each to the pound. Good when labels are liable to get damp.

CHAPTER IX.

SEED-TABLES.

1. Quantity of Seed required to sow an Acre.

Asparagus		4 or 5 lbs., or 1 oz. for 50 ft. of drill.
Beans, Dwarf	in drills	1½ bu.
" Pole	"	10 to 12 qts.
Beet	"	5 to 6 lbs.
Buckwheat	"	1 bu.
Cabbage	in beds to transplant	¼ lb.
Carrot	in drills	2 to 4 lbs.
Cauliflower	1 oz. of seed for 1000 plants	
Celery	1 oz. for 2000 plants	
Clover	for orchards	8 to 16 lbs.
" Crimson	for orchards and vineyards	8 to 16 lbs.
Corn	in hills	8 to 10 qts.
Cow-pea	broadcast	2 bu.
Cucumber	in hills	2 lbs.
Cress, Water	in drills	2 to 3 lbs.
" Upland	"	2 to 3 lbs.
Egg-plant	1 oz. of seed for 1000 plants	
Grass	for lawns	2 to 4 bu.
Kale, or Sprouts		3 to 4 lbs.
Lettuce	1 oz. of seed for 1000 plants	
Melon, Musk	in hills	2 to 3 lbs.
" Water	"	4 to 5 lbs.
Mustard	broadcast	½ bu.
Onion	in drills	5 to 6 lbs.
" Seed for Sets	"	30 lbs.
" Sets	"	6 to 12 bu.

SEED-TABLES.

Orchard Grass		20 to 30 lbs.
Parsnip	in drills	4 to 6 lbs.
Peas	"	1 to 2 bu.
"	broadcast	2 to 3 bu.
Potato (cut-tubers)		7 to 8 bu.
Pumpkin	in hills	4 to 5 lbs.
Radish	in drills	8 to 10 lbs.
Rye	for orchards	1 to 1½ bu.
Sage	in drills	8 to 10 lbs.
Salsify	"	8 to 10 lbs.
Spinage	"	10 to 12 lbs.
Squash, Bush	in hills	4 to 6 lbs.
" Running	"	3 to 4 lbs.
Tomato	to transplant	¼ lb.
Turnip	in drills	1 to 2 lbs.
"	broadcast	3 to 4 lbs.
Vetch		1 bu.

2. Average Time required for Garden Seeds to germinate.

	Days.		Days.
Bean	5–10	Lettuce	6–8
Beet	7–10	Onion	7–10
Cabbage	5–10	Pea	6–10
Carrot	12–18	Parsnip	10–20
Cauliflower	5–10	Pepper	9–14
Celery	10–20	Radish	3–6
Corn	5–8	Salsify	7–12
Cucumber	6–10	Tomato	6–12
Endive	5–10	Turnip	4–8

3. Weight and Size of Garden Seeds.

Adapted from Vilmorin's Tables.

	Weight of a qt. of seeds in ozs.	Number of seeds in 1 grain.
Angelica	5.825	11.01
Anise	11.65	12.96

100 HORTICULTURIST'S RULE-BOOK.

	Weight of a qt. of seeds in ozs.	Number of seeds in 1 grain.
Asparagus Bean (*Dolichos sesquipedalis*)	29.90	32.40 to 42.12
Balm	21.35	129.60
Basil	20.58	51.84
Bean	24.26 to 33.01	4.86 to 5.18 in 100 gr.
Beet	9.71	3.24
Borage	18.74	4.21
Borecole	27.18	19.44
Broccoli	27.18	24.30
Cabbage	27.18	19.44
Caper	17.86	10.37
Caraway	16.34	22.08
Cardoon	24.46	1.62
Carrot with the spines	9.32	45.36
" without the spines	13.98	61.56
Catmint	30.29	77.76
Cauliflower	27.18	24.30
Celery	18.64	162.00
Chervil	14.76	29.16
" Sweet-scented	9.71	2.50
" Turnip-rooted	20.97	29.16
Chicory	15.54	45.36
Chick-pea	30.29	1.94 in 10 gr.
Coriander	12.43	5.83
Corn-salad	10.87	64.80
Cress, American	20.97	61.56
" Common Garden	28.35	29.16
" Meadow (Cuckoo-flower)	22.52	97.20
" Para	7.77	220.32
" Water	22.52	259.20
Cucumber, Common	19.42	2.14
" Globe	19.42	6.48
" Prickly-fruited Gherkin	21.36	8.42

SEED—TABLES. 101

	Weight of a qt. of seeds in ozs.	Number of seeds in 1 grain.
Cucumber, Snake (*Cucumis flexuosus*)	17.48	2.59
Dandelion	10.49	77.76 to 97.20
Dill	11.65	58.32
Egg-plant	19.42	16.20
Endive	13.20	38.88
Fennel, Common or Wild	17.48	20.09
" Sweet	9.13	8.10
Gumbo, see OKRA.		
Good King Henry	24.27	27.86
Gourds, Fancy	17.48	1.29
Hop	9.71	12.96
Horehound	26.41	64.80
Hyssop	22.33	55.08
Kohlrabi	27.18	19.44
Leek	21.36	25.92
Lettuce	16.69	51.84
Lovage	7.77	19.44
Maize, or Indian Corn	24.85	2.59 to 3.24 in 10 gr.
Marjoram, Sweet	21.35	259.20
" Winter	26.15	777.60
Martynia	11.26	1.29
Muskmelon	13.08	3.56
Mustard, Black or Brown	26.15	45.36
" Chinese Cabbage-leaved	25.63	42.12
" White, or Salad	29.12	12.96
Nasturtium, Tall	13.20	4.54 to 5.18 in 10 gr.
" Dwarf	23.30	9.7 in 10 gr.
Okra	24.08	9.7 to 11.66 in 10 gr.
Onion	19.42	16.20
Orach	5.44	16.20
Pea	27.18 to 31.07	1.29 to 3.56 in 10 gr.
" Gray or Field	26.41 to 31.07	3.24 to 5.18 in 10 gr.
Peanut	15.53	1.29 to 1.94 in 10 gr.

	Weight of a qt. of seeds in ozs.	Number of seeds in 1 grain.
Pepper	17.48	9.72
Pumpkin	9.71	1.94 in 10 gr.
Purslane	23.69	162.00
Radish	27.18	7.77
Rampion	31.07	1620.00
Rhubarb	3.10 to 4.66	3.24
Rocket Salad	29.12	35.64
Rosemary	15.54	58.32
Rue	22.52	32.40
Sage	21.36	16.20
Salsify	8.93	6.48
Savory, Summer	19.42	97.20
" Winter	16.69	162.00
Scorzonera	10.09	5.83
Scurvy-grass	23.30	97.20 to 116.64
Sea-kale	8.16	9.72 to 11.66 in 10 gr.
Spinage, Prickly-seeded	14.56	5.83
" Round-seeded	19.80	7.13
" New Zealand	8.67	6.48 to 7.77 in 10 gr.
Squash, Bush-scallop	16.69	6.48
Strawberry	23.30	51.84 to 162.00
" Blite (*Blitum*)	31.07	324.00
" Tomato (*Physalis*)	25.24	64.80
Sweet Cicely	9.71	2.59
Tansy	11.65	453.60
Thyme	26.41	388.80
Tomato	11.65	19.44 to 25.92
Turnip	26.02	29.16
Valerian, African	4.27	16.20
Watermelon	17.86	3.24 to 3.88 in 10 gr.
Wax Gourd	11.65	1.36
Welsh Onion, Common	18.64	19.44
" Early White	22.91	32.40
Wormwood	25.24	745.20

SEED-TABLES. 103

1. Number of Tree-Seeds in a Pound.

FRUIT TREES.

	About.
Apple	12,000
Cherry Pits	1,000
Peach	200
Pear	15,000
Plum	600
Quince	15,000
Mulberry	200,000

FOREST TREES.

		By count.
Butternut	Juglans cinerea	15
Black Walnut	Juglans nigra	25
American Horse-Chestnut	Æsculus glabra	36
Hickory (Shellbark)	Carya alba	78
American Sweet Chestnut	Castanea vesca, var.	90
Silver-leaved Maple	Acer dascycarpum	2,421
Honey-locust	Gleditschia triacanthos	2,496
Black Cherry	Prunus serotina	4,311
Black Ash	Fraxinus sambucifolia	5,629
American Basswood	Tilia Americana	6,337
Norway Maple	Acer platanoides	7,231
Sugar Maple	Acer saccharinum	7,488
Barberry	Berberis vulgaris	8,183
Red Cedar	Juniperus Virginiana	8,321
Rock Elm	Ulmus racemosa	8,352
American White Ash	Fraxinus Americana	9,858
Osage Orange	Maclura aurantiaca	10,656
Silver Fir	Abies pectinata	12,000
Box Elder	Negundo aceroides	14,784
Hardy Catalpa	Catalpa speciosa	19,776
Ailanthus	Ailanthus glandulosus	20,161
White Pine	Pinus Strobus	20,540
Scarlet Maple	Acer rubrum	22,464

		By count.
Green Ash	Fraxinus viridis	22,656
Black Locust	Robinia Pseudacacia	28,992
Red Elm	Ulmus fulva	54,359
American White Elm	Ulmus Americana	92,352
American Mountain Ash	Pyrus Americana	108,327
White Birch	Betula alba	500,000

5. Longevity of Garden Seeds.

Adapted from Vilmorin's Tables.

The plus sign denotes that the seeds had not all lost their germinating power at the termination of the number of years recorded.

	Average years.	Extreme years.
Angelica	1 or 2	3
Anise	3	5
Asparagus Bean (*Dolichos sesquipedalis*)	3	8
Balm	4	7
Basil	8	10+
Bean	3	8
Beet	6	10+
Borage	8	10+
Borecole	5	10
Broccoli	5	10
Cabbage	5	10
Caraway	3	4
Cardoon	7	9
Carrot, with the spines	4 or 5	10+
" without the spines	4 or 5	10+
Catmint	6	10+
Cauliflower	5	10
Celery	8	10
Chervil	2 or 3	6
" Sweet-scented	1	1
" Turnip-rooted	1	1

SEED-TABLES.

	Average years.	Extreme years.
Chicory	8	10+
Chick-pea	3	8
Coriander	6	8
Corn-salad, Common	5	10
Cress, American	3	5
" Common Garden	5	9
" Meadow (Cuckoo-flower)	4	(?)
" Para	5	7+
" Water	5	9
Cucumber, Common	10	10+
" Globe	6	(?)
" Prickly-fruited Gherkin	6	7+
" Snake (*Cucumis flexuosus*)	7 or 8	10+
Dandelion	2	5
Dill	3	5
Egg-plant	6	10
Endive	10	10+
Fennel, Common or Wild	4	7
" Sweet	4	7
Gumbo, see OKRA.		
Good King Henry	3	5
Gourds, Fancy	6	10+
Hop	2	4
Horehound	3	6
Hyssop	3	5
Kohlrabi	5	10
Leek	3	9
Lettuce, Common	5	9
Lovage	3	4
Maize, or Indian Corn	2	4
Marjoram, Sweet	3	7
" Winter	5	7
Martynia	1 or 2	(?)
Muskmelon	5	10+
Mustard, Black or Brown	4	9

	Average years.	Extreme years.
Mustard, Chinese Cabbage-leaved	4	8
" White or Salad	4	10
Nasturtium, Tall	5	5
" Dwarf	5	8
Okra	5	10+
Onion	2	7
Orach	6	7
Parsnip	2	4
Parsley	3	9
Pea, Garden	3	8
" Gray or Field	3	8
Pepper	4	7
Pumpkin	4 or 5	9
Purslane	7	10
Radish	5	10+
Rampion	5	10+
Rhubarb	3	8
Rocket Salad	4	9
Rosemary	4	(?)
Rue	2	5
Sage	3	7
Salsify	2	8
Savory, Summer	3	7
" Winter	3	6
Scorzonera	2	7
Scurvy-grass	4	7
Sea-kale	1	7
Spinage, Prickly-seeded	5	7
" Round-seeded	5	7
" New Zealand	5	8
Squash, Bush-scallop	6	10+
Strawberry	3	6
" Tomato (*Physalis*)	8	10+
Sweet Cicely	1	1
Tansy	2	4

SEED—TABLES. 107

	Average years.	Extreme years.
Thyme	3	7
Tomato	4	9
Turnip	5	10+
Valerian, African	4	7
Watermelon	6	10
Wax Gourd	10	10+
Welsh Onion, Common	2 or 3	7
" Early White	3	8
Wormwood	4	6

6. Average Yields of Seed-Crops.

	When crop is as good as 20 bu. of wheat per acre would be.	When crop is very heavy.
Bean	600 lbs. per acre	1500 lbs. per acre
Pea	900 " "	2500 " "
Squash, Summer,	100 " "	700 " "
" Winter	100 " "	400 " "
Sweet Corn	1000 to 2500 " " (according to variety)	2500 to 4000 " "
Cucumber	150 " "	700 " "
Muskmelon	125 " "	600 " "
Watermelon	150 " "	1000 " "
Tomato	100 " "	400 " "
Cabbage	250 " "	800 " "

The average crop is probably 10 to 20 per cent less than the figures given in the first column.

CHAPTER X.

PLANTING-TABLES.

1. Dates for Sowing or Setting Kitchen-Garden Vegetables in Different Latitudes.

(1) LANSING, MICHIGAN.

Average of 4 and 5 years.

Bean, Bush	May 16.
" Pole	May 30.
Beet	April 20.
Broccoli	May 10.
Brussels Sprouts	May 10.
Cabbage, Early, under glass	March 15.
Cabbage, Late	May 20.
Carrot	May 7.
Cauliflower, under glass	March 15.
Celery, under glass	March 18.
" in open ground	May 20.
Corn	May 19.
Cucumber	May 23.
Egg-plant, under glass	March 15.
Kale	May 9.
Kohlrabi	May 9.
Lettuce	May 5.
Melon	May 30.
Okra	May 15.
Onion	April 17.
Parsnips	May 7.
Peas	April 15.

PLANTING-TABLES. 109

Pepper, under glass . . . . March 16.
Potato . . . . May 3.
Pumpkin . . . . May 31.
Radish . . . . April 26.
Salsify . . . . May 7.
Spinage . . . . April 10.
Squash . . . . May 28.
Tomato, under glass . . . . March 13.
Turnip . . . . April 15.

(2) BOSTON. (*Rawson.*)

Asparagus . . . . . . About the end of April.
Bean, Bush . . . . . . About the first week in May.
Bean, Pole . . . . . . From about the middle of May to the 1st of June.
Bean, Lima . . . . . . About the 1st of June.
Beet . . . . About the middle of April.
Borecole, or Kale . . . About the middle of April; plant out in June.
Brussels Sprouts . . . In March or April in hotbed.
Cabbage . . . . Transplant the last week in April or the 1st in May.
Carrots . . . . Last of May or 1st of June.
Cauliflower . . . . . . From the 1st of May until the 1st of July.
Celery . . . . The 1st week in April to the 2d in July. •
Corn, Sweet . . . . . About the 1st of May.
Cucumber . . . . . . For 1st crop, about the middle of March.
Egg-plant . . . . . . About March 15th in hotbed.
Endive . . . . June or July.
Kohlrabi . . . . May or June.
Okra . . . . About the 10th of May.
Peas . . . . During the last of April up to the 1st of May,

Pepper . . . . . . Put out of doors about the 1st of April.
Radish . . . . . . From the 1st of April to the middle of June.
Spinage . . . . . . About the 1st of September.
Tomato . . . . . . About the 25th of May set plants outdoors.
Turnips, for fall use . . Any time from July 1st to August 20th.
Watermelon . . . . About the middle of May.

(3) NEW YORK. (*Henderson.*)

Plants to sow from the middle of March to the end of April. Thermometer in the shade averaging 45 degrees.

Beet.	Cauliflower.	Parsley.
Carrot.	Endive.	Peas.
Cress.	Kale.	Radish.
Celery.	Lettuce.	Spinage.
Cabbage.	Onions.	Turnip.
	Parsnip.	

From the middle of May to the middle of June. Thermometer in the shade averaging 60 degrees.

Bean, Bush.	Bean, Runner.	Nasturtium.
Bean, Cranberry.	Corn, Sweet.	Okra.
Bean, Lima.	Cucumber.	Pumpkin.
Bean, Pole.	Melon, Musk.	Squash.
Bean, Scarlet.	Melon, Water.	Tomato.

(4) NORFOLK, VIRGINIA.

Months in which different crops are planted or sown, or set out in the open air.

Kale and Spinach Sown during August, September, and October.
Cabbage . . . The seeds are sown in August and September, and the plants are transplanted in the open air in November and December.

PLANTING-TABLES. 111

Onions	Sown in August, September, January, and February.
Leeks	The same as onions.
Lettuce	Sown in September and January.
Radish	Sown in every month in the year.
Peas	December, January, February, March, April, August, and September.
Beans	March and April.
Egg-plant	April and May.
Tomatoes	April and May.
Squash	April.
Cauliflower	March and April.
Potatoes	February, March, and July.
Sweet Potatoes	May.
Beets	February and March.
Corn	April, May, June, and July.
Oats	September, October, November, December, February, and March.
Millet	June and July; after potatoes.
Grass-seed	September, October, November, February, and March.
Carrots	February and March.
Celery	April and May.
Cucumbers	April.
Watermelons	April.
Canteloupes	April.
Peanuts	May.

(5) GEORGIA. (*Oemler.*)

Asparagus	From December 1st to the middle of March.
Bean, Bush	From the 1st to the middle of March.
Beet	Through November and December.
Cabbage	From the 1st of October to the 15th. Transplant about November 1st and later.
Cauliflower	From May to September.
Cucumber	About March 1st to the 15th.

Egg-plant . . . To prick out, about the middle of January, otherwise ten or fifteen days later.
Lettuce . . . . About the middle of September.
Onion . . . . . About January 1st.
Pea. . . . . . About December 1st.
Potato . . . . The 1st of February.
Radish . . . . From Christmas to the last of February.
Spinage . . . . From September 10th until October 15th.
Squash . . . . About the last of February up to the middle of March.
Sweet Potato . In cold frames, about the 1st of January.
Tomato . . . . About January 1st.
Watermelon . . About the 15th of March.

2. Tender and Hardy Vegetables.

Vegetables injured by a slight frost, and which should therefore be planted only after the weather has settled.

All Beans.	Egg-plant.	Pumpkin.
Corn.	All Melons.	Squash.
Cucumber.	Okra.	Sweet Potato.
	Pepper.	Tomato.

Vegetables which, when properly handled, will endure a frost.

Asparagus.	Corn-salad.	Parsley.
Beet.	Cress.	Parsnip.
Borecole.	Endive.	Pea.
Broccoli.	Horseradish.	Radish.
Brussels Sprouts.	Kale.	Rhubarb.
Cabbage.	Kohlrabi.	Salsify.
Carrot.	Leek.	Sea-kale.
Cauliflower.	Lettuce.	Spinage.
Celery.	All Onions.	Turnip.

3. Usual Distances apart for planting Fruits.

Apples . . . . 30 to 40 feet each way.
" Dwarf . . . . 10 " 15 " " "

PLANTING-TABLES.

Pears	20	to	30	feet each way.	
" Dwarf	10	"	15	" "	"
Plums	16	"	20	" "	"
Peaches	16	"	20	" "	"
Cherries	16	"	25	" "	"
Apricots	16	"	20	" "	"
Nectarines	16	"	20	" "	"
Quinces	8	"	14	" "	"
Figs	20	"	25	" "	"
Mulberries	25	"	30	" "	"
Japanese Persimmons	20	"	25	" "	"
Loquats	15	"	25	" "	"
Pecans	35	"	40	" "	"
Grapes	8	"	12	" "	"
Currants	4 × 5 feet.				
Gooseberries	4 × 5 "				
Raspberries, Black	3 × 6 "				
" Red	3 × 5 "				
Blackberries	4 × 7 to 6 × 8 feet.				
Cranberries	1 or 2 ft. apart each way.				
Strawberries	1 × 3 or 4 feet.				
Oranges and Lemons	25 to 30 feet each way.				

Distances recommended for Orange Trees in California.

Dwarfs, as Tangerines	10	to	12	feet.
Half-dwarfs, as Washington Navel .	24	"	30	"
Mediterranean Sweet, Maltese Blood, Valencia	24	"	30	"
St. Michael	18	"	24	"
Seedlings	30	"	40	"

4. Usual Distances apart for planting Vegetables.

Artichoke . . Rows 3 or 4 ft. apart, 2 to 3 ft. apart in the row.

Asparagus . . Rows 3 to 4 ft. apart, 1 to 2 ft. apart in the row.

Beans, Bush	1 ft. apart in rows 2 to 3 ft. apart.
" Pole	3 to 4 ft. each way.
Beet, Early	In drills 12 to 18 in. apart.
" Late	In drills 2 to 3 ft. apart.
Broccoli	$1\frac{1}{2} \times 2\frac{1}{2}$ ft. to 2×3 ft.
Cabbage, Early	16×28 in. to 18×30 in.
" Late	2×3 ft. to $2\frac{1}{2} \times 3\frac{1}{2}$ ft.
Carrot	In drills 1 to 2 ft. apart.
Cauliflower	2×2 ft. to 2×3 ft.
Celery	Rows 3 to 4 ft. apart, 6 to 9 in. in the row; "new celery culture," 7×7 in., each way.
Corn-salad	In drills 12 to 18 in. apart.
Corn, Sweet	Rows 3 to $3\frac{1}{2}$ ft. apart, 9 in. to 2 ft. in the row.
Cress	In drills 10 to 12 in. apart.
Cucumber	4 to 5 ft. each way.
Egg-plant	3×3 ft.
Endive	1×1 ft. to $1 \times 1\frac{1}{2}$ ft.
Horseradish	1×2 or 3 ft.
Kohlrabi	10×18 in. to 1×2 ft.
Leek	6 in. $\times$ 1 or $1\frac{1}{2}$ ft.
Lettuce	$1 \times 1\frac{1}{2}$ or 2 ft.
Melons, Musk	5 to 6 ft. each way.
" Water	7 to 8 ft. each way.
Mushroom	6 to 8 in. each way.
Okra	$1\frac{1}{2} \times 2$ or 3 ft.
Onion	In drills from 14 to 20 in. apart.
Parsley	In drills 1 to 2 ft. apart.
Parsnip	In drills, 18 in. to 3 ft. apart.
Peas	In drills; early kinds, usually in double rows, 6 to 9 in. apart; late kinds, in single rows, 2 to 3 ft. apart.
Pepper	15 to 18 in. $\times$ 2 to $2\frac{1}{2}$ ft.
Potato	10 to 18 in. $\times$ $2\frac{1}{2}$ to 3 ft.
Pumpkin	8 to 10 ft. each way.
Radish	In drills, 10 to 18 in. apart.
Rhubarb	2 to 4 ft. $\times$ 4 ft.

PLANTING-TABLES. 115

Salsify . . . In drills, 1½ to 2 ft. apart.
Sea-kale . . . 2 × 2 to 3 ft.
Spinage . . . In drills, 12 to 18 in. apart.
Squash, Bush . 3 to 4 ft. × 4 ft.
" Late . 6 to 8 ft. each way.
Sweet Potato . 2 ft. × 3 to 4 ft.
Tomato . . . 4 ft. × 4 to 5 ft.
Turnip . . . In drills, 1½ to 2¼ ft. apart.

5. Number of Plants Required to Set an Acre of Ground at Given Distances.

	Plants.		Plants.
1 in. × 1 in.	6,272,640	3 in. × 5 in.	418,175
1 " × 2 "	3,136,320	3 " × 6 "	348,480
1 " × 3 "	2,090,880	3 " × 7 "	298,697
1 " × 4 "	1,568,160	3 " × 8 "	261,360
1 " × 5 "	1,254,528	3 " × 9 "	232,320
1 " × 6 "	1,045,440	3 " ×10 "	209,088
1 " × 7 "	896,091	3 " ×11 "	190,080
1 " × 8 "	784,080	3 " ×12 "	174,240
1 " × 9 "	696,960	4 " × 4 "	392,040
1 " ×10 "	627,269	4 " × 5 "	313,632
1 " ×11 "	570,240	4 " × 6 "	261,360
1 " ×12 "	522,720	4 " × 7 "	224,022
2 " × 2 "	1,568,160	4 " × 8 "	196,020
2 " × 3 "	1,045,440	4 " × 9 "	174,240
2 " × 4 "	784,080	4 " ×10 "	156,816
2 " × 5 "	627,264	4 " ×11 "	142,560
2 " × 6 "	522,720	4 " ×12 "	130,680
2 " × 7 "	448,045	5 " × 5 "	250,905
2 " × 8 "	392,040	5 " × 6 "	209,088
2 " × 9 "	348,480	5 " × 7 "	179,218
2 " ×10 "	313,632	5 " × 8 "	156,816
2 " ×11 "	285,120	5 " × 9 "	139,392
2 " ×12 "	261,360	5 " ×10 "	125,452
3 " × 3 "	696,960	5 " ×11 "	114,048
3 " × 4 "	522,720	5 " ×12 "	104,544

	Plants.		Plants.
6 in. × 6 in.	174,240	12 in. × 18 in.	29,040
6 " × 7 "	149,348	12 " × 20 "	26,136
6 " × 8 "	130,680	12 " or 1 ft. } × 24 " or 2 ft.	21,780
6 " × 9 "	116,160		
6 " × 10 "	104,544	12 in. × 30 "	17,424
6 " × 11 "	95,040	12 " × 36 " or 3 ft.	14,520
6 " × 12 "	87,120	12 " × 42 "	12,446
7 " × 7 "	128,013	12 " × 48 " or 4 ft.	10,890
7 " × 8 "	112,011	12 " × 54 "	9,680
7 " × 9 "	99,562	12 " × 60 " or 5 ft.	8,712
7 " × 10 "	89,609	15 " × 15 "	27,878
7 " × 11 "	81,462	15 " × 18 "	23,232
7 " × 12 "	74,674	15 " × 20 "	20,908
8 " × 8 "	98,010	15 " × 24 " or 2 ft.	17,424
8 " × 9 "	87,120	15 " × 30 "	13,939
8 " × 10 "	78,408	15 " × 36 " or 3 ft.	11,616
8 " × 11 "	71,280	15 " × 42 "	9,953
8 " × 12 "	65,340	15 " × 48 " or 4 ft.	8,712
9 " × 9 "	77,440	15 " × 54 "	7,744
9 " × 10 "	69,696	15 " × 60 " or 5 ft.	6,969
9 " × 11 "	63,360	18 " × 18 "	19,360
9 " × 12 "	58,080	18 " × 20 "	17,424
10 " × 10 "	62,726	18 " × 24 " or 2 ft.	14,520
10 " × 12 "	52,272	18 " × 30 "	11,616
10 " × 15 "	41,817	18 " × 36 " or 3 ft.	9,680
10 " × 18 "	34,848	18 " × 42 "	8,297
10 " × 20 "	31,362	18 " × 48 " or 4 ft.	7,260
10 " × 24 " or 2 ft.	26,132	18 " × 54 "	6,453
10 " × 30 "	20,908	18 " × 60 " or 5 ft.	5,808
10 " × 36 " or 3 ft.	17,424	20 " × 20 "	15,681
10 " × 42 "	14,935	20 " × 24 " or 2 ft.	13,168
10 " × 48 " or 4 ft.	13,068	20 " × 30 "	10,454
10 " × 54 "	11,616	20 " × 36 " or 3 ft.	8,712
10 " × 60 " or 5 ft.	10,454	20 " × 42 "	7,467
12 " × 12 "	43,560	20 " × 48 " or 4 ft.	6,534
12 " × 15 "	34,848	20 " × 54 "	5,308

PLANTING-TABLES. 117

		Plants.			Plants.
20 in. × 60 in. or 5 ft.		5,227	4 ft. × 6 ft.		1,185
1 ft. × 1 ft.		43,560	4 " × 7 "		1,556
1 " × 2 "		21,780	4 " × 8 "		1,361
1 " × 3 "		14,520	4 " × 9 "		1,210
1 " × 4 "		10,890	4 " × 10 "		1,089
1 " × 5 "		8,712	4 " × 11 "		990
1 " × 6 "		7,260	4 " × 12 "		907
1 " × 7 "		6,223	5 " × 5 "		1,742
1 " × 8 "		5,445	5 " × 6 "		1,452
1 " × 9 "		4,840	5 " × 7 "		1,244
1 " × 10 "		4,356	5 " × 8 "		1,089
1 " × 11 "		3,960	5 " × 9 "		968
1 " × 12 "		3,630	5 " × 10 "		871
2 " × 2 "		10,890	5 " × 11 "		792
2 " × 3 "		7,260	5 " × 12 "		726
2 " × 4 "		5,445	6 " × 6 "		1,210
2 " × 5 "		4,356	6 " × 7 "		1,037
2 " × 6 "		3,630	6 " × 8 "		907
2 " × 7 "		3,111	6 " × 9 "		806
2 " × 8 "		2,722	6 " × 10 "		726
2 " × 9 "		2,420	6 " × 11 "		660
2 " × 10 "		2,178	6 " × 12 "		605
2 " × 11 "		1,980	7 " × 7 "		888
2 " × 12 "		1,815	7 " × 8 "		777
3 " × 3 "		4,840	7 " × 9 "		691
3 " × 4 "		3,630	7 " × 10 "		622
3 " × 5 "		2,904	7 " × 11 "		565
3 " × 6 "		2,420	7 " × 12 "		518
3 " × 7 "		2,074	8 " × 8 "		680
3 " × 8 "		1,815	8 " × 9 "		605
3 " × 9 "		1,613	8 " × 10 "		544
3 " × 10 "		1,452	8 " × 11 "		495
3 " × 11 "		1,320	8 " × 12 "		453
3 " × 12 "		1,210	9 " × 9 "		537
4 " × 4 "		2,722	9 " × 10 "		484
4 " × 5 "		2,178	9 " × 11 "		440

		Plants.			Plants.
9 ft. × 12 ft.	. . . .	403	15 ft. × 48 ft.	. . . .	60
9 " × 14 "	. . . .	345	15 " × 54 "	. . . .	53
9 " × 15 "	. . . .	322	15 " × 60 "	. . . .	48
9 " × 18 "	. . . .	268	18 " × 18 "	. . . .	134
9 " × 20 "	. . . .	242	18 " × 20 "	. . . .	121
10 " × 10 "	. . . .	435	18 " × 24 "	. . . .	100
10 " × 12 "	. . . .	363	18 " × 30 "	. . . .	80
10 " × 15 "	. . . .	290	18 " × 36 "	. . . .	67
10 " × 18 "	. . . .	242	18 " × 42 "	. . . .	57
10 " × 20 "	. . . .	217	18 " × 48 "	. . . .	50
10 " × 24 "	. . . .	181	18 " × 54 "	. . . .	44
10 " × 30 "	. . . .	145	18 " × 60 "	. . . .	40
10 " × 36 "	. . . .	121	20 " × 20 "	. . . .	108
10 " × 42 "	. . . .	103	20 " × 24 "	. . . .	90
10 " × 45 "	. . . .	96	20 " × 30 "	. . . .	72
10 " × 48 "	. . . .	90	20 " × 36 "	. . . .	60
10 " × 54 "	. . . .	80	20 " × 42 "	. . . .	51
10 " × 60 "	. . . .	72	20 " × 48 "	. . . .	45
12 " × 12 "	. . . .	302	20 " × 54 "	. . . .	40
12 " × 15 "	. . . .	242	20 " × 60 "	. . . .	36
12 " × 18 "	. . . .	201	24 " × 24 "	. . . .	75
12 " × 20 "	. . . .	181	24 " × 30 "	. . . .	60
12 " × 24 "	. . . .	151	24 " × 36 "	. . . .	50
12 " × 30 "	. . . .	121	24 " × 42 "	. . . .	43
12 " × 36 "	. . . .	100	24 " × 48 "	. . . .	37
12 " × 42 "	. . . .	86	24 " × 54 "	. . . .	33
12 " × 48 "	. . . .	75	24 " × 60 "	. . . .	30
12 " × 54 "	. . . .	67	30 " × 30 "	. . . .	48
12 " × 60 "	. . . .	60	30 " × 36 "	. . . .	40
15 " × 15 "	. . . .	193	30 " × 42 "	. . . .	34
15 " × 18 "	. . . .	161	30 " × 48 "	. . . .	30
15 " × 20 "	. . . .	145	30 " × 54 "	. . . .	26
15 " × 24 "	. . . .	121	30 " × 60 "	. . . .	24
15 " × 30 "	. . . .	96	36 " × 36 "	. . . .	33
15 " × 36 "	. . . .	80	36 " × 42 "	. . . .	28
15 " × 42 "	. . . .	69	36 " × 48 "	. . . .	25

PLANTING-TABLES.

		Plants.			Plants.
36 ft. × 54 ft.		22	42 ft. × 48 ft.		21
36 " × 60 "		20	42 " × 54 "		19
38 " × 38 "		30	42 " × 60 "		17
38 " × 40 "		28	48 " × 48 "		18
38 " × 42 "		27	48 " × 54 "		16
38 " × 48 "		23	48 " × 60 "		15
38 " × 50 "		22	50 " × 50 "		17
38 " × 54 "		21	50 " × 54 "		16
38 " × 60 "		19	50 " × 60 "		14
40 " × 40 "		27	54 " × 54 "		14
40 " × 42 "		25	54 " × 60 "		13
40 " × 48 "		22	60 " × 60 "		12
40 " × 50 "		21	70 " × 70 "		8
40 " × 54 "		20	80 " × 80 "		6
40 " × 60 "		18	90 " × 90 "		5
42 " × 42 "		24	100 " × 100 "		4

To find the number of plants required to set an acre, multiply together the two distances, in feet, at which the trees stand apart, and divide 43,560 by the product; the quotient will be the number of plants required.

QUINCUNX PLANTING. — To find the number of plants required to set an acre by the quincunx method, ascertain from the above tables the number required at the given rectangular distances, and then increase the number by one-half.

6. Model Kitchen Garden.

(*W. W. Tracy; D. M. Ferry & Co.*)

It is important to have the garden so arranged that most of the work can be done by horse power. We can best point out the things to be considered in the arrangement by means of the accompanying diagram. The points gained by this plan are:

First. — Ability to cultivate the ground. All but a strip seven and one-half feet wide between the beets and bush beans can be worked by any common one-horse cultivator.

120   HORTICULTURIST'S RULE-BOOK.

Second. — Placing those vegetables which may stay out all winter side by side, where they will not interfere with next season's plowing.

EAST.

Width	Vegetable
6 ft.	Asparagus.
6 ft.	Rhubarb. Artichoke. Parsnip. Salsify.
4 ft.	Cucumbers, followed by Fall Spinage. Peas.
4 ft.	Early Potatoes or Peas, followed by Celery. Early Cabbage and Cauliflower.
3 ft.	Beets. Turnips.
3 ft.	Lettuce, early and late. Winter Radish. Endive.
2½ ft.	Onions, with early Radish sown in row.
2½ ft.	Bush Beans. Parsley.
2½ ft.	Late Cabbage.
4 ft.	Early Corn and Summer Squash.
4 ft.	Late Corn.
4 ft.	Tomatoes and Pole Beans.
4 ft.	Musk and Water Melon.
6 ft.	Winter Squash.
8 ft.	
8 ft.	

WEST.

PLANTING—TABLES. 121

Third. — Arranging the vegetables very nearly in the order in which they should be planted or set out in the spring. This would be nearly perfect, except in case of the cucumbers, if the late cabbage were to follow the tomatoes.

Fourth. — Providing for easy rotation of crops by simply reversing (with the exception of the permanent row of asparagus and that of the parsnip and salsify) the plan.

The number of rows of each vegetable, and the relative proportion of each, may be varied, according to the wants of the family, but the proportion given here will be found to suit most families who depend upon the garden for both winter and summer vegetables.

If necessary, the turning-ground at both ends may be filled with winter squashes, as they are planted so late and at such a distance apart that they would not seriously hinder the turning of a steady horse with a careful driver.

7. Self-Fertile and Self-Sterile Fruits.

Some varieties of fruits are more or less completely unable to pollinate themselves, and they should be planted near other varieties to ensure fruitfulness. Any variety will fertilize any other variety of the same species, so far as known, if the bloom occurs at the same time. In general, in planting a self-sterile variety, every second or third row should be planted to some other variety. The subject is little understood, but the following lists represent the best of our knowledge.

PEARS (*Waite*).

Varieties more or less self-sterile. — Anjou, Bartlett, Boussock, Clairgeau, Clapp, Columbia, De la Chêne, Doyenne Sieulle, Easter, Gansels Bergamotte, Gray Doyenne, Howell, Jones, Lawrence, Louise Bonne, Mount Vernon, Pound, Sheldon, Souvenir du Congress, Superfin, Colonel Wilder, Winter Nelis.

Varieties generally self-fertile. — Angoulême, Bosc, Brockworth, Buffum, Diel, Doyenne d'Alençon, Flemish Beauty,

Heathcote, Kieffer, Le Conte, Manning Elizabeth, Seckel, Tyson, White Doyenne.

APPLES (*Waite* and *Fairchild*).

Varieties more or less self-sterile. — Bellfleur, Chenango (Strawberry), Gravenstein, King, Northern Spy, Norton Melon, Primate, Rambo, Red Astrachan, Roxbury Russet, Spitzenburgh, Talman Sweet.

Varieties mostly self-fertile. — Baldwin, Codlin, Greening.

"The varieties of apples are more inclined to be sterile to their own pollen than the pears. With the former, in the great majority of cases, no fruit resulted from self-pollination. The results as a rule, however, were less clear-cut than in the pear, because, with most of the self-sterile varieties, an occasional fruit will set under self-pollination, and none of the varieties were very completely self-fertile." — WAITE.

OTHER FRUITS.

"The quince seems to fruit nearly as well with its own pollen as with that of another variety." — WAITE.

Many of the native plums are notoriously self-sterile, particularly Wild Goose. Other self-sterile varieties are Miner, Wazata, Minnetonka, Itaska. Varieties more or less self-fertile are Moreman, Newman, Wayland, Golden Beauty, Marianna, Deep Creek, Purple Yosemite.

Strawberries often lack stamens altogether, whilst others, like Crescent, have so few and so poor stamens that they are practically self-sterile. Ordinarily, there should be a row of a perfect-flowered variety for every two rows of a pistillate or infertile variety.

GRAPES (*Beach*).

Unfruitful when planted by themselves. — Black Eagle, Brighton, Eumelan, Massasoit, Wilder, Rogers' No. 5, Gaertner, Merrimac, Requa, Aminia, Essex, Barry, Herbert, Salem.

Able to set fruit of themselves. — Concord, Diamond, Niagara, Winchell or Green Mountain, Rogers' Nos. 13, 24, and 32, Agawam, Delaware.

CHAPTER XI.

MATURITIES, YIELDS, AND MULTIPLICATION.

1. **Time required for Maturity of Different Garden Crops, reckoned from the Sowing of the Seeds.**

Beans, String	45– 65	days from seed.
" Shell	65– 70	" " "
Beets, Turnip	65	" " "
" Long Blood	150	" " "
Cabbage, Early	105	" " "
" Late	150	" " "
Cauliflower	110	" " "
Corn	75	" " "
Egg-plant	150–160	" " "
Lettuce	65	" " "
Melon, Water	120–140	" " "
" Musk	120–140	" " "
Onion	135–150	" " "
Pepper	140–150	" " "
Radish	30– 45	" " "
Squash, Summer	60– 65	" " "
" Winter	125	" " "
Tomatoes	150	" " "
Turnips	60– 70	" " "

2. **Time required, from Setting, for Fruit-Plants to bear. (For northern and central latitudes.)**

Apple — 3 years. Good crop in about 10 years.
Blackberry — 1 year. Good crops in 2 and 3 years.
Citrous fruits (oranges, lemons, etc.) — 2 to 3 years. Good crop in 2 or 3 years later.

Cranberry — 3 years gives a fair crop.
Currant — 1 year. Good crops in 2 and 3 years.
Gooseberry — 1 year. Good crops in 2 and 3 years.
Grape — Fair crop in 4 years.
Peach — 2 years. Good crop in 4 and 5 years.
Pear — 3 or 4 years. Fair crop in 6 to 12 years; dwarfs in 5 to 7 years.
Persimmon, or Kaki — 1 to 3 years.
Quince — 2 years. Good crop in 4 years.
Raspberry — 1 year. Good crop in 2 and 3 years.
Plum — 3 years. Good crop in 5 or 6 years.
Strawberry — 1 year. Heaviest crop usually in 2 years.

3. Average Profitable Longevity of Fruit-Plants under High Culture.

Apple	25–40 years.		Pear	50–75 years.
Blackberry	6–12 "		Persimmon, or Kaki, as long as an apple tree.	
Currant	20 "			
Gooseberry	20 "		Plum	20–25 years.
Orange and Lemon, 50 or more.			Raspberry	6–12 "
Peach	8–12 years.		Strawberry	1– 3 "

When serious trouble from diseases is to be apprehended, the plantation may be brought into early fruiting and then destroyed before the disease makes great headway. This is particularly applicable to blackberries, raspberries, and strawberries.

4. Average Full Yields per Acre of Various Crops.

The yields of those crops in which the salable products are equal in number to the number of plants per acre, and in which the product is sold by the piece, are to be calculated from the planting-tables in Chap. X. — such as cabbage, celery, and the like.

Apples — A tree 20 to 30 years old may be expected to yield from 25 to 40 bushels every alternate year.

MATURITIES, YIELDS, AND MULTIPLICATION. 125

Artichoke — 200 to 300 bushels.
Beans, Green or Snap — 75 to 120 bushels.
" Lima — 75 to 100 bushels of dry beans.
Beets — 400 to 700 bushels.
Carrots — 400 to 700 bushels.
Corn — 50 to 75 bushels, shelled.
Cranberry — 100 to 300 bushels. 900 bushels have been reported.
Cucumber — About 150,000 fruits per acre.
Currant — 100 bushels.
Egg-plant — 1 or 2 large fruits to the plant for the large sorts like New York Purple, and from 3 to 8 fruits for the smaller varieties.
Gooseberry — 100 bushels.
Grape — 3 to 5 tons. Good raisin vineyards in California, 15 years old, will produce from 10 to 12 tons.
Horseradish — 3 to 5 tons.
Kohlrabi — 500 to 1000 bushels.
Onion, from seed — 300 to 800 bushels. 600 bushels is a large average yield.
Parsnips — 500 to 800 bushels.
Pea, green in pod — 100 to 150 bushels.
Peach — In full bearing, a peach tree should produce from 5 to 10 bushels.
Pear — A tree 20 to 25 years old should give from 25 to 45 bushels.
Pepper — 30,000 to 50,000 fruits.
Plum — 5 to 8 bushels may be considered an average crop for an average tree.
Potato — 100 to 300 bushels.
Quince — 100 to 300 bushels.
Raspberry and Blackberry — 50 to 100 bushels.
Salsify — 200 to 300 bushels.
Spinage — 200 barrels.
Strawberry — 75 to 250 or even 300 bushels.
Tomato — 8 to 16 tons.
Turnip — 600 to 1000 bushels.

5. Tabular Statement of the Ways in which Plants are Propagated.*

A. By Seeds. — *Seedage.*

B. By Buds.
- I. On their own roots.
  - I. By undetached parts. — *Layerage.*
    1. Root-tips.
    2. Stolons and Runners.
    3. Layers proper.
       - Simple.
       - Serpentine.
       - Mound or Stools.
       - Pot or Chinese.
  - II. By detached parts.
    1. By undivided parts. — *Separation.* (Bulbs, corms, bulblets, bulb-scales, tubers, etc.)
    2. By divided parts. — *Cuttage.*
       - Division.
       - Cuttings proper.
         - Of stems.
           - Growing wood.
           - Ripened wood.
         - Of tubers.
         - Of roots.
         - Of leaves.
- II. On roots of other plants. — *Graftage.*
  - I. By detached scions.
    1. Budding: Shield, flute, veneer, ring, annular, whistle or tubular.
    2. Grafting: Whip, saddle, splice, veneer, cleft, bark, herbaceous, seed, double, cutting.
  - II. By undetached scions. — *Inarching.*

---

* Modified from a synopsis prepared by B. M. Watson, Jr., Bussey Institution.

MATURITIES, YIELDS, AND MULTIPLICATION.

6. Particular Methods by which Various Fruits are multiplied.

Barberry . . . . . . Cuttings of mature wood; seeds.
Orange . . . . . . Seeds; seedlings budded or grafted.
Figs . . . . Cuttings, either of soft or mature wood.
Mulberry . . . . . Cuttings of mature wood. Some varieties are root-grafted, and some are budded.
Olive . . . . Cuttings of mature or even old wood. Chips from the trunks of old trees are sometimes used.
Pomegranate . . . Cuttings, layers, and seeds.
Apple and Pear . . . Seeds; seedlings budded or grafted.
Peach and other stone-fruits —
        Seeds; seedlings budded. Peach trees are sold at one year from the bud, but other stone-fruit trees are planted when two or three years old.
Quince. . . . . . . Cuttings, usually; the cuttings often grafted.
Grape . . . . Cuttings of from one to three buds; layers.
Currant and Gooseberry —
        Cuttings.
Raspberries, red . . Suckers from the root; root-cuttings.
    "   black . . Layers from tips of canes; root-cuttings.
Blackberry . . . . Root-cuttings; suckers from the root.
Dewberry. . . . . . Layers of tips of the canes; root-cuttings.
Dwarf Juneberry . . Sprouts or suckers from the root.
Cranberry . . . . . Layers or divisions.
Strawberry . . . . Runners; tip-cuttings.

7. Stocks used for Various Fruits.

Almond . . . . . . Peach, hard-shelled almond, plum.
Apple . . . . Common apple seedlings, Paradise and Doucin stocks, crab-apple and wild crab.

Apricot	Apricot and peach in mild climates, and plum in severe ones. Marianna.
Cherry	Mazzard stocks are preferred for standards; Mahaleb stocks are used for dwarfing. The wild pin-cherry (*Prunus Pennsylvanica*) is sometimes used as stock in the Northwest, on account of its hardiness. Seedlings of Morello cherries are also used there.
Medlar	Hawthorn, medlar, quince.
Mulberry	Seedlings of white and Russian mulberry; cuttings of Downing.
Orange	Seedlings; Otaheite orange, shaddock; *Citrus trifoliata*, particularly for dwarfs.
Peach and Nectarine .	Peach. Plum is often used when dwarfs are wanted, or when the peach must be grown in a too severe climate or upon heavy soil.
Pear	Pear (seedlings of common pear and the Chinese type). Quince (rarely mountain ash, or thorn) for dwarfs. Apple temporarily.
Persimmon, Japanese .	Native persimmon.
Plum	Plum, myrobalan plum, peach; Marianna.
Quince	The finer varieties are sometimes grafted upon strong-growing kinds like the Angers. When cuttings are difficult to root, they are sometimes grafted upon apple roots, the foster-root being removed upon transplanting, if it does not fall away of itself.

CHAPTER XII.

COMPUTATION TABLES.

I. TABLES OF CUSTOMARY WEIGHTS AND MEASURES.

1. Avoirdupois or Commercial Weight.

$27\frac{11}{32}$	grains	= 1 dram.
16	drams	= 1 ounce.
16	ounces	= 1 pound.
25	pounds	= 1 quarter.
4	quarters, or 100 pounds	= 1 hundredweight.
20	hundredweight, or 2000 lbs. . . .	= 1 ton.
480	pounds	= 1 imperial quarter
100	pounds is also called	1 cental.

```
   t.   cwt.   lb.     oz.       dr.      gr.
   1  = 20  = 2000 = 32,000  = 512000
          1  =  100  =  1,600  =  25600
                  1  =    16  =    256 = 7000
                           1  =    16  = 4375
```

2. Troy or Jewelers' Weight.

24 grains	= 1 pennyweight.
20 pennyweights	= 1 ounce.
12 ounces	= 1 pound.

```
         lb.   oz.   pwt.   gr.
         1  = 12 = 240 = 5760
              1  =  20 =  480
                    1  =   24
```

3. Apothecaries' Weight.

20 grains	= 1 scruple.
3 scruples	= 1 dram.

8 drams . . . . = 1 ounce.
12 ounces . . . . = 1 pound.

$$\begin{array}{cccc} \text{lb.} & \text{oz.} & \text{dr.} & \text{scr.} & \text{gr.} \\ 1 = & 12 = & 96 = & 288 = & 5760 \\ & 1 = & 8 = & 24 = & 480 \\ & & 1 = & 3 = & 60 \\ & & & 1 = & 20 \end{array}$$

4. Table of Comparative Weights.

Avoirdupois.	Troy.	Apothecaries.
7000 gr. = 1 lb.	5760 gr. = 1 lb.	5760 gr. = 1 lb.
1 lb. =	$1\frac{31}{111}$ lbs. =	$1\frac{31}{144}$ lbs.
or 144 lbs. =	175 lbs. =	175 lbs.
1 oz. =	$1\frac{75}{192}$ oz. =	$1\frac{75}{192}$ oz.
or 192 oz. =	175 oz. =	175 oz.

5. Dry Measure.

2 pints . . . . = 1 quart.
8 quarts . . . . = 1 peck.
4 pecks . . . . = 1 bushel.
8 bushels (480 pounds) . . . . . . = 1 quarter.
36 bushels . . . . = 1 chaldron.

$$\begin{array}{cccc} \text{bu.} & \text{pk.} & \text{qt.} & \text{pt.} \\ 1 = & 4 = & 32 = & 64 \\ & 1 = & 8 = & 16 \\ & & 1 = & 2 \end{array}$$

6. Liquid Measure.

4 gills . . . . = 1 pint.
2 pints . . . . = 1 quart.
4 quarts . . . . = 1 gallon.
31½ gallons . . . . = 1 barrel.
2 barrels, or 63 gallons . . . . . . = 1 hogshead.

$$\begin{array}{cccc} \text{gal.} & \text{qt.} & \text{pt.} & \text{gi.} \\ 1 = & 4 = & 8 = & 32 \\ & 1 = & 2 = & 8 \\ & & 1 = & 4 \end{array}$$

COMPUTATION TABLES. 131

7. Apothecaries' Fluid Measure.

60 minims . . . . = 1 fluid dram.
8 fluid drams . . . . = 1 fluid ounce.
16 fluid ounces . . . . = 1 pint.
8 pints . . . . = 1 gallon.

```
      cong.  o.   f.℥.   f.℈.      m.
      1  =  8  =  128  =  1024  =  61,440
             1  =   16  =   128  =   7,680
                     1  =     8  =     480
                             1  =      60
```

1 minim equals 1 drop of water.

8. Line or Linear Measure.

12 inches . . . . = 1 foot.
3 feet . . . . = 1 yard.
5½ yards, or 16½ feet . . . . . = 1 rod or pole.
40 rods . . . . = 1 furlong.
8 furlongs (320 rods) . . . . . = 1 mile (statute mile).
3 miles . . . . = 1 league.

```
      l.   mi.   fur.    rd.      yd.         ft.           in.
      1 =  3  =  24  =  960  =   5280    =  15,840    =  190,080
           1  =   8  = 320  =   1760    =   5,280    =   63,360
                  1  =  40  =    220    =     660    =    7,920
                         1  =    5½     =    16½     =      198
                                  1     =     3      =       36
                                                 1   =       12
```

9. Surveyors' or Chain Measure.

7.92 inches . . . . = 1 link.
25 links . . . . = 1 rod or pole
4 rods, or 66 feet . . . . . . = 1 chain.
80 chains . . . . = 1 mile.

```
      mi.   ch.     rd.       l.         in.
      1  =  80  =  320  =   8000  =   63,360
             1  =   4   =    100  =      792
                     1  =     25  =      198
                                1 =      7.92
```

10. Square or Surface Measure.

144 square inches . . . . = 1 square foot.
9 square feet . . . . = 1 square yard.
30¼ square yards . . . . = 1 sq. rod or perch.
160 square rods . . . . = 1 acre.
640 acres . . . . = 1 sq. mile or section.

sq.m.	a.	sq. rd.	sq. yd.	sq. ft.	sq. in.
1 =	640 =	102,400 =	3,097,600 =	27,878,400 =	4,014,489,600
	1 =	160 =	4,840 =	43,560 =	6,272,640
		1 =	30¼ =	272¼ =	39,204
			1 =	9 =	1,296
				1 =	144

11. Surveyors' Square Measure.

625 square links . . . . = 1 square rod or pole.
16 poles . . . . = 1 square chain.
10 square chains . . . . = 1 acre.
640 acres . . . . = 1 sq. mile or section.
36 square miles (6 miles square) . . = 1 township.

tp.	sq. mi.	a.	sq. ch.	sq. rd.	sq. l.
1 =	36 =	23,040 =	230,400 =	3,686,400 =	2,304,000,000
	1 =	640 =	6,400 =	102,400 =	64,000,000
		1 =	10 =	160 =	100,000
			1 =	16 =	10,000
				1 =	625

12. Solid or Cubic Measure.

1728 cubic inches . . . . = 1 cubic foot.
27 cubic feet . . . . = 1 cubic yard.
16 cubic feet . . . . = 1 cord foot.
8 cord feet, or 128 cubic feet . . = 1 cord of wood.
24¾ cubic feet . . . . = 1 perch.

cu.yd.	cu.ft.	cu. in.	cd.	cd. ft.	cu. ft.	cu. in.
1 =	27 =	46,656 =	1 =	8 =	128 =	221,184.

13. Miscellaneous Measures.

$\frac{1}{12}$ of an inch . . . . = a line (American).
$\frac{1}{10}$ of an inch . . . . = a line (French).

COMPUTATION TABLES. 133

$\frac{1}{3}$ of an inch . . . . = a size (of shoes).
3 inches . . . . = a palm.
4 inches . . . . = a hand.
9 inches . . . . = a span.
18 inches . . . . = a cubit.
2$\frac{1}{2}$ feet . . . . = a military pace.
3 (or 3.3) feet . . . . = a pace.
A wine gallon . . . . = 231 cubic inches.
A dry gallon . . . . = 268.8 "
An imperial gallon . . . . = 277.274 "
An imperial or English bushel . . . = 2,218.192 "
A U. S. bushel . . . . = 2,150.42 "
A U. S. bushel heaped (heaped to a
cone 6 inches high) . . . . . . = 2,747.7 "
1 pint of water weighs 1.0431 pounds.
1 gallon of water weighs 8.3448 pounds.
1 cubic foot of water weighs 62.425 pounds at 39.2° F.
An English (statute) mile is . . . . 1760 yards.
A Scotch mile is . . . . 1984 "
An Irish mile is . . . . 2249 "
A Dutch mile is . . . . 8101 "
A Roman mile is . . . . 1628 "
A German mile is . . . . 6859 "
A Russian mile is . . . . 1100 "
An Arabian mile is . . . . 2148 "
A sea (nautical) mile is . . . . 2026 "
1 tael (Chinese) is . . . . 1$\frac{1}{3}$ oz. avoir.
1 Danish pound is . . . . 1.102 lb. avoir.
1 Russian pound is . . . . .9 "
1 libra (Spanish) is . . . . 1.014 "
100 pounds nails . . . . = 1 keg.
196 pounds flour . . . . = 1 barrel.
150 pounds potatoes . . . . = 1 barrel of freight.

14. Approximate value of household measures:

45 drops of water is a teaspoonful.
1 teaspoonful equals 1 fluid dram.

1 dessertspoonful equals 2 teaspoonfuls, or 2 drams.
1 tablespoonful equals 2 dessertspoonfuls, or 4 teaspoonfuls.
2 tablespoonfuls equal 8 teaspoonfuls, or 1 fluid ounce.
1 common-size wineglassful equals 2 ounces, or $\frac{1}{2}$ gill.
1 common-size tumbler holds $\frac{1}{2}$ pint.
A small tea-cup is estimated to hold 4 fluid ounces, or 1 gill.
1 pound of wheat is equal to about 1 pint.
1 pound and 2 ounces of Indian meal is equal to 1 quart.
1 pound of soft butter is equal to about 1 pint.
1 pound of sugar is equal to about 1 pint.
A pint of pure water is about a pound.

II. Metric Weights and Measures.

15. Weight.

Names.	Number of Grams.	Equivalents in Denominations of Avoirdupois Weight.
Millier or Tonneau,	1,000,000	2204.6 pounds.
Quintal,	100,000	220.46 pounds.
Myriagram,	10,000	22.046 pounds.
Kilogram or Kilo,	1,000	2.2046 pounds.
Hectogram,	100	3.5274 ounces.
Dekagram,	10	0.3527 ounce.
Gram,	1	15.432 grains.
Decigram,	$\frac{1}{10}$	1.5432 grains.
Centigram,	$\frac{1}{100}$	0.1543 grain.
Milligram,	$\frac{1}{1000}$	0.0154 grain.

1 gram is the weight of 1 cubic centimeter of distilled water at its maximum density (39.1° Fahr.) in a vacuum. As a matter of fact, however, the gram now in use is the one-thousandth part of the weight of a kilogram of platinum, which was deposited in the Palace of the Archives in Paris, in 1799, by the international commission, which was appointed to fix the standards of what is now known as the metric system.

COMPUTATION TABLES. 135

16. Capacity.

NAMES.	NUMBER OF LITERS.	EQUIVALENTS IN DRY MEASURE.	EQUIVALENTS IN LIQUID OR WINE MEASURE.
Kiloliter or Stere,	1,000	1.308 cubic yards.	264.17 gallons.
Hectoliter,	100	2 bush. and 3.35 pecks.	26.417 gallons.
Dekaliter,	10	9.08 quarts.	2.6417 gallons.
Liter,	1	0.908 quart.	1.0567 quarts.
Deciliter,	$\frac{1}{10}$	6.1022 cubic inches.	0.845 gill.
Centiliter,	$\frac{1}{100}$	0.6102 cubic inch.	0.338 fluid oz.
Milliliter,	$\frac{1}{1000}$	0.061 cubic inch.	0.27 fluid dr,

1 liter is equivalent to 1 cubic decimeter.

17. Length.

		EQUIVALENTS IN DENOMINATIONS IN USE.
Myriameter,	10,000 meters.	6.2137 miles.
Kilometer,	1,000 meters.	0.62137 mile, or 3.280 ft. 10 in.
Hectometer,	100 meters.	328 ft. 1 in.
Dekameter,	10 meters.	393.7 inches.
Meter,	1 meter.	39.37 inches.
Decimeter,	$\frac{1}{10}$ of a meter.	3.937 inches.
Centimeter,	$\frac{1}{100}$ of a meter.	0.3937 inch.
Millimeter,	$\frac{1}{1000}$ of a meter.	0.0397 inch.

Surface.

Hectare,	10,000 square meters.	2.471 acres.
Are,	100 square meters.	119.6 square yards.
Centare,	1 square meter.	1550 square inches.

18. Cubic Measure.

Myriaster	10,000 cu. meters.
Kiloster	1,000 cu. meters.
Hectoster	100 cu. meters.
Decaster	10 cu. meters.
Ster	1 cu. meter.
Decister	$\frac{1}{10}$ cu. meter.
Centister	$\frac{1}{100}$ cu. meter.
Millister	$\frac{1}{1000}$ cu. meter.

The word *ster* is seldom used. The names of solid measures are commonly made by adding *cubic* to the denominations of linear measure; as cubic meter, cubic decimeter, and the like.

19. Equivalents of Common Measures in Metric Terms.

LENGTH.

		Approximately.		Exactly.
1 inch	is	$2\frac{1}{2}$ centimeters		(2.54)
1 foot	"	0.3 of meter		(.3048)
1 yard	"	0.9 "		(.9144)
1 rod	"	5 meters		(5.029)
1 chain	"	20 "		(20.117)
1 furlong	"	200 "		(201.17)
1 mile	"	1600 "		(1609.3)

AREA.

1 sq. inch	is	$6\frac{1}{4}$ sq. centimeters		(6.451)
1 sq. foot	"	0.09 of sq. meter		(.0929)
1 sq. yard	"	0.83 " "		(.8361)
1 sq. rod	"	25 sq. meters		(25.29)
1 rood	"	1000 " "		(1011.7)
1 acre	"	0.4 of hectare		(.4047)
1 sq. mile	"	258 hectares		(258.99)

BULK.

1 cubic inch is	$16\frac{1}{3}$	cubic centimeters	(16.387)
1 cubic foot "	0.028	of cubic meter	(.028316)

COMPUTATION TABLES.   137

1 cubic yard	is	0.76	of cubic meter	. . .	(.7645)
100 cubic feet	"	2.8	cubic meters	. . .	(2.8316)
1 M board meas.	"	2¼	" "	. . .	(2.36)
1 cord	"	3.6	" "	. . .	(3.624)
1 U. S. liq. pint	"	0.47	of liter	. . . . .	(.473)
1 " quart	"	0.9	"	. . . . .	(.946)
1 " gallon	"	3.7	liters	. . . . .	(3.785)
1 peck	"	9	"	(U. S. 8.81.	Eng. 9.08)
1 bushel	"	36	"	(U. S. 35.24.	Eng. 36.35)

WEIGHT.

1 grain	is	0.06½	of gram	. . . . .	(.0648)
1 troy oz.	"	31	grams	. . . . .	(31.103)
1 avoir. oz.	"	28	"	. . . . .	(28.35)
1 avoir. pound	"	0.45	of kilo	. . . . .	(.4536)
60 lbs. (wheat bu.)	"	27	kilos	. . . . .	(27.216)
80 lbs. (coal bu.)	"	36	"	. . . . .	(36.287)
1 cental	"	45	"	. . . . .	(45.36)
112 lbs. (cwt.)	"	50	"	. . . . .	(50.8)
1 net ton	"	0.9	metric ton	. . . .	(.9072)
1 gross ton	"	1	" "	. . . .	(1.016)

III. MONEY TABLES.

20. English Money.

4 farthings (qr.) . . . . = 1 penny (d.).
12 pence . . . . = 1 shilling (s.).
20 shillings . . . . = 1 pound or sovereign (£).
21 shillings . . . . = 1 guinea (g.).

$$\begin{array}{cccc} \pounds. & s. & d. & qr. \\ 1 = & 20 = & 240 = & 960 \\ & 1 = & 12 = & 48 \\ & & 1 = & 4 \end{array}$$

1 pound is about $4.86.

21. French Money.

10 millimes (*m.*) . . . . = 1 centime (*c.*).
10 centimes . . . . = 1 decime (*d.*).
10 decimes . . . . = 1 franc (*fr.*).

$$\begin{array}{cccc} \text{fr.} & \text{d.} & \text{c.} & \text{m.} \\ 1 = & 10 = & 100 = & 1000 \\ & 1 = & 10 = & 100 \\ & & 1 = & 10 \end{array}$$

1 franc is nearly 20 (19.3) cents.

22. German Money.

100 pfennige (*pf.*) . . . . = 1 mark (*R.M.*).

A mark is about 24 cents.

23. Dutch Money.

100 cents . . . . = 1 florin or guilder.

A florin is 40 cents.

24. Italian Money.

100 centesimi . . . . = 1 lira.

A lira is nearly 20 (19.3) cents.

25. Spanish Money.

100 centimos . . . . = 1 peseta.

1 peseta is nearly 20 (19.3) cents.

26. Russian Money.

100 copecks . . . . = 1 rouble.

A rouble is about 54 cents.

27. Austrian Money.

100 kreutzer . . . . = 1 florin.

A florin is about 33 cents.

COMPUTATION TABLES. 139

28. Money Table. (*Baedeker.*)

ENGLISH.			DUTCH.		FRENCH AND BELGIAN.		GERMAN.		AMERICAN.	
£.	s.	d.	florin.	cent.	franc	cent.	mark.	pfg.	dollar.	cent.
1			12		25		20		4	76
	19		11	40	23	75	19		4	53
	18		10	80	22	50	18		4	29
	17		10	20	21	25	17		4	5
	16		9	60	20		16		3	81
	15		9		18	75	15		3	57
	14		8	40	17	50	14		3	34
	13		7	80	16	25	13		3	10
	12		7	20	15		12		2	86
	11		6	60	13	75	11		2	62
	10		6		12	50	10		2	38
	9		5	40	11	25	9		2	14
	8		4	80	10		8		1	91
	7		4	20	8	75	7		1	67
	6		3	60	7	50	6		1	43
	5		3		6	25	5		1	19
	4		2	40	5		4			95
	3		1	80	3	75	3			71
	2		1	20	2	50	2			48
	1	8½	1		2	15	1	70		41
	1	7		96	2		1	60		38
	1			60	1	25	1			24
		9¾		48	1			80		19
		9		45		94		75		18
		8		40		83		66		16
		7		35		73		58		14
		6		30		62		50		12
		5		25		52		41		10
		4		20		42		33		8
		3		15		31		25		6
		2		10		21		16		4
		1		5		10		8		2

IV. Legal and Standard Measures of the Various States (Corrected to the Close of 1894).

29. Legal or Customary Weights of a Bushel of Produce in Various States.

States.	Apples.	Apples, dried.	Beans, Castor.	Beans, White.	Buckwheat.	Corn, ear.	Corn, shelled.	Onions.	Peaches.	Potatoes, Irish.	Potatoes, Sweet.	Peas.	Bluegrass Seed.	Turnips.	Wheat.
Arkansas	..	24	..	60	52	70	56	57	..	60	50	60	14	57	60
California	..	..	..	..	40	..	52	..	..	..	..	..	..	..	60
Colorado	..	..	..	60	52	70	56	57	..	60	..	..	14	..	60
Connecticut	..	..	..	60	48	..	56	50	..	60	..	60	..	50	..
Delaware	..	..	..	..	..	..	56	..	..	..	..	..	..	..	60
Georgia	..	24	..	60	52	70	56	57	38	60	55	60	14	55	60
Illinois	..	24	46	60	52	70	56	57	33	60	50	..	14	55	60
Indiana	..	25	66	60	50	68	56	48	33	60	55	..	..	..	60
Iowa	48	48	46	60	52	70	56	57	33	60	46	..	14	..	..
Kansas	..	24	44	60	50	70	56	57	33	60	50	..	14	55	60
Kentucky	24	24	45	60	56	70*	56	57	39	60	55	60	14	60	60
Louisiana	..	..	..	..	..	..	56	..	..	..	..	..	..	..	60
Maine	44	..	60	60	48	..	56	52	..	60	..	60	..	50	60
Maryland	..	28	60	60	48	70	56	56	40	56	56	62	14	56	60
Massachusetts	48	25	..	60	48	..	56	57	..	60	54	60	..	..	60
Michigan	48	22	46	60	48	70	56	54	28	60	56	60	14	58	60
Minnesota	..	28	..	..	42	..	56	..	28	60	..	..	..	..	60
Missouri	48	24	46	60	52	..	56	57	33	60	56	60	14	42	60
Montana	..	..	..	..	42	..	56	57	..	..	60	..	..	50	60
Nebraska	..	24	46	60	52	70	56	57	33	60	50	60	14	55	60
Nevada	..	..	..	60	..	..	56	..	..	..	..	..	..	..	..
New Hampshire	..	..	..	60	..	..	56	..	..	60	..	60	..	..	60
New Jersey	50	25	60	60	50	..	56	57	..	60	54	60	..	50	..
New York	..	..	..	62	48	..	58	..	..	60	..	60	..	..	..
North Carolina	..	..	..	..	50	..	56	..	..	60	..	60	..	..	60
Ohio	48	22	..	60	50	68	56	50	48	60	50	60	..	60	60
Oregon	45	..	..	..	42	..	56	..	..	60	..	..	..	..	60
Pennsylvania	..	..	..	..	48	..	56	..	..	56	..	..	..	..	..
Rhode Island	..	..	..	..	..	..	56	52	..	60	..	..	..	..	..
Tennessee	50	24	..	60	50	70	56	56	50	60	50	60	14	50	60
Texas	..	..	..	60	42	..	56	57	..	60	55	..	..	55	60
Vermont	46	..	60	62	48	..	56	52	..	60	..	60	..	..	60
Virginia	..	28	..	60	52	70	56	57	40	60	56	60	14	55	60
West Virginia	..	25	..	60	52	..	56	..	33	60	..	..	..	..	60
Wisconsin	57	28	..	60	50	..	56	50	28	60	..	..	..	42	..
Washington	45	..	..	..	42	..	56	50	..	60	..	60	..	50	60

*70 pounds from Nov. 1 to May 1; 68 pounds May 1 to Nov. 1.

COMPUTATION TABLES. 141

30. Miscellaneous Legal Weights per Bushel.

BEETS, MANGELS, and RUTA BAGAS: 60 pounds in Maine, Vermont, Connecticut; 56 in Wisconsin; 50 in Missouri. CARROTS: 50 pounds in Maine, Vermont, Massachusetts, Wisconsin, Missouri, Montana; 55 in Connecticut. PARSNIPS: 45 pounds in Connecticut; 44 in Wisconsin, Missouri; 50 in Montana; 55 in Indiana. BOTTOM ONION SETS, 36 pounds in Kentucky. RICE CORN, 56 pounds in Kansas. BERRIES, 32 pounds in Rhode Island. CHERRIES, GRAPES, CURRANTS, GOOSEBERRIES, 40 pounds in Iowa. BLACKBERRIES, STRAWBERRIES, RASPBERRIES, 32 pounds in Iowa. PEACHES, QUINCES, 48 pounds in Iowa. DRIED PEACHES: 33 pounds in Massachusetts; 39 in Kentucky. DRIED PLUMS, 28 pounds in Michigan. CRANBERRIES, 40 pounds in Michigan. " WILD PEACHES," 33 pounds in Ohio. In the DAKOTAS, a bushel of wheat is 60 pounds; corn, 56 pounds; buckwheat, 42 pounds; onions, 52 pounds; potatoes, 60 pounds; turnips, 60 pounds; sweet potatoes, 46 pounds. In RHODE ISLAND, WISCONSIN, WASHINGTON, and MONTANA, a bushel of ROOT CROPS is 50 pounds.

31. Miscellaneous Legal Sizes.

The heap bushel contains 2564 cubic inches in Connecticut and Kansas; 2150.42 inches in New Jersey, Pennsylvania, Nebraska, Tennessee, Missouri, Washington.

The bushel measure must be $19\frac{1}{2}$ inches in outside diameter, the half-bushel $15\frac{1}{2}$ inches, the peck $12\frac{1}{2}$ inches, in New York and California.

The bushel measure must be $18\frac{1}{2}$ inches in inside diameter, the half-bushel $13\frac{3}{4}$ inches, the peck $10\frac{3}{4}$ inches, and the half-peck 9 inches, in New Hampshire and Minnesota.

Produce sold by dry measure must be heaped as full as the measure will hold in Ohio, Illinois, Michigan, Wisconsin, Minnesota, California, Oregon, and Washington.

Heap measures must be cylindrical, with a plane bottom, in New York and California.

The half-bushel is $13\frac{39}{40}$ inches in interior diameter and $7\frac{1}{27}$ inches deep in Ohio. It contains $1075\frac{1}{5}$ cubic inches in Indiana.

In New Jersey the cranberry box, to hold a bushel, must be $12 \times 8\frac{3}{4} \times 22$ inches in the clear.

In Wisconsin, cranberry packages must conform to the following sizes: "The legal and standard cranberry barrel in this State shall be twenty-three and three-quarters inches high, sixteen and one-fourth inches in diameter at the head, and eighteen inches in diameter at the bilge, inside measure. Every manufacturer of barrels for cranberries shall stamp or brand his name with the letters W. S. on such barrels, to indicate that they are the Wisconsin Standard in size. All sales of cranberries in packages less than a barrel should be by the bushel or quart, struck or level dry measure. A standard bushel crate for cranberries shall be twenty-two inches long, twelve and one-fourth inches wide by seven and one-half inches deep, inside measure."

In New York a barrel of apples, quinces, pears, or potatoes shall contain 100 quarts of grain or dry measure, except that potatoes, when sold by weight, shall be 172 pounds to the barrel.

In New York the measure for fruit shall be the half-bushel, which shall be made cylindrical, the diameter outside to outside $15\frac{1}{2}$ inches. The standard half-bushel has $1075\frac{21}{100}$ cubic inches.

In Michigan the quantity known as a box or a basket of peaches shall contain $716\frac{2}{3}$ cubic inches or $\frac{1}{3}$ of a bushel, strict measure.

Michigan Standard Measure. — The half-bushel or parts thereof shall be the standard measure for fruits customarily sold by heaped measure; and in measuring said commodities, the half-bushel or other small measure shall be heaped as high as may be, without special effort or design.

Michigan Standard Barrel. — A barrel of fruit, roots, or vegetables is the quantity contained in a barrel made from staves 27 inches in length, and each head $16\frac{1}{2}$ inches in diameter, or ordinary flour-barrel size.

COMPUTATION TABLES. 143

In Maine a barrel of potatoes is 165 pounds.

In Tennessee a barrel of apples contains $2\frac{1}{2}$ bushels. A liquid barrel contains 42 gallons.

In Wisconsin a barrel of apples shall contain 100 quarts dry measure.

The avoirdupois pound bears to the troy pound the relation of 7000 to 5760 in New York, New Jersey, Pennsylvania, Ohio, Iowa, Nebraska, Tennessee, and California.

In Ohio and Rhode Island, standard dry measure shall be used for berries and other small fruits.

The New Jersey standard legal peach basket is 16 quarts. Height, $12\frac{1}{4}$ inches. Width across top, $13\frac{1}{2}$ inches. Inside measurement, 1075.1 cubic inches. Shall be marked "Standard, N. J.," in Roman letters upon the staves just below the rim, either burned in or painted in permanent red paint, and each letter shall be not less than 1 inch in length and $\frac{1}{2}$ inch in width. (Laws of 1892.)

V. SOCIETY AND CUSTOMARY STANDARDS.

32. Fruit Packages in Florida and Georgia.

The standard orange box adopted by the Florida Fruit Exchange measures $12 \times 12 \times 26\frac{5}{8}$ inches, with partition in the middle. The Exchange issues the following instructions:

We recommend the following classifications for oranges: Fancy, Choice Bright, Bright Russet, Choice Russet, Russet.

Oranges classed as Fancy should be extra-bright, with very smooth, thin skin. Rough, thick-skinned fruit, being ever so bright, should never be classed as Fancy.

Oranges classed as Choice Bright should be strictly bright and fairly smooth skin, and of desirable size.

Oranges classed as Bright should be bright, and free from rust.

Oranges classed as Bright Russet should be at least *two-thirds bright*, with smooth skin and of desirable size.

Oranges classed as Choice Russet should be of quite smooth skin and of desirable size.

Oranges of a common dark variety should be classed as Russet.

Never pack bright and rusty oranges in the same box. Never pack large and small oranges in the same box.

One of the most important features in the packing of oranges is the uniform neatness of the packages. Buyers will pay more for fruit that is neatly and properly packed than they will pay for such as is carelessly put up. A box of oranges neatly packed, strapped, and marked, naturally attracts the attention of buyers.

After your fruit has been carefully packed in accordance with above instructions, please mark the boxes as follows:

Place the stencil of the Florida Fruit Exchange on one end of the box in centre of head.

In the *upper left-hand* corner of the box-head stencil the quality of orange the box contains — *Fancy, Choice Bright, Bright, Bright Russet, Choice Russet, Russet, Mandarin, Tangerine,* or *Navel,* as the case may be.

In the *upper middle* of the box-head stencil the number of oranges the box contains — "128," "176," "200," as the case may be.

In the *upper right-hand* corner stencil the *letters* according to the following schedule:

All sizes under 128, mark A.
Sizes 128 to 138, mark B.
Sizes 146 to 160, mark C.
Sizes 176 to 200, mark D.
All sizes over 200, mark E.

The Georgia Horticultural Society adopts the one-third bushel oblong crate for peaches and similar fruits. The dimensions of this crate are about $8 \times 12\frac{1}{2} \times 22$ inches.

33. California. Sizes in Common Use for Local Markets.
(*Wickson.*)

APPLE AND PEAR. — Top, bottom, and sides of $\frac{1}{4}$-inch and ends of $\frac{5}{8}$-inch stuff. The length is 22 inches; ends 10 by 12 inches. This is called a 50-pound box, but it contains less weight.

COMPUTATION TABLES. 145

Cherry. — 15½ inches in length; ends 8½ by 3½.

Fig. — The two-layer fig box is 20 inches long; ends 2 by 3½ inches, and holds about 20 pounds. The single layer is the same length and width, but 2 inches deep, and holds about 12 pounds.

Grapes. — The same as that used for plums in distant shipment, except that the depth is usually 5 inches, and the contents about 25 pounds of fruit. Grapes are also shipped in 4-pound splint baskets, of which 4 go in a half crate, or 8 in a whole crate.

Melons. — Cantaloupe crates 38 inches long, 16 inches wide, and 15 inches deep. Watermelons come in bulk in cars, or in large cases of all descriptions.

Oranges. — Flat boxes 22 inches long, ends 7¾ by 17½ inches. It is divided into two parts by a central partition. The prevailing orange box at present is about 26½ inches long, ends 11¼ inches square, with a central partition.

Small Fruits. — Chests or crates which contain 10, 15, or 20 drawers. The drawers are 15½ inches long, ends 8¼ by 1¾ inches. The sizes have been constantly decreasing. The old drawers held 5 pounds of strawberries; the present weight is about 4 pounds.

Packages for Dried Fruits. — 25-pound box: Inside measurements — length, 13¾ inches; width, 9¾ inches; depth, 5½ inches. Outside measurements — length, 15¼ inches; width, 10¼ inches; depth, 6½ inches; top, bottom, and sides, ⅜ of an inch thick; ends, ¾ of an inch thick.

A More Flat Package: Inside measurements — length, 16 inches; width, 9 inches; depth, 5 inches. Outside measurements — length, 17¼ inches; width, 9¾ inches; depth, 5¾ inches; top, bottom, and sides, ⅜ of an inch thick; ends, ⅝ of an inch thick.

Fifty-Pound Box: Inside measurements — length, 15¼ inches; width, 9 inches; depth, 9 inches. Outside measurements — length, 17¼ inches; width, 10 inches; depth, 10 inches; top, bottom, and sides, ½ inch thick; ends, 1 inch thick.

Sacks for Dried Fruit. — White cotton sacks, made of what

is called heavy export goods, are used for shipment of dried fruits. They are 20 by 36 inches, and hold about 80 pounds of fruit.

RAISINS. — 20-pound raisin box, $19\frac{7}{8}$ inches long, ends 9 by $4\frac{3}{4}$ inches. Half box, same length and width, depth, $2\frac{3}{4}$ inches. Quarter box, same length and width ; depth, $1\frac{1}{4}$ inches. Eighth box, $15\frac{1}{2}$ inches long, ends 6 by $1\frac{1}{4}$ inches.

34. California Packages for Eastern Shipment as adopted by the Fruit Union of that State.

The ends of all boxes should be made of $\frac{3}{4}$-inch stuff, and all cleats of $\frac{3}{8}$-inch stuff. The sides, tops, and bottoms of cherry boxes should be $\frac{1}{4}$-inch stuff: the sides made of two strips, each of $\frac{1}{4}$-inch stuff and $\frac{7}{8}$ of an inch in width. Peach, pear, and plum boxes should be made of $\frac{3}{16}$-inch stuff. All the lumber used should be dressed as smooth as possible.

Cherry boxes, capacity 10 pounds. Outside measurements — 18 inches in length, $10\frac{7}{8}$ inches in width, 3 inches in depth. Inside measurements — length, $16\frac{1}{2}$ inches ; width, $10\frac{3}{8}$ inches ; depth, $2\frac{1}{4}$ inches.

Plum boxes, capacity 20 pounds. Outside measurements — $19\frac{3}{4}$ inches in length, $12\frac{1}{4}$ inches in width, $4\frac{3}{8}$ inches in depth. Inside measurements — length, $8\frac{1}{2}$ inches ; width, $11\frac{3}{4}$ inches ; depth, 4 inches.

There are 4 sizes of peach and apricot boxes :

First, capacity 22 pounds. Outside measurements — $19\frac{3}{4}$ inches in length, $12\frac{1}{4}$ inches in width, $4\frac{3}{8}$ inches in depth. Inside measurements — length, $18\frac{1}{2}$ inches ; width, $11\frac{3}{4}$ inches ; depth, $4\frac{3}{8}$ inches.

Second, capacity 25 pounds. Outside measurements — $19\frac{3}{4}$ inches in length, $12\frac{1}{4}$ inches in width, $5\frac{1}{4}$ inches in depth. Inside measurements — length, $18\frac{1}{2}$ inches ; width, $11\frac{3}{4}$ inches ; depth, $4\frac{7}{8}$ inches.

Third, capacity 27 pounds. Outside measurements — $19\frac{3}{4}$ inches in length, $12\frac{1}{4}$ inches in width, $5\frac{3}{4}$ inches in depth. Inside measurements — length, $18\frac{1}{4}$ inches ; width, $11\frac{3}{4}$ inches ; depth, $5\frac{3}{8}$ inches.

COMPUTATION TABLES.

Fourth, capacity 30 pounds. Outside measurements — 19¾ inches in length, 12⅛ inches in width, 6¼ inches in depth. Inside measurements — length, 18½ inches; width, 11¾ inches; depth, 5⅞ inches.

Pear boxes, capacity 40 pounds. Outside measurements — 19¾ inches in length, 12⅛ inches in width, 8⅞ inches in depth. Inside measurements — length, 18½ inches; width, 11¾ inches; depth, 8½ inches.

35. California Prunes.

Prunes are graded by running them over screens of various degrees of coarseness. The meshes should be oblong, 2 inches or more in length for all the sizes, the widths varying as stated in the table below. The California French prunes are usually sorted in six sizes, by using the following methods:

Grade.	Width of mesh for green prunes.	Width of mesh for dried prunes.
Extras, 40 to 50 to pound	1⅜ inches	1¼ inches.
No. 1, 50 to 60 "	1¼ "	1⅛ "
No. 2, 60 to 70 "	1⅛ "	1 "
No. 3, 70 to 80 "	1 "	⅞ "
No. 4, 80 to 90 "	⅞ "	¾ "
No. 5, 90 to 100 "	¾ "	⅝ "

36. Covent Garden (London) Measures.

SEA-KALE PUNNETS. — 8 inches diameter at the top, 7½ inches at the bottom, and 2 inches deep.

RADISH PUNNETS. — 8 inches in diameter and 1 inch deep, if to hold 6 hands; or 9 inches by 1 inch, if for 12 hands.

MUSHROOM. — 7 inches by 1 inch.

SALAD PUNNETS. — 5 inches by 1 inch.

SIEVE. — Contains 7 imperial gallons. Diameter, 15 inches; depth, 8 inches. A sieve of peas is equal to 1 bushel. A sieve of currants, 12 quarts.

HALF-SIEVE. — Contains 3½ imperial gallons. It averages 12½ inches in diameter and 6 inches in depth.

BUSHEL SIEVE — 10½ imperial gallons. Diameter at top, 11¾ inches ; at bottom, 17 inches ; depth, 11¼ inches.

BUSHEL BASKET ought, when heaped, to contain an imperial bushel. Diameter at bottom, 10 inches ; at top, 14½ inches ; depth, 17 inches. Walnuts, nuts, apples, and potatoes are sold by this measure. A bushel of the last named, cleansed, weighs 56 pounds, but 4 pounds additional are allowed if they are not washed.

A JUNK contains ⅔ of a bushel.

POTTLE. — A long tapering basket that holds rather over a pint and a half. A pottle of strawberries should hold ½ a gallon, but never holds more than 1 quart. A pottle of mushrooms should weigh 1 pound.

HAND applies to a bunch of radishes, which contains 12 to 30 or more, according to the season.

BUNDLE contains from 6 to 12 or 20 heads of broccoli, celery, etc.; sea-kale, 12 to 18 heads ; rhubarb, 20 to 30 stems, according to size ; asparagus from 100 to 150.

GRAPES are put up in 2-pound and 4-pound punnets ; new potatoes by the London growers in 2-pound punnets. Apples and pears are put up in bushel sieves or half-sieves. A hundred-weight of Kentish filberts is 104 pounds. Weights are always 16 ounces to the pound.

BUNCH. — Radishes, 12 to 24 ; carrots, 12 and upwards ; turnips, 12 and upwards ; leeks, 6 and upwards.

A ROLL of celery contains 6, 8, to 12 heads or roots.

A SCORE of lettuce or endive is 22.

A TALLY is 5 dozen.

37. What constitutes Wholesale Quantities.

The wholesale fruit-dealers of Washington, D.C., have adopted the following rules to govern the least quantities of fruits to be sold at wholesale rates :

BANANAS. — Not less than 1 bunch.

APPLES. — Not less than 1 barrel or box as received ; no packages to be broken.

PINEAPPLES. — Not less than 25.

COMPUTATION TABLES. 149

ORANGES. — Not less than 1 box; no packages to be broken.
LEMONS. — Not less than 1 box; no packages to be broken.
GRAPES OF ALL KINDS. — Not less than 5 baskets.
MALAGA GRAPES. — By the keg only.
PEACHES. — Not less than 1 box or 1 bushel crate, or not less than 5 baskets; no packages to be broken. If in half-bushel lots, not less than 2.
PEARS. — One box or barrel; if in baskets, not less than 5.
WATERMELONS. — Not less than 25.
MUSKMELONS. — Not less than 25.
STRAWBERRIES AND ALL OTHER BERRIES. — Not less than a 32-quart crate, unless small quantity received. A 60-quart crate may be halved. An exception made with raspberries: not less than 15 quarts. In February and March, strawberries, not less than 15 quarts.

VI. MISCELLANEOUS WEIGHTS AND ESTIMATES.

38. Weights of Various Varieties of Apples per Bushel.

The following varieties, just from the trees in October, gave the following weights for a heaped bushel (Michigan):

	Pounds.		Pounds.
Baldwin	50	Fallawater	48
Belmont	50	Golden Russet	53
Ben Davis	47	Lawver	47
Bunker Hill	49	Nickajack	51
Cabashae	57	Northern Spy	46
Esopus Spitzenburgh	44	Pennock	47
Rambo	50	Swaar	51
Rhode Island Greening	52	Sweet Bough	39
Roxbury Russet	50	Talman Sweet	48
Rubicon	46	Tompkins King	44
Stark	50	Yellow Bellefleur	46

39. Dried Fruit and Cider.

A bushel of average apples gives from 6 to 7½ pounds of evaporated product. Seven pounds to the bushel is a good average.

PRODUCT OF DRIED RASPBERRIES (*W. J. Green*):

Ohio . . . 9 lbs. to the bu.	Ada . . . 8½ lbs. to the bu.
Gregg . . 8¼ " "	Tyler . . . 8¼ " "
Hilborn . . 8½ " "	Shaffer . . 8 " "

In general, 3¼ quarts (about 4 pounds) of fresh black-cap raspberries are required for a pound of marketable dried berries.

A pound of dried peaches may be made from 4 or 5 pounds of fresh fruit, if the variety has a dry flesh; but 6 or 7 pounds is often required.

In California, 20 pounds of grapes produce 6 or 7 pounds of raisins.

From 7 to 12 bushels of apples are required for a barrel of cider.

40. Various Estimates.

Raspberries contain from 1½ to 3 pounds of seeds to the bushel.

A pint of garden blackberries weighs about one pound.

Good clusters of American grapes weigh on an average from one-half to three-fourths pound, while extra-good clusters will reach a pound and a half. Clusters have been reported which weighed two pounds.

A bushel of sweet-corn ears, "in the milk," with the husks which come from it, weighs from 50 to 70 pounds.

There are about 5000 honey-bees in a pound.

Watermelons are usually sorted into three grades. Of the largest size, about 6 melons are placed in a barrel. Of medium size, about 8 (4 melons in each of two layers), and of the smallest size, 10 to 12. A truck-load of melons comprises about 200 fair-sized fruits. A car-load numbers from 1000 to 1500.

Cocoanuts are packed for shipment in bags which hold 100.

"Ekimis" branded upon boxes of Smyrna figs means A. No. 1, or Superior Selected. "Eleme" means Selected, the second grade.

To find the bushels of apples, potatoes, shelled corn, etc.,

COMPUTATION TABLES. 151

in bins, divide the cubic contents in inches by 2747.7 (the cubic inches in a heaped bushel). If the corn is in the ear, deduct one-third from the result.

To find the tons of hay in a mow or stack, divide the cubic contents by about 510, if the hay is not well settled; or by about 400, if the hay is well packed.

VII. CAPACITIES OF PIPES AND TANKS.

41. Quantity of Water held by Pipes of Various Sizes.

Diameter of Bore.	Contents of 100 Feet in Length.
$\frac{1}{2}$ inches.	.84 gallons.
1 "	3.39 "
$1\frac{1}{2}$ "	7.64 "
2 "	13.58 "
$2\frac{1}{2}$ "	21.22 "
3 "	30.56 "
4 "	54.33 "
5 "	84.90 "
6 "	122.26 "

42. Number of Gallons in Circular Tanks and Wells.

To find the contents in gallons of circular tanks, etc., square the diameter in feet, multiply by the depth, and then multiply by 5.875.

Diameter.	GALLONS WHEN THE DEPTH IS									
	3 ft.	4 ft.	5 ft.	6 ft.	7 ft.	8 ft.	9 ft.	10 ft.	11 ft.	12 ft.
4 ft.	282.00	376.00	470.00	564.00	658.00	752.00	846.00	940.00	1034.00	1128.00
5 "	440.63	587.50	734.38	881.25	1028.13	1175.00	1321.89	1468.76	1615.63	1762.50
6 "	634.50	846.90	1057.50	1269.00	1480.50	1692.00	1903.50	2115.00	2326.50	2538.00
7 "	863.63	1151.50	1439.38	1727.25	2015.13	2303.00	2590.89	2878.76	3166.63	3454.50
8 "	1128.00	1504.00	1880.00	2256.00	2632.00	3008.00	3384.00	3760.00	4136.00	4512.00
9 "	1427.63	1903.50	2379.38	2855.26	3331.13	3806.00	4282.89	4758.76	5234.63	5710.52
10 "	1762.52	2350.00	2937.52	3525.00	4112.52	4700.00	5287.56	5875.04	6461.52	7050.00
11 "	2132.63	2843.50	3554.38	4265.26	4976.12	5687.00	6397.89	7108.76	7819.43	8530.52
12 "	2538.00	3384.00	4230.00	5076.00	5922.00	6768.00	7614.00	8460.00	9306.00	10152.00

43. Number of Gallons in Square-Built Tanks.

To find the number of gallons in any square or oblong vessel multiply the number of cubic feet contained in it by 7.4805.

Size of Tank.			3 ft. deep.	4 ft. deep.	5 ft. deep.
6 by	3	feet	403.9	538.5	673.2
6 "	4	"	538.5	718.0	897.6
6 "	5	"	673.2	897.6	1122.0
6 "	6	"	807.8	1077.1	1346.4
7 "	4	"	628.3	837.7	1047.2
7 "	5	"	785.4	1047.2	1309.0
7 "	6	"	942.4	1256.6	1570.8
7 "	7	"	1099.5	1466.0	1832.6
8 "	4	"	717.0	957.4	1196.8
8 "	5	"	897.6	1196.8	1496.0
8 "	6	"	1077.1	1436.1	1683.0
8 "	7	"	1256.6	1675.5	2094.4
8 "	8	"	1436.1	1914.8	2393.6
9 "	5	"	1009.8	1346.4	1683.0
9 "	6	"	1211.7	1615.6	2019.6
9 "	7	"	1413.7	1884.9	2356.2
9 "	8	"	1615.6	2154.2	2692.8
9 "	9	"	1817.6	2423.5	3029.4
10 "	5	"	1122.0	1496.0	1870.0
10 "	6	"	1346.4	1795.2	2244.0
10 "	7	"	1570.8	2094.4	2618.0
10 "	8	"	1795.2	2393.6	2992.0
10 "	9	"	2019.6	2692.8	3366.0
10 "	10	"	2244.0	2992.0	3740.0
11 "	6	"	1481.0	1974.7	2468.4
11 "	7	"	1727.8	2303.8	2879.8
11 "	8	"	1974.7	2632.9	3291.2
11 "	9	"	2221.5	2962.0	3702.6
11 "	10	"	2468.4	2521.2	4114.0
11 "	11	"	2715.2	3620.3	4525.4
12 "	6	"	1660.5	2154.2	2692.8

COMPUTATION TABLES. 153

Size of Tank.	3 ft. deep.	4 ft. deep.	5 ft. deep.
12 by 7 feet	1884.9	2513.2	2141.6
12 " 8 "	2154.2	2872.3	3590.4
12 " 9 "	2423.5	3231.3	4039.2
12 " 10 "	2692.8	3590.4	4488.0
12 " 11 "	2962.0	3949.4	4936.8
12 " 12 "	3231.3	4308.4	5385.6

VIII. THERMOMETER SCALES.

Fahrenheit.—The freezing-point is taken as the 32d degree of the scale, and 180 degrees are made between that and the boiling-point, which therefore becomes 212°.

Centigrade or **Celsius.**—The freezing-point of water is taken as zero, and boiling-point as 100°.

Reaumur.—The freezing-point of water is taken as zero, the boiling-point as 80°.

A degree Centigrade is therefore greater than a degree of Fahrenheit as nine is greater than five; and a degree of Reaumur is greater, as nine is greater than four.

To reduce Fahrenheit degrees to Centigrade, subtract 32 from the given degree of Fahrenheit and multiply the remainder by 5 and divide it by 9: $(F.° - 32) \frac{5}{9}$.

To reduce Centigrade to Fahrenheit, multiply the given degree of Centigrade by 9 and divide the product by 5, then to the quotient add 32: $(\frac{9}{5}C.° + 32)$.

To reduce Fahrenheit to Reaumur, subtract 32 from the given degree of Fahrenheit and multiply the remainder by 4 and divide by 9: $(F.° - 32) \frac{4}{9}$.

To reduce Reaumur to Fahrenheit, multiply the given degree of Reaumur by 9 and divide by 4, then add 32: $(\frac{9}{4}R.° + 32)$.

CHAPTER XIII.

GREENHOUSE AND WINDOW-GARDEN WORK AND ESTIMATES.

I. THE HEATING OF GREENHOUSES.
(By Professor R. C. Carpenter.)

1. Methods of proportioning Radiating Surface for heating of Greenhouses.

Radiating surface, whether from steam or hot-water pipes, is estimated in square feet of exterior surface. All projections, ornaments, etc., on the exterior of pipes or radiators are counted as efficient surface. Formerly, cast-iron pipe of about 4 inches in diameter was used almost altogether for greenhouse work; it is still used to some extent for hot-water heating, but the great majority of houses are now piped with wrought iron, which is made of standard size and thickness, and is a regular article of trade.

The *heating surface* in a boiler or hot water heater is that portion of the boiler, or heater, which is exposed to the direct heat of the fire or of the heated gases.

Grate surface is the number of square feet of grate in the boiler or heater.

In estimating the heat required for greenhouses, the area expressed in square feet of glass in the roof and walls is taken as the basis from which computations are made. Certain rules of practice have been adopted and appear to give fairly good results in proportioning radiating surface, grate surface, and heating surface. The ratio of heating surface to grate surface will depend upon the kind of coal to be burned and the economy desired. The more heating surface provided per unit of grate

GREENHOUSE AND WINDOW-GARDEN WORK. 155

surface, the higher the economy, but the greater the first cost of the heater. The usual practice is to employ 40 square feet of heating surface to 1 of grate surface for hard coal, and 80 feet of heating surface to 1 of grate surface for soft coal.* One foot of heating surface in a steam boiler or in a hot-water heater will supply heat for about 8 square feet of radiating surface, under mean conditions. It will usually give a heater ample in size for the work required, but if more radiating surface is added it may in some instances prove to be small. The table following gives more exact proportions.

To maintain the temperature of the greenhouse 70 degrees

(I.) TABLE SHOWING RELATION OF GLASS SURFACE, RADIATING SURFACE, AND HEATING SURFACE.†

Temperature of radiating suface.	HOT-WATER HEATING.			STEAM HEATING.	
				(5 lbs. Pressure)	(10 lbs. Pressure)
	160°	180°	200°	220°	240°
	Square feet of glass for 1 square foot radiating surface.				
Temp. 100° F. above surrounding air	2.3	2.7	3.2	3.5	4.2
" 90° " " "	2.55	3.0	3.55	3.9	4.66
" 80° " " "	2.75	3.38	4.0	4.37	5.25
" 70° " " "	3.2	4.0	4.5	5.0	6.0
" 60° " " "	3.8	4.5	5.25	5.85	7.0
" 50° " " "	4.5	5.4	6.4	7.0	8.4
" 40° " " "	5.7	6.7	8.0	8.7	10.5
" 30° " " "	7.7	9.0	10.6	11.6	14.0
Heat units given off 1 square foot radiating surface	230	270	320	350	420
Radiating surface supplied by 1 square foot of heating surface in boiler or heater	12.2	10.5	8.8	8.0	6.8

*25 per cent less for small upright heaters.
† From Carpenter's work on Warming by Hot Water and Steam.

above that of the surrounding air, there should be 1 square foot of radiating surface for 4 square feet of glass for hot-water heating, in which the maximum temperature of the water is maintained at 180 degrees; there should be 1 square foot of radiating surface for 5 square feet of glass for low-pressure (under 5 pounds) steam heating. These numbers are given somewhat greater by some authorities, and there is no doubt that if the house is not much exposed, these higher proportions will give most satisfactory results.

The following table gives more exact values for these quantities and will be found to accord with the best practice in heating of greenhouses, either by steam or hot water. It is to be noted that for steam at 5 pounds pressure the temperature will be about 220° F. For steam at 10 pounds pressure, the temperature will be about 240° F.

2. Size of Pipes connecting Radiating Surface and Boiler or Heater.

Various empirical rules have been given for proportioning main-supply and return pipes, which have proved quite satisfactory in practice. Mr. George A. Babcock gives the following rule, which will be found very satisfactory for greenhouse heating, whether with low-pressure steam or with water:

The diameter of main pipe leading to the radiating surface should be equal in inches to 0.1 the square root of radiating surface in square feet. The main pipes should not be less than 1¼ inches in diameter, return pipes for water heating the same size as mains, and, for steam heating, one size less than mains, but never less than ¾ inch in diameter. The following table shows the radiating surface supplied by various sizes of main pipe.

(II.) SIZE OF PIPES.   RADIATING SURFACE SUPPLIED.

Size	Radiating Surface Supplied
1¼ in.	155 square feet.
1½ "	225 " "
2 "	400 " "
2½ "	620 " "
3 "	900 " "
3½ "	1220 " "
4 "	1600 " "

GREENHOUSE AND WINDOW-GARDEN WORK. 157

3. Table of Dimensions of Standard Wrought-iron Pipe.

(III.) WROUGHT-IRON WELDED PIPE.—For Steam and Water.

1 inch and below, butt-welded; proved to 300 pounds per square inch, hydraulic pressure.
1¼ inch and above, lap-welded; proved to 500 pounds per square inch, hydraulic pressure.

TABLE OF STANDARD SIZES.

Inside Diameter. Nominal.	Price-List.*		Internal Area in one Lineal Inch.	Circumference of Pipe in inches.	Length of Pipe per Square Foot of Radiating Surface.	Number Square Feet in one Lineal Foot of Pipe.	Contents in Gallons, per foot.	No. of Threads per inch of Screw.
	Black, per foot.	Galvanized, per foot.						
½	$.05½	$.07¼	.3048	2.652	4.502 ft.	.221	.0102	14
¾	.07½	.09½	.533	3.299	3.637 "	.274	.0230	14
1	.10½	.13½	.8627	4.134	2.903 "	.344	.0408	11½
1¼	.14	.18½	1.496	5.215	2.301 "	.434	.0638	11½
1½	.23	.26	2.038	5.969	2.010 "	.497	.0918	11½
2	.30	.34	3.355	7.461	1.611 "	.621	.1632	11½
2½	.47	.53	4.783	9.032	1.328 "	.752	.2550	8
3	.62	.68	7.368	10.99	1.091 "	.916	.3673	8
3½	.74	.88	9.837	12.56	.955 "	1.044	.4998	8
4	.88	1.03	12.730	14.13	.849 "	1.178	.6528	8
4½	1.06	1.31	15.939	15.70	.765 "	1.309	.8263	8
5	1.28	1.60	19.990	17.47	.629 "	1.656	1.0200	8

Manufacturers' revised price-list. Adopted Sept. 18, 1889.

*Subject to large discount.

The preceding table gives the standard sizes and principal dimensions of wrought-iron pipe. From this table the amount required for a given amount of radiating surface can be readily computed. This pipe can be purchased of any dealer.

4. To design heating Surface.

1st. Find radiating surface by dividing area of glass in square feet by results in Table II. Hot-water pipes can be kept at a temperature of 180° F. if desired.

2d. Find the amount of pipe by dividing amount of radiating surface by number of feet required per square foot of radiating surface, as given in Table III. Do not use pipe less than 1½ inches in diameter for radiating surface.

3d. Find size of main pipes by Table II., using size next larger when radiating surface comes between numbers given. It is usually better to have several main and return pipes, and divide the radiating surface in sections.

II. VARIOUS ESTIMATES AND RECIPES.

5. Effects of Wind in cooling Glass. (*Leuchars.*)

Velocity of Wind per hour.	Time required to lower Temperature from 120 to 100 Fahr.
3.26 miles	2 : 58 minutes.
5.18 "	2 : 16 "
6.54 "	1 : 01 "
8.86 "	1 : 06 "
10.90 "	1 : 50 "
13.36 "	1 : 25 "
17.97 "	1 : 08 "
20.45 "	1 : 00 "
24.54 "	: 91 "
27.27 "	: 81 "

6. Per Cent of Rays of Light reflected from Glass Roofs at Various Angles of Divergence from the Perpendicular. (*Bouguer.*)

1°	2.5 per cent.
10°	2.5 "

GREENHOUSE AND WINDOW-GARDEN WORK. 159

20°	2.5 per cent.
30°	2.7 "
40°	3.4 "
50°	5.7 "
60°	11.2 "
70°	22.2 "
80°	41.2 "
85°	54.3 "

7. Angle of Roof for Different Heights and Widths of House.

(*Taft.*)

Height—Feet.	4 ft.		5 ft.		6 ft.		7 ft.		8 ft.		9 ft.	
Width—Feet.	°	′	°	′	°	′	°	′	°	′	°	′
6	33	21	39	48	45		49	24	53	8	56	18
7	29	44	35	32	40	36	45		48	49	52	07
8	26	33	32		36	52	41	11	45		48	22
9	23	57	29	3	33	5	37	52	41	38	45	
10	21	48	26	33	30	58	35		38	39	41	59
11			24	26	28	36	32	28	36	2	39	17
12			22	57	26	33	30	15	33	41	36	52
13			21	2	24	47	28	18	31	36	34	42
14					23	12	26	34	29	44	32	44

Measuring the height directly under the ridge to a point on a level with the bottom of the sash or eaves of the roof, and measuring the width along this level to the eave, the table gives the angles which the roof makes with the horizontal.

8. Standard Flower-Pots.

AMERICAN.

The Society of American Florists has adopted a standard pot, in which all measurements are made inside, and which bears a rim or shoulder at the top. The breadth and depth of these pots are the same, so that they "nest" well.

ENGLISH. — CHISWICK STANDARDS.

	Diam. at top.	Depth.
Thimbles	2 in.	2 in.
Thumbs	2½	2½
60's	3	3½
54's	4	4
48's	4½	5
32's	6	6
24's	8½	8
16's	9½	9
12's	11½	10
8's	12	11
6's	13	12
4's	15	13
2's	18	14

9. To prevent boilers from filling with sediment or scale.

1. Exercise care to get clean water and that which contains little lime. 2. Blow it out often. It can be blown out a little every day, and occasionally it should be blown off entirely. 3. Put slippery-elm bark in the boiler tank. Or, if slippery-elm is not handy, use potato-peelings, flax-seed, oak-bark, spent tan, or coarse sawdust. 4. Put in, with the feed-water or otherwise, a small quantity of good molasses (not a chemical syrup), say ½ to 1 pint in a week, depending upon the size of boiler. This will remove and prevent incrustation without damage to the boiler. These vegetable substances prevent in a measure, by mechanical means, the union of the particles of lime into incrustations.

10. To prepare paper and cloth for hotbed sash.

1. Use a sash without bars, and stretch wires or strings across it to serve as a rest for the paper. Procure stout but thin manila

wrapping-paper, and paste it firmly on the sash with fresh flour paste. Dry in a warm place and then wipe the paper with a damp sponge to cause it to stretch evenly. Dry again and then apply boiled linseed oil to both sides of the paper, and dry again in a warm place.

2. Saturate cloth or tough, thin manila paper with pure, raw linseed oil.

3. Dissolve 1¾ pounds white soap in 1 quart water; in another quart dissolve 1½ ounces gum arabic and 5 ounces glue. Mix the two liquids, warm, and soak the paper, hanging it up to dry. Used mostly for paper.

4. 3 pints pale linseed oil; 1 ounce sugar of lead; 4 ounces white rosin. Grind and mix the sugar of lead in a little oil, then add the other materials and heat in an iron kettle. Apply hot with a brush. Used for muslin.

11. Liquid putty for glazing.

Take equal parts, by measure, of boiled oil, putty, and white lead. Mix the putty and oil, then add the white lead. If the mixture becomes too thick, add turpentine. Apply with a putty-bulb.

12. Paint for shading greenhouse roofs.

Make a paint of ordinary consistency of white lead and naphtha. It is removed from the glass by the use of a scrubbing-brush. Make it thin or it is hard to remove.

Ordinary lime whitewash is good for temporary use. If salt is added, it adheres better. It may be applied with a spray-pump.

13. To keep flower-pots clean.

When the pots are cleaned, soak them a few hours in ammoniacal carbonate of copper (recipe, p. 46). Soak them about once a year. This fungicide kills the green alga upon the pots, and prevents a new growth from appearing.

III. Greenhouse Practice.

14. Potting Earth.

Loam (decomposed sod), leaf-mold, rotted farm-yard manure, peat, and sand afford the main requirement of the plants most commonly cultivated. Seedlings, and young stock generally, are best suited by a light mixture, such as one part each of loam, leaf-mold, and sand in equal parts. The older plants of vigorous growth like a rich, heavy compost, formed of equal parts of loam and manure; and a sandy, lasting soil, made up of two parts each of peat and loam to one part of sand, is the most desirable for slow-growing sorts. A little lumpy charcoal should be added to the compost for plants that are to remain any great length of time, say a year, in the same pot. The best condition of soil for potting is that intermediate state between wet and dry. Sphagnum (moss), or fibrous peat and sphagnum in mixture and chopped, should be used for orchids and other plants of similar epiphytal character.

Cow-dung is highly prized by many gardeners for use in potting soil. It is stored under cover and allowed to remain until dry, being turned several times in the meantime to pulverize it. Manure-water is made either from this dried excrement or from the fresh material. When made from the fresh material, the manure-water should be made weaker than in the other case.

15. Suggestions for Potting Plants.

The pots should be perfectly dry and clean, and well drained. However one-sided a plant may be, it is advantageous to have the main stem as near the centre of the pot as possible, and the potted plant is usually in the best position when perfectly erect. Soft-wooded plants of rapid growth, such as coleus, geraniums, fuchsias, and begonias, thrive most satisfactorily when the soil is loose rather than hard about the roots. Ferns should have it moderately firm, and hard-wooded stock, azaleas, ericas, acacias, and the like, should be potted firmly. In repotting plants, more especially those of slow growth, the **ball of soil and** roots should never be sunk to any great extent below the original level, and it is always preferable to pot a plant twice, or even three times, rather than place it in a pot too large.

16. Watering Greenhouse and Window Plants.

Plants cannot be satisfactorily watered just so many times a day, week, or month. All plants should be watered when necessary — when they are dry. This is indicated by a tendency to flag or wilt, or by the hollow sound of the pots when tapped. The latter is the safest sign, as, after a prolonged period of dull weather, many plants wilt on exposure to bright sunshine, although still wet at the roots. But a growing plant should not be allowed to become so dry as to wilt, nor should the soil ever reach a condition as dry as powder. This is a condition, however, which is essential to some plants, more particularly the bulbous and tuberous kinds, during their resting period. Incessant dribbling should be avoided; water thoroughly and be done with it until the plants are again dry. Plants under glass should not be sprayed overhead while the sun is shining hot and full upon them. The evening is the best time of the day for watering in summer, and morning in winter. In watering with liquid manure, the material should not come in contact with the foliage. Plants recently potted should not be watered heavily at the roots for a week or ten days; spray them frequently overhead.

17. Liquid Manure for Greenhouses.

Most of the artificial fertilizers may be used in the preparation of liquid manure, but a lack of knowledge as to their strength and character lessens their value in the minds of gardeners. Pure cow-manure, which varies little in stimulating property, is considered by gardeners to be the safest and most reliable material to use for a liquid fertilizer. A bushel measure of the solid manure to 100 gallons of water makes a mixture which can be used with beneficial results on the tenderest plants; and for plants of rank growth, the compound may be gradually increased to thrice that strength with safety. Soot may be added with advantage, using it at the rate of 1 part to 10 parts of the manure. The mixture should stand for a few days, stirring it occasionally, before application.

IV. Lists of Plants.

18. Twenty-five Plants adapted to Window-gardens.

POTS.

Adiantum cuneatum, particularly the form known as *A. gracillimum*.
Aloysia citriodora.
Begonia metallica, and many others.
Cocos Weddelliana.
Ficus elastica.
Freesia refracta.
Fuchsia, varieties.
Mahernia odorata.
Myrtus communis.
Pelargoniums, in variety.
Primrose, Chinese.
Pteris serrulata.
Vallota purpurea.

BASKETS.

Epiphyllum truncatum.
Fragaria Indica.
Fuchsia procumbens.
Othonna crassifolia (*Othonnopsis cheirifolia*).
Oxalis violacea.
Pelargonium peltatum.
Saxifraga sarmentosa, beefsteak geranium.
Sedum Sieboldii.
Tradescantia zebrina, wandering Jew (*Zebrina pendula*).

WATER.

Eichhornia crassipes (*E. speciosa*).
Hyacinths.
Narcissus Tazetta, var. orientalis, Chinese sacred lily.

In selecting plants for a window-garden or house conservatory, those plants should be omitted which are much subject to the attacks of aphis and mealy-bug. Amongst the common plants which are much infested, are coleus, German ivy (*Senecio scandens*), calla, Vinca variegata, Cyperus alternifolius,

GREENHOUSE AND WINDOW-GARDEN WORK.

fuchsia, and carnation. Those which are nearly exempt are most kinds of geraniums, begonias, wandering Jew, and most ferns. (For insects, see p. 17.)

19. Vegetables used for Forcing under Glass.

Asparagus.
Bush Bean.
Carrot.
Cauliflower; generally matured under glass, as a late spring crop.
Cress.
Cucumber; there are two types of forcing cucumbers, the common, or White Spine type and the English or frame varieties.
Lettuce.
Muskmelon; generally grown as a late fall or late spring crop.
Parsley.
Pea.
Radish.
Rhubarb.
Sweet herbs, particularly spearmint.
Tomato.

Lettuce, tomato, cucumber, asparagus, and bean are generally the most profitable forced crops in this country, in about the order named.

20. Twenty-five Useful Aquatic and Sub-aquatic Plants for Out-door Use.

T denotes those which do not endure the winter.

Acorus gramineus, variegated.
Aponogeton distachyum.
Azolla Caroliniana.
Caltha palustris.
Cyperus alternifolius; *t.*
Eichhornia crassipes or azurea, (properly *E. speciosa*); *t.*
Limnanthemum Indicum; *t.*
" nymphoides.
Limnocharis Humboldtii (*Hydrocleys Commersonii*).
Myriophyllum proserpinacoides; *t.*
Nelumbium (*Nelumbo*). Many species and varieties. Some *t.*
Nuphar advena.
Nymphæa. Many species and varieties. Some *t.*
Ouvirandra fenestralis (*Aponogeton fenestrale*); *t.*
Papyrus (*Cyperus Papyrus*); *t.*

Pistia Stratiotes; t.
Pontederia cordata.
Sagittaria Montevidensis; t.
Salvinia natans.
Sarracenia purpurea.
Scirpus Tabernæmontani ze-
brina (*Juncus effusus*, variegated).
Trapa natans.
Typha latifolia.
Victoria regia; t.
Zizania aquatica.

21. Commercial Plants and Flowers, or "Florists' Plants."

The following are chiefly grown by florists in this country:

Adiantum.
Alyssum.
Anemone.
Asparagus plumosus.
Aster, China.
Bouvardia.
Calla.
Carnation.
Cattleya.
Chrysanthemum.
Coreopsis.
Cypripedium.
Daisy (*Bellis perennis*).
Freesia.
Gaillardia.
Gladiolus.
Gypsophila.
Helianthus.
Heliotrope.
Hyacinth.
Iris.
Lilium Harrisii (*L. longiflorum*, var. *eximium*).
Lily of the Valley.
Marguerite or Paris Daisy (*Chrysanthemum frutescens*, and *C. fœniculaceum*).
Mignonette.
Narcissus.
Nymphæa.
Pansy.
Pæonia.
Phlox.
Rose.
Smilax (*Asparagus medeoloides*).
Spirea.
Stevia (*Piqueria trinervia*).
Swainsonia.
Sweet Pea.
Tuberose.
Tulip.
Violet.

The following plants can be grown in houses which are adapted to the carnation:

Alyssum.
Asparagus (edible).
Asparagus plumosus.
Calla.

GREENHOUSE AND WINDOW-GARDEN WORK. 167

Cauliflower.
Chrysanthemum.
Cress.
Daisy.
Freesia.
Gladiolus.
Hyacinth.
Iris.
Lettuce.
Lily of the Valley (not forcing).

Mignonette.
Narcissus.
Pansy.
Pea.
Radish.
Rhubarb.
Stevia.
Sweet Pea.
Tulip.
Violet.

22. Customary temperatures in which plants are grown under glass.

	Day.	Night.
Asparagus (edible)	85°	85°
Asparagus plumosus	70°	60°
Bean	75°	65°
Carnation	60°	50°
Cauliflower	50°	40°
Chrysanthemum	55°	45°
Cucumber	80°	70°
Lettuce	55°	40°
Lily (Easter)	65°	55°
Lily of the valley (forcing)	90°	90°
Melon	80°	70°
Mushroom (under benches or in cellars)	65°	65°
Radish	55°	45°
Rose	65°	55°
Smilax	60°	50°
Tomato	75°	60°
Violet	50°	40°

CHAPTER XIV.

METHODS OF KEEPING AND STORING FRUITS AND VEGETABLES. MARKET DATES.

Apples. —
1. Keep the fruit as cool as possible without freezing. Select only normal fruit, and place it upon trays in a moist but well-ventilated cellar. If it is desired to keep the fruit particularly nice, allow no fruits to touch each other upon the trays, and the individual fruits may be wrapped in tissue paper. For market purposes, pack tightly in barrels after the apples have shrunk and store the barrels in a very cool place.

2. Some solid apples, like Spitzenburgh and Newtown Pippin, are not injured by hard freezing, if they are allowed to remain frozen until wanted and are then thawed out very gradually.

3. Many apples, particularly russets and other firm varieties, keep well when buried after the manner of pitting potatoes. Sometimes, however, they taste of the earth. This may be prevented by setting a ridge-pole over the pile of apples in forked sticks, and making a roof of boards in such a manner that there will be an air-space over the fruit. Then cover the boards with straw and earth. Apples seldom keep well after removal from a pit in spring.

4. Apples may be kept by burying in chaff. Spread chaff — buckwheat-chaff is good — on the barn-floor, pile on the apples and cover them with chaff and fine broken or chopped straw 2 feet thick, exercising care to fill the interstices.

Cabbage. — The most satisfactory method of keeping cabbages is to bury them in the field. Select a dry place, pull the cabbages and stand them head down on the soil. Cover them with soil to the depth of 6 or 10 inches, covering very lightly at first to prevent heating — unless the weather should quickly become severe — and as winter sets in cover with a good dressing of straw or coarse manure. The cabbages should be allowed to stand where they grew until cold weather approaches. The storing beds are usually made about 6 or 8 feet wide, so that the middle of the bed can be reached from either side, and to prevent heating if the weather should remain open. Cabbages quickly decay in the warm weather of spring.

Cabbage for family use is most conveniently kept in a barrel or box half buried in the garden. Cabbages and turnips should never be kept in the house cellar, as when decaying they become very offensive.

Celery. — For market purposes, celery is stored in temporary board pits, in sheds, in cellars, and in various kinds of earth pits and trenches. The points to be considered are, to provide the plants with moisture to prevent wilting, to prevent hard freezing, and to give some ventilation. The plants are set loosely in the soil. There are several methods of keeping celery in an ordinary cellar for home use. The following methods are good:

Select a shoe or similar box. Bore one-inch holes in the sides, four inches from bottom. Put a layer of sand or soil in the box, and stand the plants, trimmed carefully, upon it, closely together, working more sand or soil about the root part, and continuing until the box is full. The soil should be watered as often as needed, but always through the holes in the side of the box. Keep the foliage dry.

Celery may also be stored and well blanched at the same time, in a similar way, by standing it in a barrel upon a layer of soil. Some roots and soil may be left adhering to the plants. Crowd closely, water through holes near the bottom as in case of box storage, and keep the plants in the dark.

Blanched celery can also be preserved for a long time by

trimming closely and packing upright in moss inside of a box. A large quantity of the vegetable may thus be stored in a small space.

Crystallized or **Glacé Fruit.**—The principle is to extract the juice from the fruit and replace it with sugar syrup, which hardens and preserves the fruit in its natural shape. The fruit should be all of one size and of a uniform degree of ripeness, such as is best for canning. Peaches, pears, and similar fruits are pared and cut in halves; plums, cherries, etc., are pitted. After being properly prepared, the fruit is put in a basket or bucket with a perforated bottom and immersed in boiling water to dilute and extract the juice. This is the most important part of the process, and requires great skill. If the fruit be left too long, it is over-cooked and becomes soft; if not long enough, the juice is not sufficiently extracted, and this prevents perfect absorption of the sugar. After the fruit cools, it may again be assorted as to softness. The syrup is made of white sugar and water. The softer the fruit, the heavier the syrup required. The fruit is placed in earthen pans, covered with syrup and left about a week. This is a critical stage, as fermentation will soon take place, and when this has reached a certain stage the fruit and syrup are heated to the boiling-point, which checks the fermentation. This is repeated, as often as may be necessary, for about six weeks. The fruit is taken out of the syrup, washed in clean water, and either glacéd or crystallized, as desired. It is dipped in thick syrup, and hardened quickly in the open air for glacing, or left to be hardened slowly if to be crystallized. The fruit is now ready for packing, and will keep in any climate.

Figs.—After the figs are gathered and dried in the same way as peaches or apricots, wash to remove all grit, and spread in shallow pans and set them in the oven to become thoroughly heated, taking care to prevent scorching. Then roll in powdered sugar, which has been rolled to remove all lumps. When cold, pack away, preferably in paper bags.

They make a delicious lunch with a bowl of milk. They are also excellent for the dessert.

Gooseberries keep well if kept tight in common bottles filled with pure water. Be sure that none but perfect berries are admitted, and keep in a cool place. The berries should be picked before they are ripe, or edible from the hand, — in the stage at which they are used for culinary purposes.

Grapes. —

1. The firm grapes usually keep best — as Catawba, Vergennes, Niagara, Diana, Jefferson, etc. Thickness of skin does not appear to be correlated with good keeping qualities. Always cut the bunches which are to be stored on a dry day, when the berries are ripe, and carefully remove all soft, bruised, and imperfect fruits and all leaves. Keep the fruit dry, cool, and away from currents of air. Many varieties keep well if simply placed in shallow boxes or baskets and kept undisturbed in a cool, rather moist place.

2. Pack the bunches in layers of dry, clean sand.

3. Pack in layers of some small grain, as wheat, or oats, or barley.

4. Cork-dust is also excellent for use in packing grapes. This cork can be had from grocers who handle the white Malagas, which are packed in this material.

5. Pack the bunches in finely cut, soft, and dry hay, placing the grapes and hay in consecutive layers.

6. Dry hardwood sawdust is also good for packing.

7. Place on shelves in a cool, airy room. After a few days wrap the bunches separately in soft paper and pack in shallow pasteboard boxes, not more than two or three layers deep. Keep in a cool, dry room that is free from frost.

8. Cut the bunches with sharp scissors, place in shallow baskets, but few in a basket, and after reaching the house dip the cut end of stems in melted wax. Now take tissue paper or very thin manila paper cut just to the right size, and carefully wrap each cluster of grapes. Secure shallow tin boxes; place a layer of cotton-batting at the bottom, then

a layer of grapes, then batting; three layers of grapes are enough for one box, alternating with cotton-batting, and topping with batting; then gently secure the lid to each box, and when done place in cold storage for use in April or even later. If cold storage cannot be had, put in a dry, cool room, and when cold weather approaches cover in an interior closet with just sufficient covering to prevent freezing; warmth will cause over-ripening and deterioration.

9. ROE'S METHOD.— In a stone jar place alternate layers of grapes and straw paper, the paper being in double thickness. Over the jar place a cloth and bury below frost in a dry soil. The grapes will keep until New Year's.

KEEPING GRAPES FOR MARKET (W. M. Pattison, Quebec). — It is the generally received opinion that the thick-skinned native seedlings are the only keepers. This is correct as regards preserving flavor, but several hybrids of foreign blood are the best keepers known. Before giving results of this and former trials, instructions in packing may be of service. The varieties intended to be laid up for winter use should be those alone which adhere well to the stem and are not inclined to shrivel. These should be allowed to remain on the vines as long as they are safe from frost. A clear, dry day is necessary for picking, and careful handling and shallow baskets are important. The room selected for the drying process should be well ventilated, and the fruit laid out in single layers on tables or in baskets where the air circulates freely, the windows being closed at night and in damp weather. In about ten days the stems will be dried out sufficiently to prevent molding when laid away. When danger from this is over, and the stems resemble those of raisins, the time for packing has arrived. In this, the point to be observed is to exclude air proportionately with their tendency to mold. I have used baskets for permanent packing, but much prefer shallow trays or boxes of uniform size to be packed on each other, so that each box forms a cover for the lower, the uppermost only needing one. Until very cold weather, the boxes can be piled so as to allow the remaining moisture to escape through a crevice about the width of a knife-blade. Before packing, each bunch should be examined and all injured, cracked, and rotten berries removed with suitable scissors. If two layers are packed in a box, a sheet of paper should intervene. The boxes must be kept in a cool, dry room or passage, at an even temperature. If the thermometer goes much below freezing-point, a blanket or newspaper can be thrown over them, to be removed in mild weather. Looking over them once in the winter and removing defective berries will suffice, the poorest keepers being placed accessible. Under this treatment the best keepers will be in good edible order as late as February, after which they deteriorate.

The following is a list of grapes worth noticing, that have been tested for keeping:

Description.	List of Grapes to be Recommended.
Nov. 1st.	Lady, Antoinette, Carlotta, Belinda.
Dec. 1st.	Lady Washington, Peter Wiley, Mason, Worden, Senasqua, Romell's Superior, Ricketts' No. 546, Concord, Delaware.
Jan. 1st.	Duchess, Essex, Barry, Rockland, Favorite, Aminia, Garber, Massasoit, Demsey's No. 5, Burnett, Undine, Allen's Hybrid, Agawan, Gen. Pope, Francis Scott.
Jan. 15th.	Salem, Vergennes, El Dorado.
Feb. 1st.	Wilder, Herbert, Peabody, Rogers' No. 30, Gærtner, Mary and Owosso.

(Varieties keeping well until—)

Onions demand a dry cellar, and the bulbs should be thoroughly dried in the sun before they are stored. All tops should be cut away when the onions are harvested. If a cellar cannot be had, the bulbs may be allowed to freeze, but great care must be exercised or the whole crop will be lost. The onions must not be subjected to extremes of temperature, and they should not thaw out during the winter. They can be stored on the north side of a loft, being covered with two or three feet of straw, hay, or chaff to preserve an equable temperature. They must not be handled while frozen, and they must thaw out very gradually in the spring. This method of keeping onions is reliable only when the weather is cold and tolerably uniform, and it is little used.

Orange. — Aside from the customary wrapping of oranges in tissue paper and packing them in boxes, burying in dry sand is sometimes practised. The fruit is first wrapped in tissue paper, and it should be buried in such manner that the fruit shall not be more than three tiers deep.

Pears. — Pears should be picked several days or a couple of weeks before they are ripe, and then placed in a dry and well-ventilated room, like a chamber. Make very shallow piles, or, better, place on trays. They will then ripen up well. The fruits are picked when full grown but not ripe, and when the stem separates readily from the fruit-spur if the pear is lifted up. All pears are better for being prematurely picked in this way. Winter pears are stored in the same manner as winter apples.

Quinces are kept in the same way as winter apples and winter pears. Some varieties, particularly the Champion, may be kept until after New Year's in a good cellar.

Roots of all sorts, as beets, carrots, salsify, parsnips, can be kept from wilting by packing them in damp sphagnum moss, like that used by nurserymen. They may also be packed in sand. It is an erroneous notion that parsnips and salsify are not good until after they are frozen.

Squashes should be stored in a dry room in which the temperature is uniform and about 50°. Growers for market usually build squash houses or rooms and heat them. Great care should be taken not to bruise any squashes which are to be stored. Squashes procured from the market have usually been too roughly handled to be reliable for storing.

Sweet potatoes. — IN THE NORTH. — Dig the potatoes on a sunny day, and allow them to dry thoroughly in the field. Sort out the poor ones and handle the remainder carefully. Never allow them to become chilled. Then pack them in barrels in layers, in dry sand, and store in a warm cellar. They are sometimes stored in finely broken charcoal, in charcoal-dust, wheat-chaff, and similar substances.

Sometimes they are kept in small and open crates, without packing-material, the crates being stacked so as to allow thorough ventilation. The Hayman or Southern Queen keeps well in this way.

A warm attic is often a good place in which to store sweet potatoes. A tight room over a kitchen is particularly good when it is so arranged that the heat from the kitchen can be utilized in warming it.

IN THE SOUTH (Berckmans). — Digging the tubers should be delayed until the vines have been sufficiently touched by frost to check vegetation. Allow the potatoes to dry off in the field, which will take but a few hours. Then sort all those of eating size to be banked separately from the smaller ones. The banks are prepared as follows: Make a circular bed 6 feet in diameter, in a sheltered corner of the garden, throwing up the earth about a foot high. Cover this with straw and bank up the tubers in shape of a cone, using from 10 to 20 bushels to each bank. A triangular pipe made of narrow planks to act as a ventilator should be placed in the middle of the cone. Cover the tubers with straw 6 to 10 inches thick and bank the latter with earth, first using only a small quantity, but increasing the thickness a week or ten days afterwards. A board should be placed upon the top of the ventilating pipe to prevent water from reaching the tubers. Several banks are usually made in a row, and a rough shelter of boards built over the whole. The main point to be considered in putting up sweet potatoes for winter is entire freedom from moisture and sufficient covering to prevent heating. It is therefore advisable to allow the tubers to undergo sweating (which invariably occurs after being put in heaps) before covering them too much; and if the temporary covering is removed for a few hours, a week after being heaped, the moisture generated will be removed and very little difficulty will follow from that cause. If covered too thickly at once, the sweating often engenders rapid fermentation, and loss is then certain to follow. Sand is never used here in banking potatoes. Some varieties of potatoes keep much better than others. The Yellow Sugar Yam and the Pumpkin Yam are the most difficult to carry through; while the Trinidad potato keeps as readily as Irish potatoes, only requiring to be kept free from frost and light by a slight covering of straw, if the tubers are placed in a house. Next in keeping quality come the Hayti Yam, the Red-skinned, Brimstone, Nigger Killer; and the last of the potato section is the Nansemond.

Tomatoes. — Pick the firmest fruits just as they are beginning to turn, leaving the stems on, exercising care not to bruise them, and pack in a barrel or box in clean and thoroughly dry sand, placing the fruits so that they will not touch each other. Place the barrel in a dry place.

In the autumn when frosts appear, tomatoes, if carefully picked and laid on straw under the glass of cold frames, will continue to ripen until near Christmas. Fruit ripened in this way seems to be as good as that ripened naturally on the vines. Green but full-grown tomatoes may be gradually ripened by placing them in cupboards or bureau drawers.

The ripening of tomatoes may be hastened ten days by bagging them as grapes are bagged.

Grading and packing fruit. — A first-class apple, pear, or other tree fruit is one which is full grown, of normal size, symmetrical, characteristic of the variety, wholly free of blemishes of insects or fungi, and not overripe. In apples, pears, and plums, the stem must be left on if the specimen is to be first-class, but in peaches, apricots, quinces, and oranges, the stem remains upon the tree or, at least, is not necessary to a first-class fruit.

Second-class fruits are generally considered to be those which fall below first-class and which are good enough for marketing. They are sound enough to keep well, are fairly uniform in size and shape, but may have more or less surface blemishes. A small, dry worm-hole in the blossom end of an apple or pear makes the fruit second-class.

The greatest care should be exercised in packing fruits for market. Apples and pears which are to be shipped in barrels are commonly packed as soon as they leave the trees, but if the fruit is to be used for winter storage, it should be allowed to sweat and shrink before barrelling. These processes may be allowed to take place in piles in the orchard or in bins under cover, but the fruit should generally be kept cool. The piles should be in the shade of trees if possible, or, if under cover, in a cool shed or barn, as under a north or a shaded roof. The first layer of fruit on either end of the barrel should be "faced," by placing the fruits in concentric rings around the head with the stem end next the head. After the lower end is faced, fruit of uniform grade is carefully poured or placed in, the barrel being lightly shaken once or twice to settle the fruit. The upper end should usually be faced like the lower one, and the fruit should stand an inch or less above the rim of the barrel before the head is pressed in. The shipping-mark is usually placed on the opposite head, or the one which stood on the ground whilst the packing proceeded, and this then becomes the top end. Merchants frequently turn the barrel over and open the other end, however; hence this should be faced as advised. Sprayed fruits shrink less and keep longer than unsprayed samples.

Perishable and dessert fruits which are shipped in baskets or other small packages, should be carefully laid in one by one, in layers. They will then ship without settling. See that the packages are full when they leave the packing-house. Care must be exercised not to rub the bloom off grapes and plums. Grape clusters should have all imperfect berries cut away before packing. If berries are picked when dry, and cooled off before packing, they may be shipped in tight unventilated packages.

Chautauqua grape figures. — The grapes are shipped in 9-pound Climax baskets, which weigh, when not filled, including cover, 24 ounces, holding $7\frac{1}{2}$ pounds of grapes. A carload is 2800 to 3000 baskets. The railroads count 222 baskets to the ton. A girl will pack from 100 to 150 baskets per day. One cent per basket is paid for packing. An average acre of Concord grapes yields about 500 baskets. The average annual cost of cultivating the vineyard up to picking time is $8. The expense of picking, packing, packages, and carting is about $28 for the 500 baskets. The bunches are cut from the vines with shears made for the purpose. In the packing-house the bunches are trimmed.

Dates at which Various Fruits and Nuts appear in Northern Markets. (*From New England Grocer.*)

NUTS. — Peanuts, about the first of November.

Walnuts — French, Naples, and Grenoble — about the middle of November.

Pecans, about the same time as walnuts.

Filberts, about the first of November.

Castanas (Bertholletia or Brazil-nut), early in March.

Almonds, shelled about October first, and Ivica and Princess about forty-five days later.

Shellbarks, October first.

Baracoa cocoanuts begin to come during the latter part of March and the first of April.

Chestnuts, late in September.

DRIED FRUITS. — Citron (Leghorn), October first.

Currants, the middle of October.

Dates, Fard about the middle of November, and Persian about December 12.

Prunes, French, about the middle of October, and Turkish a month or so later.

Raisins, Malaga fruit — which includes loose Muscatels, 2, 3, 4, and 6-crown, and Imperial Cabinet layers, B. B., Empire Cluster, Royal, and Imperial — begin to put in appearance about the first of November. California raisins begin to come early in October. Sultana raisins are due about October first, and New Valencias about the same time.

FOREIGN GREEN FRUIT. — Oranges — Messina, Valencia, and Palermo, and all Mediterranean fruit, early in December.

Florida oranges generally begin to arrive the first of November. Jamaicas get here the middle of September.

Lemons — Messina, Valencia, and Palermo, and all Mediterranean fruit, December first.

Aspinwall, Cuban, Jamaica, and Baracoa bananas come the year round, every month in the year, and about every day in the month a portion of the time — certainly every week in each month.

Pineapples, mostly Havanas, come whenever there is a demand for them, the year round. Florida pines come during the latter part of May and the first of June.

Grapes, Malagas, are due about October first.

New figs begin to come along about the same time.

DOMESTIC GREEN FRUIT — Apples, new, early in August. Russets generally make their appearance upon the market early in the winter, and Gravensteins in December.

Pears, September.

Peaches, Jersey, latter part of August and early in September. Delawares early in August.

Plums, all along from August first to the middle of November.

Grapes, Hamburgs, are in the market about all the year round, save, perhaps, three or four months. Catawbas arrive about the middle of August, and Ives about the same time.

Berries. Blueberries, usually in July. Blackberries are liable to arrive any time in June.

Watermelons are with us from the first of June to the first of September.

Cantaloupes, early in July, lasting about three months.

CHAPTER XV.

COLLECTING AND PRESERVING SPECIMENS FOR CABINETS OR EXHIBITION. PERFUMERY. LABELS. PRESERVING WOOD.

1. Collecting and Preserving Plants.

Collect samples of all parts of the plant, — lower and upper leaves, stem, flowers, fruit, and in most cases roots. In small species, those two feet high or less, the whole plant should be taken. Of larger plants, take portions about a foot long. Press the plants between papers or "driers." These driers may be any thick porous paper, as blotting-paper or carpet-paper, or, for plants that are not succulent or very juicy, newspapers in several thicknesses may be used. It is best to place the specimens in sheets of thin paper — grocer's tea-paper is good — and place these sheets between the driers. Many specimens can be placed in a pile. On top of the pile place a short board and a weight of 30 or 40 pounds, or a lighter weight if the pile is small and the plants are soft. Change the driers every day. The plants are dry when they become brittle, and when no moisture can be felt by the fingers. Some plants will dry in two or three days, while others require as many weeks. If the pressing is properly done, the specimens will come out smooth and flat, and the leaves will usually be green, although some plants always turn black in drying.

Specimens are usually mounted on single sheets of white paper of the stiffness of very heavy writing-paper or thin Bristol-board. The standard size of sheet is $11\frac{1}{2} \times 16\frac{1}{2}$ inches. The plants may be pasted down permanently and entirely to the sheet, or they may be held on by strips of gummed paper. In the former case, Denison's fish-glue is the best gum to use.

Only one species or variety should be placed on a sheet. Specimens which are taller than the length of a sheet should be doubled over when they are pressed. The species of a genus are collected into a genus cover. This cover is a folded sheet of heavy manila or other firm paper, and the standard size, when folded, is 12 × 16½ inches. On the lower left-hand corner of this cover the name of the genus is written. A label should accompany each specimen upon the separate sheets, recording the name, date of collecting, name of collector, and any notes which may be of interest. The specimens are now ready to be filed away on shelves in a horizontal position. If insects attack the specimens, they may be destroyed by fumes of bisulphide of carbon (see Chap. I.) or chloroform. In this case it is necessary to place the specimens in a tight box and then insert the liquid. Lumps of camphor placed in the cabinet are useful in keeping away insects. Usually, however, specimens are dipped in poison, and then dried before being mounted.

Herbarium Poisons. — 1. 120 grains of arsenic acid dissolved in a quart of alcohol. The arsenic acid is very deliquescent and the bottle must be kept tightly corked. This is Dr. Gray's favorite preparation for use in the herbarium at Harvard University.

2. Place as much corrosive sublimate in alcohol as the liquid will dissolve. If the poison is applied with a brush, care must be taken to avoid one with iron trimmings, as the sublimate corrodes the iron.

3. Dissolve 1¾ ounces of corrosive sublimate in 1 pint of alcohol; add 2½ fluid drams of carbolic acid, and apply with a paint-brush.

4. 1 pound of corrosive sublimate, 1 pound of carbolic acid to 4 gallons of methylated spirit (wood alcohol).

2. Preserving, Printing, and Imitating Flowers and Other Parts of Plants.

To Preserve the Color of Dried Flowers. — 1. Immerse the stem of the fresh specimen in a solution of 32 parts by weight of alum, 4 of nitre, and 186 of water for two or three days until the liquid is thoroughly absorbed, and then press in the ordinary way, except that dry sand is sifted over the specimen and the packet submitted to the action of gentle heat for 24 hours.

2. Make a varnish composed of 20 parts of powdered copal and 500 parts of ether, powdered glass or sand being used to make the copal dissolve more readily. Into this solution the plants are carefully dipped; then they are allowed to dry for 10 minutes, and the same process is repeated four or five times in succession.

3. Plants may also be plunged in a boiling solution of 1 part of salicylic acid and 600 of alcohol, and then dried in bibulous paper. But this should be done very rapidly, violet flowers especially being decolorized by more than an instantaneous immersion.

4. Red flowers which have changed to a purplish tint in drying may have their color restored by laying them on a piece of paper moistened with dilute nitric acid (1 part to 10 or 12 parts of water), and then submitting them to moderate pressure for a few seconds; but the solution must not touch the green leaves, as they are decolorized by it.

5. *With Sulphur.* (Quin.) Procure a chest about 3 or 4 feet square, with a small opening in the under part of one side, to be closed by a bar, through which the basin containing brimstone must be put into the chest; this opening must be covered inside with perforated tin, in order to prevent those flowers which hang immediately over the basin from being spoiled. Paper the inside to render it air-tight. When the chest is ready for use, nail small laths on two opposite sides of the interior, at a distance of about 6 inches apart, and on these lay thin round sticks upon which to arrange the flowers; these should not be too close together, or the vapor will not circulate freely through the vacant spaces around the flowers. When the chest is sufficiently full of flowers, close it carefully, place a damp cloth on the sides of the lid, and some heavy stones upon the top of it; then take small pieces of brimstone, put them in a small flat basin, kindle and put through the opening in the bottom of the chest and shut the bar. Leave the chest undisturbed for 24

hours, after which time it must be opened, and if the flowers be sufficiently smoked they will appear white, if not, they must be smoked again. When sufficiently smoked, take the flowers out carefully and hang them up in a dry, airy place in the shade, and in a few days or even hours they will recover their natural color, except being only a shade paler.

To give them a very bright and shining color, plunge them into a mixture of 10 parts of cold water and 1 of good nitric acid; drain off the liquid, and hang them up again the same as before. The best flowers for this process are asters, roses, fuchsias (single ones), spireas (red-flowered kinds, such as callosa, Douglasi, etc.), ranunculus, delphiniums, cytisus, etc. The roses should be quite open, but not too fully blown.

6. *In Sand.* (Quin.) Dry the plants in clean silver sand, free from organic matter (made so by repeated washing, until the sand ceases to discolor the water). Heat the sand rather hot, and mix with it by constant stirring with a small piece of wax candle, which prevents the sand from adhering to the flowers. Have a box not higher than 3 inches, but as broad as possible; this box should have instead of a bottom a narrow-meshed iron-wire net at a distance of $\frac{3}{4}$ inch from where the bottom should be. Place the box on a board and fill with sand till the net is just covered with a thin layer of sand; upon this layer of sand place a layer of flowers, on that a layer of sand, then flowers, and so on; the layers of sand should vary in thickness according to the kind of flowers, from $\frac{1}{8}$ inch to $\frac{1}{4}$ inch.

When the box contains about three layers of flowers, it must be removed to a very sunny dry place, the best being close under the glass in an empty greenhouse, exposed to the full influence of the sun. After a week, if the weather is sunny and dry, the flowers will be perfectly dried; then the box is lifted a little, the sand falls gently through the iron net, and the flowers remain in their position over the net without any disturbance whatever.

They should then be taken out carefully and kept in a dry and, if possible, dark place, where no sun can reach them, and afterwards they will keep very well for many years.

Care should be taken that the flowers are cut in dry weather, and that while lying in the sand no part of a flower shall touch another part, as this always spoils the color and causes decay. Sand should be filled in between all the parts of the flower; therefore it is necessary to insert the double flowers in an erect position, in order to fill the sand between the petals, while most of the single flowers must be put in with the stalks upwards.

PRINTING PLANTS.—1. First, lightly oil one side of paper, then fold in four, so that the oil may filter through the pores, and the plant may not come into direct contact with the liquid. The plant is placed between the leaves of the second folding, and in this position pressed (through other paper) all over with the hand, so as to make a small quantity of oil adhere to its surface. Then it is taken out and placed between two sheets of white paper for two impressions, and the plant is pressed as before. Sprinkle over the invisible image remaining on the paper a quantity of black lead or charcoal, and distribute it in all directions; the image then appears in all its parts. With an assortment of colors the natural colors of plants may be reproduced. To obtain fixity, rosin is previously added to the black lead in equal parts. Expose to heat sufficient to melt the rosin.

2. The best paper to use is ordinary wove paper, without watermarks; if it can be afforded, use thin drawing-paper. First select the leaves, then carefully press and dry them. If they be placed in a plant-press, care must be taken not to put too great pressure on the specimens at first, or they will be spoiled for printing. An old book is the best for drying the samples to be used. Take printers' or proof ink, and a small leather dabber; work a bit of ink about the size of a pea on a small piece of slate or glass, with the dabber, until it is perfectly smooth. A drop or two of linseed oil will assist the operation. Then give the leaf a thin coating, being careful to spread it equally; now lay the leaf ink downwards on a sheet of paper and place it between the leaves of an old book, which must then be subjected to a moderate pressure in a copying-press, or passed between the rollers of a wringing-machine. Impressions can be taken with greater rapidity by laying the book on the

floor and standing upon it for a few seconds. Soft book-paper is the best. Previous to using it, place a few sheets between damp blotting-paper, which causes it to take the ink still more readily. At first you will find that you lay on too much ink. If the impression is too black, use the leaf again. If the midrib of the leaf is too thick, it must be shaved down with a sharp knife.

3. *Leaf-Prints.* (Engle.) 1. A small ink-roller, such as printers use for inking type. 2. A quantity of printers' green ink. 3. A pane of stout window-glass (the larger the better) fastened securely to an evenly planed board twice the size of the glass. A small quantity of the ink is put on the glass and spread with a knife, after which it is distributed evenly by going over in all directions with the ink-roller. When this has been carefully done, the leaf to be copied is laid on a piece of waste paper and inked by applying the roller once or twice with moderate pressure. This leaves a film of ink on the veins and network of the leaf, and by placing it on a piece of blank paper and applying considerable pressure for a few moments the work is done, and when the leaf is lifted from the paper the impress remains with all its delicate tracery, faithful in color and outline to the original.

To make the ink of proper consistency, add several drops of balsam copaiba to a salt-spoonful of ink. In case the leaf sticks, the ink is too thick.

SKELETONIZING PLANTS.— 1. *By Maceration.* Place the leaves in water and allow them to remain in the same water for from 3 to 4 months, until the soft matter decays, and the stem may be taken in the hand and the refuse shaken away. There remains behind a network or skeleton of the original object, which can be bleached with a little lime. Leaves and pods may both be treated satisfactorily in this manner. The pod of the "Jimson weed" or *Datura Stramonium* is a favorite for this purpose.

2. *By Chemicals.* Chloride of lime, $\frac{1}{4}$ pound; washing soda, $\frac{1}{2}$ pound. Put the soda into $1\frac{1}{2}$ pints boiling water (rainwater is best) and let it thoroughly dissolve. Put the

chloride of lime in a large pitcher, and add same quantity of cold water. Stir well and cover closely to prevent the escape of the chlorine. When the soda-water is cool, pour it on the chloride of lime, stir well together and cover tightly, leaving it for an hour or more. Then pour off very gently the clear liquid, which must be bottled tightly.

This solution will remove fruit-stains from white goods, and will bleach any vegetable substances. When used for cotton or linen, it must be considerably diluted, and the goods well rinsed afterwards.

WATERPROOF PAPER FOR ARTIFICIAL FLOWERS.— Waterproof paper, transparent and impervious to grease, is obtained by soaking good paper in an aqueous solution of shellac and borax. It resembles parchment paper in some respects. If the aqueous solution be colored with aniline colors, very handsome paper, of use for artificial flowers, is prepared.

TO KEEP FLOWERS FRESH.— If cut flowers are not needed immediately, wet them and then wrap them in paper and place in a tight box in a cool place. Keep as cool as possible without freezing.

The disagreeable odor which comes from flowers in vases is due to the decay of the leaves and stems in the water. Therefore remove all the lower leaves before putting flowers in vases.

Flowers that have stood in a vase for a day or so can be greatly refreshed if taken from the vase at night, thoroughly sprinkled and wrapped, stems, blossoms, and all, as closely as possible in a soaked cloth, and laid aside until the morning. They will be much fresher than if they had been left in their vases, yet will not have bloomed out so much. Before thus laying them aside, and again in the morning, a bit of each stem should be cut off, as the end soon hardens. This ought also to be done once or twice a day, even if the flowers are kept constantly in their vases. Roses which have drooped before their time — as, for example, when worn on the dress — may be revived if the stems, after being thus cut, are placed for ten minutes in almost boiling water and then removed to cold water.

It is also well to add a little charcoal or ammonia to the water in which flowers are standing.

If salt is added to the water in which cut flowers are kept, it will delay wilting and decay.

3. Preserving Fruits for Exhibition.

1. Corrosive sublimate — which is a violent poison — is prepared at the rate of half an ounce to a gallon of water. Renew the liquid every year or two. Distilled or other very pure water should be used if it is desired to retain the color of the fruit, and glycerine may be added to prevent the fruit from shrinking.

2. Sulphur is sometimes used as follows: Put 30 gallons of water in a 40-gallon barrel; float on top of the water a tin pan, in which put a little sulphur. Set the sulphur on fire and cover the barrel tightly until the fire goes out; renew the sulphur several times, opening the barrel for renewal of air between the doses. The water absorbs the sulphurous acid, and the fluid is then used as a preservative.

Better results are generally obtained if the prepared sulphurous acid is purchased. It costs about 35 cents per pound in 5-pound bottles. Two ounces of the acid is added to a gallon of water.

3. Place an ounce of salicylic acid in 5 gallons water, and then add a little glycerine. The amount of glycerine will depend upon the juiciness of the fruit. The greater the juiciness, the more glycerine must be added. From 8 to 15 per cent may be considered an average.

Another recipe, and one particularly useful for dark-colored grapes, is as follows: Dissolve an ounce of salicylic acid in 8 ounces of alcohol, and add this to 2 gallons of water. Allow it to stand for a short time before using.

4. Boric acid may be used as a preservative by dissolving a half pound in 50 pounds of water. If the liquid is not clear, filter it. Useful for colored fruits.

5. A solution of zinc chloride, for preserving light-colored and yellow fruits, is made by dissolving 1 pound of the chloride in 50 pounds of water. Filter if the solution is not clear.

6. Bisulphite of soda, ½ ounce of the pure, dry, commercial article, to a gallon of water, to which is added 4 ounces of alcohol, makes a good preservative. It is best to dissolve the bisulphite in a half pint of water, before adding the remainder of the water and the alcohol. Filter if necessary. The alcohol is added to prevent the fruit from bursting.

7. Pure kerosene is excellent in which to preserve strawberries and blackcap raspberries. Be sure that no drops of water adhere to the fruits before they are placed in the oil.

8. Alcohol preserves fruits almost perfectly, except that it destroys the color. High-grade alcohol is usually diluted one-half with pure water before using.

9. Formic acid is an excellent preservative, particularly for pulpy and colored fruits. The commercial formalin is generally used, in 2 or 3 per cent solution, usually the latter strength. Formalin may be added to alcohol (8).

4. Collecting and Preserving Insects.

Flying insects are caught in a net made of mosquito-bar, after the fashion of the minnow-net. The material is made into a bag about a yard deep, and about a foot in width at the top. The opening is fastened upon a wire hoop, which is secured to a pole—as a broomstick. Insects are killed by placing them in a "cyanide-bottle." This is prepared by placing 2 or 3 lumps of cyanide of potassium the size of a quail's egg in a museum-bottle or glass jar, covering the lumps with dry plaster of Paris, and then adding just enough water to make the plaster set. The fumes of the poison coming through the plaster quickly kill the insects. Keep the bottle corked. The cyanide is very poisonous and the fumes should not be inhaled. A very broad-mouthed bottle with glass stopple is necessary. Bugs and beetles can be pinned and mounted as soon as they are dead. It is customary to pin beetles through the right wing-cover, and bugs—as squash-bugs—through the triangular space between the wings. Butterflies, moths, bees, flies, etc., must be pressed to preserve the wings. This is done by placing on a "setting-board." This apparatus is a little trough with a crack at the bottom The sides of the trough are made of thin bits of board, 3 or 4 inches wide and a foot or more long. These sides have very little slant. The crack in the bottom of the trough is left about a half-inch wide, and it is covered beneath with a strip of cork. The body of the insect is now placed lengthwise the crack, a pin is thrust through the thorax, or middle division of the insect, into the cork, and the wings are laid out on the sides of the trough. The wings are held in place by strips of cardboard pinned over them. Take care not to stick the pins through the wings. In about two weeks the insects will be dry and stiff.

Insects must be kept in tight boxes to keep other insects from devouring them. Cigar boxes are good. Tight boxes with glass covers are generally used by collectors. Place sheets of cork in the bottom of the box to receive the pins. If insects attack the specimens, expose them in a tight box to vapors of bisulphide of carbon (see Chap. I.) or benzine.

5. Preparing Old Bottles for Specimens.

CUTTING GLASS BOTTLES. — 1. Pass 5 or 6 strands of coarse packing-twine round the bottle on each side of the line where you want it divided, so as to form a groove $\frac{1}{8}$ inch wide ; in this groove pass one turn of a piece of hard-laid white cord, extend the two ends, and fasten to some support. Saw the bottle backwards and forwards for a short time ; after a minute's friction, by a side motion of the bottle throw it out of the cord into a tub of water, and then tap on the side of the tub and the bottom will fall off.

2. Fill the bottle the exact height you wish it to be cut, with oil of any kind ; dip, very gradually, a red-hot iron into the oil. The glass suddenly chips and cracks all round, then the upper surface may be lifted off at the surface of the oil.

3. For cutting off bottoms of bottles, make a slight nick with a file, and then mark round with a streak of ink where you want it to come off. Make an iron red-hot and lay it on the nick. This will cause it to expand and crack ; then, by moving the rod round, the crack will follow.

6. Perfumery.

PERMANENT ATTAR OR OTTO OF ROSES (Ellwanger).—The roses employed should be just blown, of the sweetest-smelling kinds, gathered in as dry a state as possible. After each gathering, spread out the petals on a sheet of paper and leave until free from moisture; then place a layer of petals in a jar, sprinkling with coarse salt; then another layer of coarse salt alternating until the jar is full. Leave for a few days, or until a broth is formed; then incorporate thoroughly and add more petals and salt, mixing thoroughly daily for a week, when fragrant gums and spices should be added, such as benzoin, storax, cassia-buds, cinnamon, cloves, cardamon, and vanilla-bean. Mix again and leave for a few days, when add essential oil of jasmine, violet, tuberose, and attar of roses, together with a hint of ambergris or musk, in mixture with the flower ottos, to fix the odor. Spices, such as cloves, should be sparingly used.

PERFUME JAR.—1. 1 pound of dried rose-petals bought at a drug-store, 4 ounces of salt, and 2 ounces of saltpeter, on which put 8 drops of essence of ambergris, 6 drops of essence of lemon, 4 drops of oil of cloves, 4 drops of oil of lavender, and 2 drops of essence of bergamot.

2. One-half pound of common salt, ¼ pound saltpeter, ¼ ounce storax, ½ dozen cloves, a handful of dried bay-leaves, and another handful of dried lavender-flowers. This basis will last for years, and petals of roses and other fragrant flowers gathered on dry days may be added annually, or powered benzoin, chips of sandalwood, cinnamon, orris-root, or musk may be added.

LAVENDER BAG.—One-half pound lavender-flowers, ½ ounce dried thyme and mint, ¼ ounce ground cloves and caraway, 1 ounce common salt. Tie up in a linen bag, which is hung in a wardrobe.

Orris-root is a good medium in which to place delicate perfumes for perfumery bags.

7. Labels.

TREE LABELS may be made of various kinds of material. The commonest and cheapest label is made of clean white pine, primed with thin white lead. These can be purchased of dealers in nurserymen's supplies. The ordinary nursery tree label is 3½ inches long.

The Cornell tree label is made from the "package label" used by nurserymen. It is a pine notched tally 6 inches long and 1¼ inches wide. (Cost, painted, about $1.30 per thousand.) These are wired with heavy stiff wire not less than 18 inches long, so that the loop is 5 or 6 inches across. The labels are hung on one of the lower limbs of the tree where they are very conspicuous. The ends of the wire are hooked together around the limb by means of pincers, and, being stiff, it is not readily removed by careless or mischievous persons. The name is written firmly with a very soft black lead-pencil, and when the label is hung upon the tree, it is dipped in thin white lead, which fixes the writing and preserves it almost indefinitely; or the name may be written firmly into a fresh coat of white lead.

Labels made of small strips of common zinc are often used, the name being written on the metal with a lead-pencil. The label is wound about a limb, and it expands as the part grows. The label is so inconspicuous and so easily removed that it is unsatisfactory.

Thick tallies of lead with the name stamped in with dies, are very durable.

Thin metal labels which hang on a wire are often broken or torn out at the eyelet by the wind.

STAKE LABELS, made of pine or other soft clear wood, are most satisfactory for garden use, unless, perhaps, in botanic gardens, or other permanent exhibition grounds where a more conspicuous and ornamental label is wanted. The label should be primed with white lead, after which it takes a permanent mark from a medium soft lead-pencil.

A good label for grounds which are cultivated by horses, and which are therefore likely to be broken by the whiffletrees, is a pine stake 2 feet long, 3½ inches wide, and 1½ inches thick, sawed to a taper at the lower end. Give them two coats of thin white lead, taking care not to pile them on their faces whilst drying. Make the record with a soft large lead-pencil. When the writing wears off, or the label is wanted for other uses, plane a shaving off the face, paint again and it is as good as new.

To Preserve Wooden Labels. — Thoroughly soak the pieces of wood in a strong solution of copperas (sulphate of iron); then lay them, after they are dry, in lime-water. This causes the formation of sulphate of lime, a very insoluble salt, in the wood.

Black Ink for Zinc Labels. — Verdigris, 1 ounce; sal ammoniac, 1 ounce; lampblack, ½ ounce; rain water, ½ pint. Mix in an earthenware mortar or jar and put up in small bottles. To be shaken before use and used with a clean quill pen on bright zinc.

8. To Preserve Posts in the Ground.

Dip them in hot coal-tar.

Char them.

Use the copperas solution mentioned above for labels.

Into boiled linseed oil stir pulverized coal until the mixture is the thickness of paint. Apply a heavy coat to the post.

Posts may be kyanized by soaking them in a liquid made by dissolving 1 pound of blue vitriol in 20 pounds of water.

CHAPTER XVI.

RULES.

1. Loudon's Rules for Gardeners.

1. Perform every operation in the proper season and in the best manner.
2. Complete every operation consecutively.
3. Never, if possible, perform one operation in such a manner as to render another necessary.
4. When called off from any operation, leave your work and tools in an orderly manner.
5. In leaving off work, make a temporary finish, and clean your tools and carry them to the tool house.
6. Never do that in the garden or hothouses, which can be equally well done in the reserve ground or in the back sheds.
7. Never pass a weed or insect without pulling it up or taking it off, unless time forbid.
8. In gathering a crop, take away the useless as well as the useful parts.
9. Let no plant ripen seeds, unless they are wanted for some purpose, useful or ornamental, and remove all parts which are in a state of decay.

2. Rules of Nomenclature.

1. RULES FOR NAMING FRUITS, ADOPTED BY THE AMERICAN POMOLOGICAL SOCIETY.

1. The originator or introducer (in the order named) has the prior right to bestow a name upon a new or unnamed fruit.
2. The society reserves the right, in case of long, inappropriate, or otherwise objectionable names, to shorten, modify, or

wholly change the same when they shall occur in its discussions or reports; and also to recommend such names for general adoption.

3. The names of fruit should, preferably, express as far as practicable by a single word, the characteristics of the variety, the name of the originator, or the place of its origin. Under no ordinary circumstances should more than a single word be employed.

4. Should the question of priority arise between different names for the same variety of fruit, other circumstances being equal the name first publicly bestowed will be given preference.

2. RULES FOR NAMING KITCHEN-GARDEN VEGETABLES, ADOPTED BY THE COMMITTEE ON NOMENCLATURE OF THE ASSOCIATION OF AMERICAN AGRICULTURAL COLLEGES AND EXPERIMENT STATIONS (1889).

1. The name of a variety shall consist of a single word, or at most of two words. A phrase, descriptive or otherwise, is never allowable; as, *Pride of Italy, King of Mammoths, Earliest of All.*

2. The name should not be superlative or bombastic. In particular, such epithets as *New, Large, Giant, Fine, Selected, Improved,* and the like, should be omitted. If the grower or dealer has a superior stock of a variety, the fact should be stated in the description immediately after the name, rather than as a part of the name itself; as, "*Trophy,* selected stock."

3. If a grower or dealer has secured a new select strain of a well-known variety, it shall be legitimate for him to use his own name in connection with the established name of the variety; as, *Smith's Winnigstadt, Jones's Cardinal.*

4. When personal names are given to varieties, titles should be omitted; as, *Major, General,* etc.

5. The term "hybrid" should not be used except in those rare instances in which the variety is known to be of hybrid origin.

6. The originator has the prior right to name the variety, but the oldest name which conforms to these rules should be adopted.

7. This committee reserves the right, in its own publications, to revise objectionable names in conformity with these rules.

3. RULES OF THE SOCIETY OF AMERICAN FLORISTS.

This society commends (through its nomenclature committee) the rules adopted by the American Pomological Society and the Station Horticulturists (as given above), and further urges "upon those originating plants requiring new names, the employment of short, appropriate, and neat vernacular names; the avoidance of misleading, long, high-sounding, or vulgar names, and the use of Latinized names exclusively in connection with species and natural varieties."

The rules adopted by the society are as follows (1893):

1. Natural species and varieties shall bear the Latin names assigned to them in Nicholson's Dictionary, so far as they are named, except that where differences exist between the Dictionary and Kew Index, the name adopted by the latter shall be chosen. Species first published or reinstated subsequent to the date of the latter (1885) shall be treated in accordance with botanical custom, especially that of the Kew Gardens. In all cases where the application of this rule shall cause the displacement of a commonly used and well-known name, the latter shall be added as a synonym.

2. Florists' varieties, races and forms, shall be named in accordance with the recommendations of the nomenclature committee (stated above); but the greatest conservatism is counseled in all changes which are likely to cause confusion or detriment to legitimate business interests.

4. RULES FOR THE NAMING OF ORCHIDS, ADOPTED BY THE COUNCIL OF THE ROYAL HORTICULTURAL SOCIETY OF ENGLAND.

SECTION I. — *Genera, species, well-marked varieties, and natural hybrids.*

1. The names of natural genera, species, and well-marked hybrids, as well as of presumed wild hybrids, shall be written

so as to accord with botanical language and ways, and to conform with the laws of botanical nomenclature, as adopted at the International Botanical Congress at Paris, in 1867.

2. Exhibitors showing, for the first time, a plant under a Latin name, shall be required to furnish the name of the botanist who has described the plant.

SECTION II. — *Artificial hybrids between genera.*

3. Every bigener shall receive a generic name in Latin, formed by combining the names of the parent genera, and a specific name also in Latin, the sign of hybridity (×) being always added.

SECTION III. — *Artificial hybrids between species.*

4. Hybrids between species, raised artificially, shall be named in Latin, with the addition of the word "hybrid," or of the sign of hybridity (×).

SECTION IV. — *Artificial crosses between varieties.*

5. Crosses between varieties, raised artificially, should receive suitable vernacular names.

SECTION V. — *General recommendations.*

6. The orchid committee shall decline to recognize any unauthorized name, or any name that is deemed unsuitable, or is not applied in conformity with the preceding rules.

7. A name once authoritatively adopted shall not be altered, unless in case of material error.

8. An award may be made to any plant that is considered by the committee worthy of such distinction, even though it be unnamed, or not named in accordance with the preceding regulations, providing that, within a reasonable time, to be determined by the committee, a proper name be given. Any award made under the circumstances shall be suspended until the plant has been properly named.

9. The operation of these rules shall be prospective, not retrospective.

10. The Council wishes to impress upon orchid growers the desirability of obtaining drawings or photographs of all new and certified orchids, and of depositing such drawings in the library of the society, for reference.

11. The Council also desires to remind cultivators of the great importance of preserving specimens for future reference and comparison, and suggests that, wherever practicable, specimens should be sent for this purpose to the Director of the Royal Gardens, Kew.

5. PARIS CODE OF BOTANICAL NOMENCLATURE.

At an international botanical congress held in Paris in 1867, a series of general rules for the nomenclature of plants was adopted, which has been more or less closely followed by botanists until the present time. The code assumes that botanical names, like other language, are determined by custom or general consensus of opinion. .It also asserts that the name of a species consists of two inseparable parts, the generic and specific, and that the author of the combination of these two, rather than the author of either part separately, should be quoted as the authority for the complete name of the species. In opposition to these assertions, some botanists now contend (see Caption 6) that the first single name applied to a species should always follow that species, in whatever genus it may be placed, and that the citation of authority following any combination should comprise the name of the person who first used the specific appellation and also the name of the person who placed the given generic and specific appellations together, in case a subsequent combination has occurred. The Paris Code comprises 68 articles, of which only the following are of direct interest here:

ARTICLE 2. The rules of nomenclature should neither be arbitrary, nor imposed by authority. They must be founded on considerations clear and forcible enough for every one to comprehend and be disposed to accept.

ART. 15. Each natural group of plants can bear in science but one valid designation, namely, the most ancient, whether adopted or given by Linnæus, or since Linnæus, provided it be consistent with the essential rules of nomenclature. [The exact work of Linnæus from which names may start is not designated.]

ART. 31. All species, even those that singly constitute a genus, are designated by the name of the genus to which they belong, followed by a name termed specific, more commonly of the adjective kind.

ART. 35. No two species of the same genus can bear the same specific name, but the same specific name may be given in several genera.

ART. 37. Hybrids whose origin has been experimentally demonstrated are designated by the generic name, to which is added a combination of the specific names of the two species from which they are derived, the name of the species that has supplied the pollen being placed first with final i or o, and that of the species that has supplied the ovulum coming next with a hyphen between (*Amaryllis vittato-reginæ*, for the Amaryllis proceeding from *A. reginæ* fertilized by *A. vittata*.

Hybrids of doubtful origin are named in the same manner as species. They are distinguished by the absence of a number (in descriptive works), and by the sign × being prefixed to the generic name (× *Salix capreola*, Kern).

ART. 38. Names of sub-species and varieties are formed in the same way as specific names, and are added to them according to relative value, beginning by those of the highest rank. Half-breeds (*mules* of florists) of doubtful origin are named and ranked in the same manner.

Sub-varieties, variations, and sub-variations of uncultivated plants may receive names analogous to the foregoing, or merely numbers or letters, for facilitating their arrangement.

ART. 39. Half-breeds (*mules* of florists) of undoubted origin are designated by a combination of the two names of the sub-species, varieties, sub-varieties, etc., that have given birth to them, the same rules being observed as in the case of hybrids.

Art. 40. Seedlings, half-breeds of uncertain origin, and sports should receive from horticulturists fancy names in common language, as distinct as possible from the Latin names of species or varieties. When they can be traced back to a botanical species, sub-species, or variety, this is indicated by a succession of names (*Pelargonium zonale*, Mrs. Pollock).

Art. 41. The date of a name or of a combination of names is that of its actual and irrevocable publication.

Art. 42. Publication consists in the sale or the distribution among the public of printed matter, plates, or autographs. It consists, likewise, in the sale or the distribution, among the leading public collections, of numbered specimens, accompanied by printed or autograph tickets, bearing the date of the sale or distribution.

Art. 48. For the indication of the name or names of any group to be accurate and complete, it is necessary to quote the author who first published the name or combination of names in question.

Art. 51. When a group is moved, without alteration of name, to a higher or lower rank than that which it held before, the change is considered equivalent to the creation of an entirely new group, and the author who has effected the change is the one to be quoted.

Art. 55. In case two or more groups of the same nature are united into one, the name of the oldest is preserved. If the names are of the same date, the author chooses.

Art. 59. Nobody is authorized to change a name because it is badly chosen or disagreeable, or another is preferable or better known, or for any other motive either contestable or of little import.

Art. 68. Every friend of science ought to be opposed to the introduction into a modern language of names of plants that are not already there, unless they are derived from a Latin botanical name that has undergone but a slight alteration.

6. RULES FOR BOTANICAL NOMENCLATURE ADOPTED BY THE BOTANICAL CLUB OF THE AMERICAN ASSOCIATION FOR THE ADVANCEMENT OF SCIENCE.

(*Combined Rules of Rochester and Madison Meetings.*)

The Paris Code of 1867 is adopted except where it conflicts with the following:

The Law of Priority. — Priority of publication is to be regarded as the fundamental principle of botanical nomenclature.

Beginning of Botanical Nomenclature. — The botanical nomenclature of both genera and species is to begin with the publication of the first edition of Linnæus' "Species Plantarum," in 1753.

Stability of Specific Names. — In the transfer of a species to a genus other than the one under which it was first published, the original specific name is to be retained.

Precedence of Publication. — In determining the name of a genus or species to which two or more names have been given by an author in the same volume, or on the same page of a volume, precedence shall decide.

Homonyms. — The publication of a generic name or a binomial invalidates the use of the same name for any subsequently published genus or species respectively.

Publication of Genera. — Publication of a genus consists only (1) in the distribution of a printed description of the genus named; (2) in the publication of the name of the genus and the citation of one or more previously published species as examples of types of the genus, with or without diagnosis.

Publication of Species. — Publication of a species consists only (1) in the distribution of a printed description of the species named; (2) in the publishing of a binomial with reference to a previously published species as a type.

Similar Generic Names. — Similar generic names are not to be rejected on account of slight differences, except in the spelling of the same word; for example, *Apios* and *Apium* are to be retained, but of *Epidendrum* and *Epidendron*, *Asterocarpus* and *Astrocarpus*, the latter is to be rejected.

Citation of Authorities. — In the case of a species which has been transferred from one genus to another, the original author must always be cited in parenthesis, followed by the author of the new binomial.

To this code the Committee on Nomenclature of the Botanical Club adds the following working rules :

1. That the original name is to be maintained, whether published as a species, sub-species, or variety.
2. That varieties are to be written as trinomials.
3. That specific or varietal names derived from persons or places, or used as the genitive of generic names or substantives, are to be printed with a capital initial letter.
4. That no comma is to be inserted between the specific or varietal name and the name of the author cited.

3. Rules for Exhibition.

In order to guide societies in the formation of laws governing the exhibition of horticultural products, the codes of three prominent societies are here inserted as samples.

1. AMERICAN POMOLOGICAL SOCIETY RULES.

For Exhibitors.

1. A plate of fruit must contain six specimens — no more, no less — except in the case of single varieties not included in collections.
2. To insure examination by the proper committees, all fruits must be correctly and distinctly labeled, and placed upon the tables during the first day of the exhibition.
3. The duplication of varieties in a collection will not be permitted.
4. In all cases of fruits intended to be examined and reported by committees, the name of the exhibitor, together with a complete list of the varieties exhibited by him, must be delivered to

the secretary of the society on or before the first day of the exhibition.

5. The exhibitor will receive from the secretary an entry-card, which must be placed with the exhibit, when arranged for exhibition, for the guidance of committees.

6. All articles placed upon the tables for exhibition must remain in charge of the society till the close of the exhibition, to be removed sooner only upon express permission of the person or persons in charge.

7. Fruits or other articles intended for testing, or to be given away to visitors, spectators, or others, will be assigned a separate hall, room, or tent, in which they may be dispensed at the pleasure of the exhibitor, who will not, however, be permitted to sell and deliver articles therein, or to call attention to them in a boisterous or disorderly manner.

For the Guidance of Examining and Awarding Committees.

1. In estimating the comparative values of collections of fruits, committees are instructed to base such estimates strictly upon the varieties in such collections which shall have been correctly named by the exhibitor prior to action thereon by the committee on nomenclature.

2. In instituting such comparison of value, committees are instructed to consider: 1st, the values of the varieties for the purposes to which they may be adapted; 2d, the color, size, and evenness of the specimens; 3d, their freedom from the marks of insects and from other blemishes; 4th, the apparent carefulness in handling, and the taste displayed in the arrangement of the exhibit.

2. MASSACHUSETTS HORTICULTURAL SOCIETY RULES.

Special Rules of the Fruit Committee. — 1. All collections and single dishes of fruit offered for prizes at any exhibition *must have marked upon the cards the numbers of the prizes for which they are offered.*

2. All fruits offered for premiums must be correctly named.

Indefinite appellations, such as "Pippin," "Sweeting," "Greening," etc., will not be considered as names.

3. All fruits offered for premiums must be composed of exactly the number of specimens or quantity named in the schedule. A "dish" of apples, pears, peaches, plums, nectarines, quinces, figs, apricots, etc., is understood to contain twelve specimens, and this number will be required of all fruits when not otherwise specified.

4. The whole quantity required of any one variety of fruit must be shown in a single dish or basket.

5. Contributors of fruits for exhibitions or prizes must present the same in the society's dishes. All small fruits must be shown in baskets, not more than an inch and three-quarters in depth, which will be furnished to the exhibitors by the superintendent, at cost. Market-baskets will not be allowed on the tables.

6. No person can compete for more than one prize with the same variety or varieties of fruit, except that a single dish may be of the same variety — but not the same specimens — as one of a collection; and also that the same variety — but not the same specimens — may compete for both special and regular prizes.

7. Grapes grown on girdled vines cannot compete for a premium.

8. All fruits offered for prizes [exceptions noted], and those for foreign grapes must be of outdoor culture.

The Fruit Committee, in making its awards, will consider the flavor, beauty, and size of the specimens, comparing each of these properties with a fair standard of the variety. The adaptation of the variety to general cultivation will also be taken into account. Other things being equal, specimens most nearly in perfection as regards ripeness will have the preference.

Special Rules of the Vegetable Committee. — 1. The specimens offered must be well-grown, and placed on the tables clean, correctly labeled, and fully complying with the Rules and Regulations of the society.

2. Special gratuities will be awarded for well-grown varieties from under glass, previous to the opening exhibition.

3. All vegetables offered for premiums must be composed of exactly the number of specimens or quantity named in the schedule.

4. All vegetables offered for premiums at any exhibition *must have marked upon the cards the numbers of the prizes for which they are offered.*

5. Prizes will not be awarded when the articles are judged unworthy.

6. Non-compliance with the rules will cause the rejection of the articles offered for premium.

Special Rules of the Flower Committee. — 1. All named varieties of plants or flowers exhibited for premiums must have the name *legibly* and correctly written on stiff card, wood, or some other permanent substance; and each separate plant or flower must have its name attached.

2. All plants, flowers, bouquets, designs, etc., offered for prizes at any exhibition, *must have marked upon the cards the numbers of the prizes for which they are offered.*

3. Plants in pots, to be entitled to prizes, must evince skillful culture in the profusion of bloom, and the beauty, symmetry, and vigor of the specimens.

4. All exhibitors not strictly complying with the above rules will be excluded from competition for premiums.

5. No gratuities will be awarded on other than regular prize days, except for objects of special merit.

3. MICHIGAN HORTICULTURAL SOCIETY RULES.

For Exhibitors. — Entries may be made for exhibition without competition; and, if worthy, the awarding committee is expected to notice them properly in its reports.

No article entered for competition in one class will be permitted to compete for a premium in any other, except as hereinafter expressly provided.

Each entry of collection of fruits must be accompanied by a correct list of the varieties of each class of fruits, named in the order of their maturity as nearly as may be. No premiums will be awarded in the absence of such list.

Fruits will be valued by committees according to their adaptation to the requirements under which they are entered. A really superior dessert fruit, if entered in a market collection, can only receive credit for its value for the market, as given in the society's catalogue ; and, *vice versa*, market varieties found in a dessert or family collection must be adjudged by their proper value for family purposes.

A plate of fruit, unless otherwise specified, must contain five specimens — no more, no less. Of those usually designated " small fruits," the exhibit must be one pint of each variety. Of crab-apples and plums, one dozen of each variety. Of dried fruits, one quart of each separate variety or article. Jellies, canned, pickled, and preserved fruits may be entered and shown in glass vessels of such character and capacity as are commonly employed for family or market purposes.

Flowers, plants, evergreens, and such other articles as the fancy of the exhibitor may suggest, may be freely employed in the ornamentation of exhibits, in any manner that shall not essentially interfere with the examinations of committees or the general designs of decoration ; and full weight will be given to such ornamentation by the awarding committees in rendering their awards.

The entry-card furnished by the secretary, specifying the class and number of the entry, must in all cases be placed in connection with the articles to which it appertains, as a guide to committees.

Articles when entered, named, and arranged for exhibition will thenceforth be strictly under the control of the officers in charge of the exhibition, and neither exhibitors nor spectators will be permitted to handle them, except by permission of the proper officer.

Any exhibitor having been awarded a premium upon an article, and removing the same prior to the close of the exhibition, without permission of the officer in charge, will by so doing forfeit his right to such premium.

The name of the fruit should in no case appear on the entry-card, except only in the case of single plates or other single articles.

Entry-cards, name-cards, and the cards of the committee on nomenclature, should, for the convenience of awarding committees and other officers, be each of a different color, or otherwise printed in different-colored inks.

Exhibitors will not be permitted to sell and deliver the articles they may have entered for exhibition, or to bring fruit or any other article for the purpose of sale, on a penalty of forfeiture of all premiums, but such articles must remain in charge of the officers until the close of the exhibition.

Any exhibitor interfering with awarding committees while in discharge of their duties, will be held, by so doing, to have forfeited all premiums.

For Awarding Committees. — 1. The division superintendent will be a member and clerk of the awarding committee for his division. The remaining members of each committee will be selected with great care from the best horticulturists of this and neighboring states. The names of such persons will not be made public until the time of the fair.

2. Members of the awarding committee are requested to report to the president, at the secretary's office, on or before noon of the second day of the fair, that the places of those failing to report may be supplied.

3. The president is chairman of the committee on nomenclature; but to expedite the business of correction the superintendent of each division will correct the nomenclature of his division, appealing to the chairman in all doubtful cases, and attaching the committee's card in all cases in which corrections are made.

4. No exhibitor will be permitted to act on a committee in a class in which he shall exhibit for premiums.

5. Members of the awarding committee are requested to report to the president, at the secretary's office, at 1 o'clock P.M., on Thursday, when they will receive their committee books, together with such explanations and instructions as may at the time seem needful.

6. Upon conclusion of their labors, not later than the afternoon of Friday, awarding committees will deliver their reports

to the president, who will examine them, and in case of insufficiency or omission, will return them with instructions. When accepted by the president, they will be delivered to the secretary.

7. When an exhibit is not deemed worthy of a premium, the committee will withhold the award.

8. A majority of an awarding committee, when present, shall constitute a quorum, and of those present, the first on the list shall act as chairman, unless the committee shall arrange otherwise.

9. Awarding committees, in estimating the comparative values of exhibits, are instructed to base such estimates strictly upon the varieties in such collections that shall be correctly labeled by the exhibitors prior to the corrections of the committee on nomenclature.

10. In awarding premiums upon any and all exhibits of fruits, committees will exclude any and all unlabeled and incorrectly labeled specimens, as well as duplicates, and consider: 1st, the value of the varieties for the required purpose, as given in the society's Catalogue of Fruits; 2d, the color, size, and evenness of the specimens; 3d, their freedom from the marks of insects and other blemishes; 4th, the apparent carefulness in handling and the tastefulness of the exhibit, recollecting that the gradations of the catalogue call for perfect specimens. These gradations should, therefore, be correspondingly lowered in case of deficiencies or imperfections. A copy of the catalogue will, for this purpose, be furnished to each committee. In grading collections entered for family purposes, the dessert and culinary sub-columns should be consulted, and the gradation expressing the highest value taken. For market, the gradations of the market sub-column only should be employed.

11. In the case of fruits not named in the catalogue, for the dessert, committees should consider: 1st, quality; 2d, beauty; 3d, size. For culinary uses: 1st, flavor; 2d, texture; 3d, size. For market: 1st, productiveness; 2d, color; 3d, handling qualities; 4th, suitable, even size.

12. The true and legitimate purpose of the premiums offered is to draw out the views of both exhibitors and committees

respecting the relative values, for the purposes specified, of the varieties included in the exhibits.

13. The society desires to encourage the planting of only a sufficiently large variety of sorts for the desired purpose. Hence it is important that the committee, in their reports, specify, in the order of their value, the varieties upon which the determination of their awards is based.

14. Useful and valuable varieties only are expected to influence awards; while indifferent sorts, even though large, showy, and attractive, should not for these reasons alone be held to add to the value of an exhibit, except, possibly, as a means of education.

15. An important object of the society is to collect valuable information of a pomological character. Committees are therefore requested to gather all the information possible from the exhibitors in their classes, and to make their reports as full as time and circumstances will permit.

16. The society desires to foster a free exercise by exhibitors of the principles of correct taste in the arrangement, display, and ornamentation of their exhibits. To this end, committees will give all reasonable and proper consideration to particulars of this character.

4. REGISTRATION OF FLOWERS.

Three societies now register new varieties of plants in this country: American Chrysanthemum Society, American Carnation Society, and American Rose Society.

4. Scales of Points for Judging Fruits and Flowers.

1. WORLD'S FAIR SCALE FOR POMACEOUS FRUITS (apples, pears, quinces). — The following points were considered by the judges of pome fruits at the World's Fair, 1893: Adaptability, size, form, color, evenness, blemishes, handling (*i.e.*, how the specimens have been handled), maturity, arrangement, quantity.

WORLD'S FAIR SCALE FOR STONE FRUITS. — Size, form, color, tissue, pit or seeds, juice, sweet or dessert, acid or cooking, maturity, flavor.

2. CANADIAN SCORE CARDS, adopted by Ontario Fruit Growers' Association (Woolverton):
Plates of Apples and Pears. — Form, 10; size, 10; color, 10; freedom from blemishes, 20; uniformity, 20; quality, 30.

General Collections of Apples and Pears. — Form, 1; size, 2; color, 2; freedom from blemishes, 3; uniformity, 2.

Dessert Collections of Apples and Pears. — Form, 2; size, 1; color, 2; clearness, 3; uniformity, 2.

Cooking Collections of Apples and Pears.— Perfection of form, 1; size, 3; color, 1; uniformity, 2; freedom from blemishes, 3.

Plates of Grapes. — Flavor, 30; form of bunch, 10; size of bunch, 15; size of berry, 15; color, 10; firmness, 5; bloom, 5; freedom from blemishes, 10.

Collections of Grapes. — Flavor, 3; form of bunch, 1; size of bunch, $1\frac{1}{2}$; size of berry, $1\frac{1}{2}$; color, 1; firmness, $\frac{1}{2}$; bloom, $\frac{1}{2}$; freedom from blemishes, 1.

3. TOMATO (Bailey). — Score of a good variety: Vigor of plant, 5; earliness, 10; color of fruit, 5; solidity, 20; shape of fruit, 20; size, 10; flavor, 5; cooking qualities, 5; productiveness, 20. — 100.

4. CALIFORNIA CITROUS SCALE ADOPTED BY CALIFORNIA STATE BOARD OF HORTICULTURE.

Oranges.

The points to be considered are: Size, form, color, peel, weight, fiber, grain, seed, taste; to be considered in order named.

Counts (credits — points) to be units and tenths thereof, expressed decimally. Possible total of same to equal 100.

1. SIZE, 0 TO 10 (COUNTS).

Standards. — Large, 126's, $3\frac{1}{4}$ inches diameter; medium, 176's, $2\frac{3}{4}$ inches diameter; small, 226's, $2\frac{1}{4}$ inches diameter; Tangerines, etc., $2\frac{1}{8}$ inches diameter.

P

Three-eighths inch excess of standard allowed (without discount) to "medium" and "small" fruit; ½ inch ditto to "large." One unit discount for each deficiency in any size.

2. Form, 0 to 5 (Counts).

Standards. — Round, oval, ovate, pyriform.

Discounts for lack of symmetry and for form blemishes. Navel marks not to be discounted, except when of abnormal size or of bad form.

3. Color, 0 to 15.

Subdivisions. — Bloom, 0 to 2; of peel, 0 to 10; of flesh, 0 to 3.

Standard. — Bloom to be perceptible, and to be discounted according to degree of deficiency, or of injury thereto; peel to be of rich, deep orange color, in natural condition, and to be discounted according to degree of deviation therefrom — one or more points. Rust, scale, and smut to be discounted 5 to 10 points, and fruit that gives visible evidence of having been cleaned of the same to be subject to equal penalty. Also peel that has been rubbed or "polished," giving gloss at expense of breaking or pressing the oil cells, to suffer some discount. Flesh to be rich, clear, and uniform in any of the shades common to fine fruit.

(Omit consideration of "Flesh Color" until after concluding Division 5, "Peel.")

4. Weight, 0 to 10.

Standard. — Specific gravity 1 (equal to that of water) with buoyancy of ¾ ounces allowed to "large" fruit; ½ ounce ditto to "medium," and ¼ ounce ditto to "small," all without discount.

One point to be discounted for first ½ ounce of buoyancy in excess of allowance, and thereafter 2 points for each additional ½ ounce.

Note. — Buoyancy may be easily determined by clasping apothecaries' weights to fruit with light rubber elastics, and then placing in water.

5. PEEL, 0 TO 10.

Subdivisions. — Finish, 0 to 3; protective quality, 0 to 7.

Standards. — Of finish, smoothness and uniformity of surface and pleasant touch; protective quality, firm and elastic texture; abundant, compact, and unbroken oil cells; and $\frac{1}{8}$ to $\frac{3}{16}$ inch thickness.

Discount 1 point for first $\frac{1}{32}$ inch above maximum or below minimum, and 2 points for second ditto — provided that for too long-picked and fully "cured" oranges the minimum shall be lowered to $\frac{3}{32}$ inch; and that to fresh-picked and to slightly "cured" "large" fruit the maximum shall be raised to $\frac{1}{4}$ inch.

Breaking of oil cells, abrasions of peel, and drying of same, to be subject to 1 to 10 discounts according to degree.

(Here consider "Color of Flesh." — See Division 3.)

6. FIBER, 0 TO 8.

Standards. — Septa delicate and translucent; maximum diameter of core $\frac{3}{16}$ inch in "large" fruit, and $\frac{1}{8}$ ditto in others.

7. GRAIN, 0 TO 4.

Standards. — Fineness, firmness, compactness.

8. SEED, 0 TO 8.

Standard. — Absence of.

Discount 1 point for each of first 3 seeds; ditto thereafter $\frac{1}{2}$ point for each additional.

Each rudiment considered as a seed if any growth has been developed; otherwise allowed without discount.

9. TASTE, 0 TO 30.

Subdivisions. — Sweetness, 0 to 10; citrous quality, 0 to 10; aroma, 0 to 10.

Standards. — Clearness and definability of elements; sweetness rich, delicate rather than heavy; citrous quality pronounced; aroma pervasive and agreeable.

Deficiency or absence to be cause for discounts against any

element, and excess to be like cause against sweetness, and against acid in citrous quality.

Staleness and flavors of age or of decay to be discounted from the aggregate of points in this division.

Lemons.

Size, form, color, weight, peel, fiber, grain, seed, taste.
Rules of counts and discounts as in scale for oranges.
Total of possible counts (points), 100.

1. Size, 0 to 7.

Standards. — Large, 250's, $2\frac{3}{4}$ inches in diameter; medium, 300's, $2\frac{1}{4}$ inches diameter; small, 360's, $1\frac{7}{8}$ inches diameter.

All sizes between 250's and 300's allowed.

Larger fruit to be discounted 1 point for each $\frac{1}{4}$ inch in excess. Smaller to be discounted 1 point for 400's ($1\frac{3}{4}$ inches), and 4 points for 450's ($1\frac{1}{2}$ inches).

2. Form, 0 to 2.

Standard. — Oblong, with allowance of well-formed points at stem and tip. Symmetry required.

3. Color, 0 to 10.

Standard. — Bright, clear lemon.

Discounts according to degree for green splashes, dashes of bronze, or deep shades or for sunburn.

Rust, scale, and smut, with fruit that gives evidence of having been cleaned of the same, to be discounted 5 to 10 counts.

Rubbing or dusting, if heavy enough to press oil from the cells, to be causes for discount.

4. Weight, 0 to 10.

Standard. — Specific gravity 1 (equal to that of water), with buoyancy of $\frac{1}{2}$ ounce allowed to "large" lemons, and $\frac{1}{4}$ ounce to "medium and small," all without discount.

One point to be discounted for first $\frac{1}{2}$ ounce excess of allowance, and 2 for each $\frac{1}{2}$ ounce thereafter.

5. Peel, 0 to 10.

Subdivisions. — Finish, 0 to 3 ; protective quality, 0 to 7.

Standard. — For protective quality to be strong, elastic, and reasonably firm texture ; abundant, compact, and unbroken oil cells, and thickness of $\frac{3}{32}$ to $\frac{3}{16}$ inch.

To be discounted 2 counts for first $\frac{1}{32}$ inch below minimum, and 5 counts for second ditto; and 1 count for first $\frac{1}{32}$ above maximum, and 2 for each succeeding ditto.

Fresh picked lemons not allowed.

6. Fiber, 0 to 8.

Standard. — Septa delicate and translucent. Core not to exceed $\frac{3}{16}$ inch in "large," and $\frac{1}{8}$ inch in "medium" and "small" fruit.

7. Grain, 0 to 4.

Standards. — Fineness, firmness, compactness.

To be water-colored, shading to blue rather than to gray.

8. Seed, 0 to 8.

Standard. — Absence of.

One point to be discounted for each of first three seeds, and $\frac{1}{2}$ point thereafter for each additional.

Rudiments to be considered as seed if any growth has been developed ; otherwise allowed without discount.

9. Taste, 0 to 40.

Subdivisions. — Acidity, 0 to 20; aroma, 0 to 10; absence of bitterness, 0 to 10.

In interstate competitions the standard of acidity shall be the highest per cent of strength of acid found in any fruit, determined by chemical test. In other competitions such tests may be applied as committees or competitors may require.

Aroma shall be full and of clear quality.

Bitterness to be determined by slicing the fruit (including peel) thin, covering with hot water, and cooling slowly ; to stand 24 hours when practicable. (No sugar to be used.) Should *a trace* of bitterness appear to the taste, discount 1 point; should this be *fairly defined*, discount 2 points; if *pronounced*, discount 5 points, and if *strong*, 10 points.

5. FLOWER SCORES.

CHRYSANTHEMUM SCALES OF THE MASSACHUSETTS HORTICULTURAL SOCIETY. — 1. Size and form of plants, 25; size of bloom, 20; general effect, 30; foliage, 25.

2. Size and form of plant, 40; size of bloom, 30; foliage, 30.

NEWPORT CHRYSANTHEMUM SCALE. — Size of bloom and quality, 30; size of plants, 30; foliage, 20; distinctness of form and color, 10; general effect, 10.

F. SCHUYLER MATHEW'S SCALE FOR THE JUDGMENT OF EXCELLENCE IN FLORAL DESIGN. — Adaptability to purpose, 35; color harmony, 25; composition, 25; excellence of material, 15.

CHICAGO SCALE FOR FLORAL ARRANGEMENT. — Adaptability for purpose intended, 45; arrangement and effect, 35; quantity of material, 20.

H. H. BATTLES' SCALE FOR FLORAL DESIGNS (50 points). — Color, general effect, grace, practicability, quality of flowers, each 10.

CHAPTER XVII.

POSTAL AND IMPOST REGULATIONS.

1 Classes of Domestic Mail Matter, and Rates.

FIRST CLASS. — Letters, postal cards, and matter wholly or partly in writing, whether sealed or unsealed (except manuscript copy accompanying proof-sheets or corrected proof-sheets of the same), and all matter sealed or otherwise closed against inspection.

Rate. — Two cents per ounce or fraction thereof. Postal cards, one cent each. On "drop" letters, two cents per ounce or fraction thereof, when mailed at letter-carrier office ; and one cent per ounce or fraction thereof at other offices.

SECOND CLASS. — Newspapers and publications issued at stated intervals as often as four times a year, bearing a date of issue and numbered consecutively, issued from a known office of publication, and formed of printed sheets, without board, cloth, leather, or other substantial binding. Such publications must be originated and published for the dissemination of information of a public character, or devoted to literature, the sciences, art, or some special industry. They must have a legitimate list of subscribers, and must not be designed primarily for advertising purposes, or for free circulation at nominal rates.

Rate. — One cent per pound or fraction thereof when sent by publisher thereof and from office of publication, including sample copies, or when sent from news agency to actual subscribers or other news agents.

One cent for each four ounces or fraction thereof on newspapers and periodical publications of second class, when sent by other than publisher or news agent.

One cent each on newspapers (excepting weeklies) and periodicals not exceeding two ounces in weight, when deposited in letter-carrier office for delivery by carrier; two cents each on periodicals weighing more than two ounces.

One cent per pound on newspapers, other than weeklies, and periodicals when deposited by publisher or news agent in letter-carrier office for general or box delivery; one cent for four ounces or fraction thereof when deposited by other than publishers or news agents for general or box delivery.

One cent per pound or fraction thereof on weekly newspapers deposited by publisher or news agent in letter-carrier office for letter or box delivery, or delivery by carrier.

Free when one copy is sent to each actual subscriber residing in county where same are printed, in whole or in part, and published; but at rate of one cent per pound when delivered at letter-carrier office, or distributed by carriers.

THIRD CLASS. — Books, circulars, and pamphlets, and matter wholly in print (not included in second class), proof-sheets, corrected proof-sheets, and manuscript copy accompanying the same.

"Printed matter" is the reproduction upon paper, by any process except that of handwriting, of any words, letters, characters, figures, or images, or of any combination thereof, not having the character of an actual and personal correspondence.

A "circular" is a printed letter, which, according to internal evidence, is being sent in identical terms to several persons. It is permissible to write, in circulars, the date, the name of the person addressed, or of the sender, and to correct mere typographical errors.

Seeds, bulbs, roots, cions, and plants are also mailable at the rate of third-class postage, such as samples of wheat or other grain in its natural condition, seedling potatoes, beans, peas, acorns, etc. Cut flowers and botanical specimens go as fourth class.

Rate. — One cent for each two ounces or fraction thereof.

FOURTH CLASS. — Merchandise; namely, all matter not em-

POSTAL AND IMPOST REGULATIONS. 217

braced in the other three classes, and which is not in its form or nature liable to destroy, deface, or otherwise damage the contents of the mail bag, or harm the person of any one engaged in the postal service, and not above the weight provided by law. Includes artificial flowers, cut flowers, dried plants, botanical and geological specimens, samples of flour or other manufactured grain for food purposes, blank address tags or labels, queen bees when properly packed, dried fruit.

Rate. — One cent per ounce or fraction thereof.

2. Foreign Postage.

To Canada, Newfoundland, and Mexico, the rates are mostly the same as domestic postage. Seeds and plants to Canada are one cent an ounce.

In the Universal Postal Union, which includes nearly all the countries of the world, rates are as follows:

Letters, $\frac{1}{2}$ ounce	5 cents
Postal cards, single, each	2 "
Newspaper and other printed matter, per 2 ounces	1 cent
Commercial papers, same as "printed matter," except that lowest rate is	5 cents
Samples of merchandise, same as "printed matter," except that lowest rate is	2 "
Registration fee	8 "

3. Unmailable Matter.

Held for Postage. — Domestic matter of first class on which two cents has not been prepaid, and all other domestic matter not fully prepaid.

Misdirected. — Matter without address, or so incorrectly, insufficiently, or inelegibly addressed that it cannot be forwarded to destination, including "nixies" or matter not addressed to a post-office, or addressed to a post-office without the name of the state being given, or otherwise so incorrectly, illegibly, or insufficiently addressed that it cannot be transmitted.

Destructive. — Matter of a harmful nature, poisons, explosive or inflammable articles, live animals, or dead animals not stuffed, fruits or vegetable matter liable to decomposition, comb-honey, guano, articles exhaling a bad odor, vinous, spirituous, and malt liquors, liquids liable to explosion, spontaneous combustion, or ignition by shock or jar (for example, kerosene oil, naphtha, benzine, turpentine, etc.). Bees and dried insects or reptiles must be so put up as not to injure any one handling the mails, nor to soil mail bags or their contents.

Disease Germs. — Discharges of any kind from diseased persons, no matter how securely put up.

Coin and Jewelry. — Coin, jewelry, and other precious articles prohibited by postal treaty from being sent in the mails to foreign countries.

Scurrilous Matter. — Matter upon the envelope or outside cover or wrapper of which, or any postal card upon which, any delineations, epithets, terms, or language of an indecent, lewd, lascivious, obscene, libelous, scurrilous, defamatory, or threatening character, or calculated by the terms, or manner or style of display, and obviously intended to reflect injuriously upon the character or conduct of another, may be written or printed.

Obscene Matter. — Every obscene, lewd, or lascivious book, pamphlet, picture, paper, letter, writing, print, or other publication of an indecent character, and every article or thing designed or intended for the prevention of conception or procuring of abortion, and every article or thing intended or adapted for any indecent or immoral use, and every written or printed card, letter, circular, book, pamphlet, advertisement, or notice of any kind giving information, directly or indirectly, where or how or of whom, or by what means any of the hereinbefore-mentioned matters, articles, or things may be obtained or made.

Lottery Matter. — Letters and circulars known to be concerning lotteries, gift-concerts, etc., or concerning any scheme devised and intended to receive and defraud the public for the purpose of obtaining money under false pretenses.

Mutilated. — Matter recovered from wrecked or burned mail cars or vessels, or matter damaged so that it cannot be forwarded to destination. All matter found loose in the mails, separated from the wrapper, label, or envelope containing the address, so that the direction cannot be known; and the matter recovered from depredations on the mails and to be restored to the owners upon due proof of ownership.

Excess of Weight and Size. — Packages of domestic third and fourth class matter, weighing more than four pounds (except single books and official matter emanating from the Departments at Washington), and of foreign matter in excess of weight or size fixed by stipulation of postal treaty.

4. Customs Regulations on Various Horticultural Products.

Act of Aug. 28, 1894.

DUTIES. — Garden and agricultural seeds, not specially provided for, 10 per cent ad valorem.

Vegetables in natural state, not specially provided for, 10 per cent ad valorem.

Apples green, ripe, or dried, dates, pineapples, grapes, olives green or prepared, fruits preserved in their own juices, peanuts, cocoanuts, 20 per cent ad valorem.

Oranges, lemons, and limes, in packages, at rate of 8 cents per cubic foot of capacity; in bulk, $1.50 per thousand; and in addition thereto a duty of 30 per cent ad valorem upon the boxes or barrels.

Plums, prunes, figs, raisins, and other dried grapes, including Zante currants, $1\frac{1}{2}$ cents per pound.

Almonds, unshelled, 3 cents per pound; shelled, 5 cents per pound. Filberts and walnuts, unshelled, 2 cents per pound; shelled, 4 cents per pound.

Orchids, lily of the valley, azaleas, palms, and other plants used for forcing under glass for cut flowers or decorative purposes, 10 per cent ad valorem.

FREE LIST. — Cabbages, cider, coffee, green peas in bulk or barrels or sacks, nursery stock, yams; seeds as follows: anise, canary, caraway, cardamom, coriander, cotton, croton, cummin, fennel, fenugreek, hemp, hoarhound, mustard, rape, St. John's bread or bene, sugar beet, mangel-wurzel, sorghum or sugar cane for seed, and all flower and grass seed. Bulbs and roots not edible.

CHAPTER XVIII.

THE WEATHER.

1. Barometer Indications.

Stationary barometer indicates continuance of the present weather.

Slowly rising barometer usually indicates fair weather.

Slowly falling barometer indicates the approach of a severe storm. One-fifth to one-third of an inch is sufficient fall to give indications.

Sudden rise of the barometer indicates the approach of a storm or the breaking-up of an existing storm.

Sudden fall of the barometer indicates high winds and probable rain.

When areas of low and high barometer are near together, heavy gales may be expected.

2. Popular Weather Signs.

Long lines of clouds extending up the sky from a common starting-point often foretell a storm from that quarter.

When the fleecy or cirrus clouds settle down into horizontal bars or ribs in the upper sky, wet and foul weather may be expected. This is the " mackerel sky."

If contiguous clouds move in various directions, rain is likely to follow soon.

When small black clouds scud over an overcast sky, heavy rain and bad weather may be expected.

Cumulus clouds that preserve a well-rounded form and float high in the air indicate fair weather.

Anvil-shaped cumulus clouds usually indicate thunderstorms.

THE WEATHER.

In spring and fall, rain is often indicated by a dense bank of gray clouds in the east, in front of which are little shoals of blackish clouds.

Cirro-cumulus clouds—like bunches and fleeces of wool scattered high in the sky—are indications of still and dry weather.

When the rays of the rising sun shoot far up into the sky, fair weather may be expected.

When the ray-like shadows of clouds overlie a hazy sky in the vicinity of the sun, rain is apt to follow. This is expressed in the phrase "the sun drawing water."

Gaudy hues of blue and purple at sunset prophesy rain and wind.

A bright red sunset means fair weather for the morrow.

A pale and diffuse sun at setting portends a storm.

If the sun sets in subdued purple and the zenith is pale blue, fair weather may be expected.

A deep red morning sky is usually followed by bad weather.

A rosy or gray morning sky means good weather.

A sonorous condition of the atmosphere foretells rain.

A bank of cloud across the southern horizon in winter indicates snow. It is frequently called the "snow-bank."

If the sun rises clear but becomes overcast within half an hour, prepare for rain.

A halo about the moon indicates a rain storm.

If the sky is white or yellowish-white nearly to the zenith after sunset, prepare for rain soon.

Strong east winds indicate a storm.

Haziness is indicative of dry weather. It is due to dust in the atmosphere.

When haziness suddenly disappears and the sun sets pale and the sky is very clear, rain is probable.

When stars twinkle with unusual prominence, rain may be expected.

Heavy dew indicates fair weather.

Absence of dew for two or three mornings in succession in summer is a precursor of rain.

3. Frosts.

To Predict Frost (Kedzie). — 1. When the sunshine is very hot and the shade very cold and the shadows very deep, "there is frost in the air," because the air is very dry and radiation of heat little checked.

2. When the dew-point is more than 10° Fahrenheit above frost-point (32°), there is little danger of frost, but when it is less than this, frost may be expected. To find approximately the temperature of dew-point when the temperature of the air is between 45° and 65° Fahrenheit, multiply the difference between the wet-bulb and dry-bulb thermometers by two and subtract the product from temperature of dry-bulb. If the remainder is above 42° Fahrenheit, there is little danger of frost. The nearer this remainder comes to 32°, the greater the danger of frost, especially if the air is still and clouds disappear at sunset.

The dew-point is determined by the wet and dry bulb thermometer (or psychrometer). The instrument may be made as follows: For the frame take a board 18 inches long, 2 inches wide, and ½ inch thick, with a hole bored in one end to hang the apparatus on a nail when not in use. Get two all-glass thermometers with cylindrical bulbs, and the degrees Fahrenheit engraved on the stem. Cover the bulb of one thermometer with a thin piece of cotton cloth, fastening it securely by a thread. When this cloth covering is wet with water and exposed to evaporation in the air, it constitutes the "wet-bulb thermometer"; the other thermometer has no covering on its bulb, is not wet at any time, and constitutes the "dry-bulb thermometer."

The range of temperature of the open air in this table is from 36° Fahrenheit to 75° Fahrenheit, and of depression of temperature in the wet bulb, from 1° to 13° Fahrenheit, giving a range in both directions of sufficient scope for the needs of Northern farmers during the growing season. The temperature of the dry-bulb (or open air temperature) is found in the left-hand column of the table; the difference in degrees

THE WEATHER. 223

TABLE FOR DETERMINING THE TEMPERATURE OF DEW-POINT FROM THE READINGS OF THE DRY AND WET BULB THERMOMETERS (HAZEN).

Dry-bulb Thermometer.	Depression of the Wet-bulb Thermometer.											
	1°	2°	3°	4°	5°	6°	7°	8°	9°	10°	11°	12°	13°
75°....	74	72	71	69	68	66	64	63	61	59	57	56	54
74°....	73	71	70	68	67	65	63	62	60	58	56	54	52
73°....	72	70	69	67	66	64	62	61	59	57	55	53	51
72°....	71	69	68	66	64	63	61	59	58	56	54	52	50
71°....	70	68	67	65	63	62	60	58	56	55	53	51	48
70°....	69	67	66	64	62	61	59	57	55	53	51	49	47
69°....	68	66	64	63	61	59	58	56	54	52	50	48	46
68°....	67	65	63	62	60	58	57	55	53	51	49	46	44
67°....	66	64	62	61	59	57	55	54	52	50	47	45	43
66°....	64	63	61	60	58	56	54	52	50	48	46	44	
65°....	63	62	60	59	57	55	53	51	49	47	45	42	41
64°....	62	61	59	57	56	54	52	50	48	46	43		40
63°....	61	60	58	56	55	53	51	49	47	44	42	41	38
62°....	60	59	57	55	53	52	50	48	45	43		39	37
61°....	59	58	56	54	52	50	48	46	44	42	41	38	35
60°....	58	57	55	53	51	49	47	45	43		39	36	33
59°....	57	56	54	52	50	48	46	44		40	38	35	32
58°....	56	55	53	51	49	47	45	42	41	39	36	33	30
57°....	55	54	52	50	48	46	44		40	37	35	31	28
56°....	54	53	51	49	47	44	42	41	39	36	33	30	26
55°....	53	52	50	48	46	43		40	37	34	31	28	25
54°....	52	50	49	46	44	42	41	39	36	33	30	27	23
53°....	51	49	47	45	43		40	37	34	31	28	25	20
52°....	50	48	46	44	42	41	38	36	33	30	27	23	18
51°....	49	47	45	43		40	37	34	31	28	25	21	16
50°....	48	46	44	42	41	38	36	33	30	27	23	19	14
49°....	47	45	43		40	37	34	31	28	25	21	17	11
48°....	46	44	42	41	38	36	33	30	27	23	19	14	9
47°....	45	43		40	37	35	32	29	25	22	17	12	6
46°....	44	42	41	39	36	33	30	27	24	20	15	10	3
45°....	43		40	37	35	32	29	26	22	18	13	7	-1
44°....	42	41	39	36	33	30	27	24	20	16	11	4	-5
		40	37	35	32	29	26	23	19	14	8	1	-9
43°....	41	39	36	34	31	28	25	21	17	12	6	-2	-15
42°....	40	38	35	33	29	26	23	19	15	9	3	-6	-22
41°....	39	36	34	31	28	25	22	17	13	7	0	-11	-32
40°....	38	35	33	30	27	24	20	16	11	4	-4	-16	-74
39°....	37	34	32	29	26	22	18	14	8	2	-8	-23	
38°....	36	33	31	28	24	21	17	12	6	-1	-12	-35	
37°....	35	32	29	26	23	19	15	10	4	-5	-17		
36°....	34	31	28	25	22	18	13	8	1	-8	-25		

between the readings of the dry and wet bulb is entered in the horizontal line at the top, from 1° to 13°. To find the temperature of dew-point at any observation, find in left-hand column the temperature of dry-bulb, then follow the horizontal line opposite that figure till you reach the perpendicular column under the difference between dry and wet bulb readings, and the figures at the meeting of these two columns will give the temperature of dew-point. For example, suppose the dry-bulb stands at 65° and wet-bulb at 55°, the difference is 10°. Pass across the page in the line of 65° till you intersect the vertical column under 10° and you read 47°, which is dew-point under these conditions. If the dew-point is 10° or more above frost-point (32° Fahrenheit), there is no danger of killing frost; but if the dew-point is less than 10° above 32°, danger may be apprehended. If a line is drawn from the intersection of 43°—1° and 67°—13°, of the table, this may be called the danger line, and all dew-point temperatures below this line indicate danger of frost, and are printed in *italics*. This margin of 10° is taken because the temperature on a still night will sink a few degrees below the first dew-point, and the temperature of the air at 5 feet above the ground is several degrees above that at ground level. For these reasons combined a margin of 10° may be safely assumed as the limit of safety.

To Protect Plants from Light Frosts.—1. Make a smudge in the garden or vineyard at night when the frost is expected. Rubbish or litter and tar make the best smudge. 2. Syringe the plants thoroughly at night-fall.

"If the farmer is forewarned of the approach of a still frost, he may do something to avert the calamity. The conservative influence of watery vapor is the most hopeful means of protection, and sometimes trivial causes of this class will produce surprising results. The old plan of 'a tub of water under the fruit tree, and a rope reaching from the tub into the branches,' may serve a useful purpose. The evaporation from the water in the tub and of the water carried up by capillary action in the rope may spread the protecting folds of the water blanket

THE WEATHER. 225

over the tree. Such appliances, while of some use for a small garden, would be futile for a farm.

"If the hoed crops of the farm are cultivated with reference to securing a constant supply of moisture in the upper soil, — to draw by capillary action of the soil upon the reservoir of water in the subsoil, and at the same time keep the surface soil in such condition as to prevent the too rapid dissipation of soil moisture, — the fields may be saved from frost by a covering as impalpable as air but as effectual as eider-down. Here is a conservatism of highest importance for both farmer and fruit grower." — *Kedzie.*

4. Signals of the United States Weather Bureau.

A. FLAG SIGNALS.

No. 1, square white flag, alone, indicates fair weather, stationary temperature.

No. 2, square blue flag, alone, indicates rain or snow, stationary temperature.

No. 3, square, white above, blue below, alone, indicates local rain, stationary temperature.

No. 4, triangular black, refers to temperature.

No. 5, square white, with black center, cold wave.

No. 1, with No. 4 above it, indicates fair weather, warmer.

No. 1, with No. 4 below it, indicates fair weather, colder.

No. 2, with No. 4 above it, indicates warmer weather, rain or snow.

No. 2, with No. 4 below it, indicates colder weather, rain or snow.

No. 3, with No. 4 above it, indicates warmer weather with local rains.

No. 3, with No. 4 below it, indicates colder weather with local rains.

No. 1, with No. 5 below it, indicates fair weather, cold wave.

No. 2, with No. 5 below it, indicates wet weather, cold wave.

B. WHISTLE SIGNALS.

The warning signal, to attract attention, will be a long blast of from fifteen to twenty seconds' duration. After this warning signal has been sounded, long blasts (of from four to six seconds' duration) refer to weather, and short blasts (of from one to three seconds' duration) refer to temperature; those for weather to be sounded first.

Blasts.	Indicate.
One long	Fair weather.
Two long	Rain or snow.
Three long	Local rains.
One short	Lower temperature.
Two short	Higher temperature.
Three short	Cold wave.

Interpretation of combination blasts.

One long, alone	Fair weather, stationary temperature.
Two long, alone	Rain or snow, stationary temperature.
One long and short	Fair weather, lower temperature.
Two long and two short	Rain or snow, higher temperature.
One long and three short	Fair weather, cold wave.
Three long and two short	Local rains, higher temperature.

By repeating each combination a few times, with an interval of ten seconds between, possibilities of error in reading the forecasts will be avoided, such as may arise from variable winds, or failure to hear the warning signal.

5. Phenology.

Phenology (contraction of *phenomenology*) is that science which considers the relationship of local climate to the periodicity of the annual phenomena of nature. It usually studies climate and the progression of the seasons in terms of plant and animal life, as the dates of migrations, of blooming, leafing, ripening of fruit, defoliation, and the like. If observations are to have permanent value, they must be taken with a definite purpose. The particular objects of phenological observations are the following:

1. To determine the general oncoming of spring.
2. To determine the fitful or variable features of spring.
3. To determine the epoch of the full activity of the advancing season.
4. To determine the active physiological epoch of the year.
5. To determine the maturation of the season.
6. To determine the oncoming of the decline of fall.
7. To determine the approach of winter.
8. To determine the features of the winter epoch.
9. To determine the fleeting or fugitive epochs of the year.

Good phenological observations upon plants should satisfy the following tests, as given by Hoffmann:

1. They should represent as broad a distribution as possible of the given species, selected for observation.
2. Ease and certainty of identifying the definite phases which are to be observed.
3. The utility of the observations as regards biological questions, such as the vegetative periods, time of ripening, etc.
4. Representation of the entire vegetation period.
5. Consideration of those species which are found in almost all published observations, and especially of those whose development is not influenced by momentary or accidental circumstances, as is the dandelion.

The epochs of vegetation which should be observed for most phenological purposes are these:

1. Upper surface of the leaf first visible or spread open.
2. First blossoms open.

3. First fruit ripe.
4. All leaves, or more than half of them, colored.

Typical and average plants should always be selected for observation, and they should be few in number. A dozen well-selected species will afford more satisfactory records, year by year, than observations made at random upon a great variety of plants. For the sudden moods of spring, the peach and dandelion are useful for observation, but such plants — those which respond quickly to every fitful variation of the early season — are not reliable for the staple records of the years. Useful plants for study are the following:

Apple.	Cultivated Strawberry.
Pear.	Lilac.
Quince.	Mock Orange or Syringa.
Plum.	Horse Chestnut.
Sweet Cherry.	Red-pith Elder.
Sour Cherry.	Common Elder.
Peach.	Flowering Dogwood.
Choke Cherry.	Native Basswood.
Wild Black Cherry.	Native Chestnuts.
Japanese or Flowering Quince.	Privet or Prim.
Cultivated Raspberry.	Red Currant.
Cultivated Blackberry.	Cultivated Grape.

CHAPTER XIX.

LITERATURE.

1. **Some Current Books upon American Horticulture.**

A. GENERAL.

BAILEY, L. H. Annals of Horticulture in North America for the Year 1889. A Witness of Passing Events and a Record of Progress. Similar volumes for 1890, 1891, 1892, 1893. Rural Publishing Co. and Orange Judd Co. $1 each.

BAILEY, L. H. Plant-Breeding. Five Lectures upon the Amelioration of Domestic Plants. Macmillan & Co. $1.

BAILEY, L. H. The Nursery-Book. A Complete Guide to the Multiplication and Pollination of Plants. Rural Publishing Co. $1.

BARNARD, CHARLES. My Handkerchief Garden. Rural Publishing Co. 20 cents.

CROZIER, WILLIAM, and PETER HENDERSON. How the Farm Pays. Peter Henderson & Co. $2.50.

FOWLER, A. B. Greenhouse Heating. Published by the author, Exeter, N.H. 75 cents.

FULLER, A. S. The Propagation of Plants. Orange Judd Co. $1.50.

GRAY, ASA. Field, Forest, and Garden Botany. Revised edition, by L. H. Bailey. American Book Co.

GREENHOUSE HEATING. Articles by various authors. Florist's Exchange, N.Y. 25 cents.

HENDERSON, PETER. Garden and Farm Topics. Peter Henderson & Co. $1.

HENDERSON, PETER. Gardening for Pleasure. Orange Judd Co. $2.

HENDERSON, PETER. Handbook of Plants. Henderson & Co. $4.
LODEMAN, E. G. The Spraying of Plants. Macmillan & Co. $1. (Rural Science Series.)
ROE, E. P. Play and Profit in My Garden. Orange Judd Co. $1.50.
ROE, E. P. The Home Acre. Dodd, Mead & Co. $1.50.
SEMPERS, F. W. Injurious Insects and the Use of Insecticides. W. Atlee Burpee & Co., Philadelphia. $1.
STEWART, HENRY. Irrigation for the Farm, Garden, and Orchard. Orange Judd Co. $1.50.
TAFT, L. R. Greenhouse Construction. Orange Judd Co. $1.50.
TREAT, MRS. MARY. Insects of the Farm and Garden. Orange Judd Co. $2.
WEED, C. M. Fungi and Fungicides. Orange Judd Co.
WEED, C. M. Insects and Insecticides. Published by the author, Hanover, N.H. $1.25.
WEED, C. M. Spraying Crops. Rural Publishing Co. 50 cents.

B. FLOWERS, ORNAMENTAL AND LANDSCAPE GARDENING.

ALLEN, CHARLES L. Bulbs and Tuberous-rooted Plants. Orange Judd Co. $2.
BARKER, MICHAEL. American Chrysanthemum Annual, 1895. Mayflower Publishing Co. $1.
CAMPBELL, ELLA GRANT. Floral Designs. $3.50.
ELLIOTT, F. R. Handbook of Practical Landscape Gardening. D. M. Dewey, Rochester. $1.50.
ELLWANGER, H. B. The Rose. Dodd, Mead & Co. $1.25.
HALLIDAY, ROBERT J. Practical Azalea Culture. Published by the author, Baltimore. $2.
HALLIDAY, ROBERT J. Practical Camellia Culture. Published by the author, Baltimore. $2.
HEINRICH, JULIUS J. Window Flower Garden. Orange Judd Co. 75 cents.
HENDERSON, PETER. Practical Floriculture. Orange Judd Co. $1.50.
HENDERSON, PETER & Co. Bulb Culture. Peter Henderson & Co., New York. 25 cents.

HUNT, M. A. How to Grow Cut Flowers. Published by the author (deceased), Terre Haute, Ind. $2.
HUTCHINS, REV. W. T. All about Sweet Peas. W. Atlee Burpee & Co., Philadelphia. 20 cents.
JOHNSON, REV. E. A. Winter Greeneries at Home. Orange Judd Co. $1.
KEMP, EDWARD. How to Lay out a Garden (or Landscape Gardening). American edition. John Wiley & Son. $2.50.
LAMBORN, L. L. American Carnation Culture. Published by the author, Alliance, Ohio. $1.50.
LONG, E. A. How to Plant a Place. Rural Publishing Co. 20 cents.
LONG, E. A. Landscape Gardening (plans). Rural Publishing Co. 50 cents.
LONG, E. A. Ornamental Gardening for Americans. Orange Judd Co. $2.
LONG, E. A. The Home Florist. Charles A. Reeser, Springfield, Ohio. $1.50.
MATHEWS, F. SCHUYLER. The Beautiful Flower Garden. W. Atlee Burpee & Co., Philadelphia. 50 cents.
MORTON, JAMES. Chrysanthemum Culture for America. Rural Publishing Co. $1.
MORTON, JAMES. Southern Floriculture. W. P. Titus, Clarksville, Tenn. $1.
PARSONS, SAMUEL, JR. Landscape Gardening. G. P. Putnam's Sons. $3.50.
PARSONS, S. B. On the Rose. Orange Judd Co. $1.
POWELL, E. C., and WILLIAM MCMILLAN. Street and Shade Trees. Rural Publishing Co. 20 cents.
RAND, E. S., JR. Flowers for the Parlor and Garden. Houghton, Mifflin & Co. $2.50.
RAND, E. S., JR. Orchids. Houghton, Mifflin & Co. $3.00.
RAND, E. S., JR. Popular Flowers and How to Cultivate Them. Houghton, Mifflin & Co. $2.00.
RAND, E. S., JR. Rhododendrons. Houghton, Mifflin & Co. $1.50.

RAND, E. S. JR. The Window Gardener. Houghton, Mifflin & Co. $1.25.
REXFORD, EBEN E. Home Floriculture. James Vick, Rochester, N.Y.
SCOTT, F. J. Beautiful Homes. American Book Exchange. $2.50.
SHEEHAN, JAMES. Your Plants. Orange Judd Co. 40 cents.
SOLLY, GEORGE A. & SON. Designs for Flower Beds. Springfield, Mass. $3.
TUBEROUS BEGONIAS. Rural Publishing Co. 20 cents.
WEIDENMANN, J. Beautifying Country Homes. Orange Judd Co. $10.

C. VEGETABLES.

BRILL, F. Cauliflowers and How to Grow Them. Orange Judd Co. 20 cents.
BRILL, FRANCIS. Farm Gardening and Seed Growing. Orange Judd Co. $1.
BURPEE, W. ATLEE. How and What to Grow in a Kitchen Garden of One Acre. W. Atlee Burpee & Co., Philadelphia. 75 cents.
BURPEE, W. ATLEE, Editor. How to Grow Cabbages and Cauliflowers. By Pedersen and Howard. W. Atlee Burpee & Co., Philadelphia. 30 cents.
BURPEE, W. ATLEE, Editor. How to Grow Melons for Market. W. Atlee Burpee & Co., Philadelphia. 30 cents.
CARMAN, E. S. The New Potato Culture. Rural Publishing Co. 75 cents.
CROZIER, A. A. The Cauliflower. Register Publishing Co., Ann Arbor, Mich. $1.
DAY, J. W. Treatise on Tomato Culture. Published by the author, Crystal Springs, Miss. 25 cents.
DAY, J. W., D. CUMMINS and A. I. ROOT. Tomato Culture. A. I. Root, Medina, Ohio. 40 cents.
FALCONER, WM. Mushrooms, How to Grow Them. Orange Judd Co. $1.50.
FITZ, JAMES. Sweet Potato Culture. Orange Judd Co. 60 cents.

GREGORY, J. J. H. Cabbages, How to Grow Them. Marblehead, Mass. 30 cents.
GREGORY, J. J. H. Carrots, Mangold-Wurzels, and Sugar Beets. Marblehead, Mass. 30 cents.
GREGORY, J. J. H. Onion Raising. Rand Avery Co., Boston. 30 cents.
GREGORY, J. J. H. Squashes, How to Grow Them. Orange Judd Co. 30 cents.
GREINER, T. Celery for Profit. W. Atlee Burpee & Co., Philadelphia. 30 cents.
GREINER, T. How to Make the Garden Pay. Wm. Henry Maule, Philadelphia. $2.
GREINER, T. Onions for Profit. W. Atlee Burpee & Co., Philadelphia. 50 cents.
GREINER, T. The New Onion Culture. Published by the author, La Salle, N.Y. 50 cents.
HARRIS, JOSEPH. Gardening for Old and Young. Orange Judd Co. $1.25.
HENDERSON, PETER. Gardening for Profit. Orange Judd Co. $2.
LANDRETH, BURNET. Market Gardening and Farm Notes. Orange Judd Co. $1.
LIVINGSTON, A. W. Livingston and the Tomato. A. W. Livingston's Sons, Columbus. $1.
NIVEN, ROBERT. The New Celery Culture. Rural Publishing Co. 20 cents.
OEMLER, A. Truck Farming at the South. Orange Judd Co. $1.50.
ONION BOOK. By some 20 experienced growers. Orange Judd Co. 20 cents.
QUINN, P. T. Money in the Garden. Orange Judd Co. $1.50.
RAWSON, W. W. Celery and its Cultivation. Published by the author, Boston. 25 cents.
RAWSON, W. W. Success in Market Gardening. Published by the author, Boston. $1.
STEWART, H. L. Celery Growing. Published by the Author, Tecumseh, Mich. $1.

TERRY, T. B. A B C of Potato Culture. A. I. Root, Medina, Ohio. 40 cents.
THOMPSON, FRED S. Rhubarb Culture. Milwaukee, Wis. $1.
VAN BOCHOVE, G. AND BROTHER. Kalamazoo Celery. Published by the authors, Kalamazoo. 50 cents.
VAUGHAN, J. C. Celery Manual. J. C. Vaughan, Chicago. 50 cents.
WHITE, WM. N. Gardening for the South. Orange Judd Co. $2.
WHITNER, J. N. Gardening in Florida. C. W. DaCosta, Jacksonville. 75 cents.

D. POMOLOGY.

BAILEY, L. H. American Grape Training. Rural Publishing Co. 75 cents.
BARRY, P. The Fruit Garden. Orange Judd Co. $2.
BIGGLE, JACOB. Biggle Berry Book. Wilmer Atkinson Co., Philadelphia. 50 cents.
BLACK, J. J. The Cultivation of the Peach and the Pear, on the Delaware and Chesapeake Peninsula. James & Webb Co., Wilmington, Del. $1.50.
BUSH & SON & MEISSNER. Illustrated Descriptive Catalogue of American Grape Vines, Bushburg, Mo. 4th edition, $1.
CHORLTON, WM. Grape Growers' Guide. A Handbook of the Cultivation of the Exotic Grape. Orange Judd Co. 75 cents.
COLLINGWOOD, H. W. Fertilizers and Fruit. Rural Publishing Co. 20 cents.
DOWNING, A. J. and CHAS. Fruits and Fruit Trees of America. John Wiley & Sons, New York. $5.
EISEN, GUSTAV. The Raisin Industry H. S. Crocker & Co., San Francisco. $3.
FARMER, L. J. On the Strawberry. Published by the author, Pulaski, N.Y. 25 cents.
FITZ, JAMES. The Southern Apple and Peach Culturist. J. W. Randolph & English, Richmond. $1.50.
FULLER, A. S. Grape Culturist. Orange Judd Co. $1.50.

FULLER, A. S. Small Fruit Culturist. Orange Judd Co. $1.50.
FULLER, A. S. Strawberry Culturist. Orange Judd Co. 25 cents.
FULTON, ALEXANDER. Peach Culture. Orange Judd Co. $1.50.
GARY, THOS. A. Orange Culture in California. Pacific Rural Press, San Francisco. 75 cents.
GREEN, S. B. Amateur Fruit Growing. Farm, Stock, and Home Publishing Co., Minneapolis. $1.
GURNEY, C. W. Northwestern Pomology. Published by the author, Concord, Neb. $1.75.
HARCOURT, HELEN. Florida Fruits and How to Raise Them. John P. Morton & Co., Louisville, Ky. $1.25.
HILLS, WM. H. Small Fruits. Cupples, Upham & Co., Boston. $1.50.
HUSMANN. American Grape Growing and Wine Making. Orange Judd Co. $1.50.
HUSMANN. Grape Culture and Wine Making in California. Payot, Upham & Co. $2.
LACY, T. JAY. Fruit Culture for the Gulf States, South of Latitude 32 degrees. Washington, La. 25 cents.
LELONG, B. M. Citrus Culture in California. State Board of Horticulture, San Francisco.
MCNEIL, J. W. Fruits and Vegetables. Published by the author, Crystal Springs, Miss. 30 cents.
MANVILLE, A. H. Practical Orange Culture, including the Culture of the Orange, Lemon, Lime, and other Citrus Fruits as grown in Florida. Ashmead Bros., Jacksonville. 50 cents.
MARVIN, ARTHUR TAPPAN. The Olive. Payot, Upham & Co., San Francisco. $2.
MEECH, W. W. Quince Culture. Orange Judd Co. $1.
MITZKY, C. & Co. Our Native Grape. Rochester, N.Y.
MOORE, REV. T. W. Orange Culture in Florida, Louisiana, and California. E. R. Pelton & Co., N.Y. Ashmead Bros., Jacksonville. $1.
PHIN, JOHN. Open-air Grape Culture. Orange Judd & Co. $1.

POWELL, E. C. Fruit Packages. Rural Publishing Co. 20 cents.
QUINN, P. T. Pear Culture for Profit. Orange Judd Co. $1.
ROE, E. P. Success with Small Fruits. Dodd, Mead & Co. $1.50.
SAUNDERS, WM. Insects Injurious to Fruits. J. B. Lippincott Co., Philadelphia. $2.
SCRIBNER, F. LAMSON. Fungus Diseases of the Grape and Other Plants. J. T. Lovett Co., Little Silver, N.J. 75 cents.
SPALDING, WM. A. The Orange: its Culture in California. Riverside, Cal.
STRONG, W. C. Fruit Culture and the Laying-out and Management of a Country Home. Rural Publishing Co. $1.
TERRY, T. B., and A. I. ROOT. How to Grow Strawberries. A. I. Root, Medina, Ohio. 40 cents.
THOMAS, J. J. American Fruit Culturist. Wm. Wood & Co., New York. $2.
TRYON, J. H. A Practical Treatise on Grape Culture. Published by the author, Willoughby, Ohio. 25 cents.
WEBB, JAMES. Cape Cod Cranberries. Orange Judd Co. 40 cents.
WHITE, J. J. Cranberry Culture. Orange Judd Co. $1.25.
WICKSON, E. J. California Fruits and How to Grow Them. Dewey and Co., San Francisco. $3.
WOODWARD, GEO. E. & F. W. Graperies and Horticultural Buildings. Orange Judd Co. $1.

The Rural Science Series, edited by L. H. Bailey and published by Macmillan, is designed to present in readable form the latest fundamental science related to rural life. "The Soil," by King, and "The Spraying of Plants," by Lodeman, are now issued. Many others are in preparation, some of them treating specifically of horticultural subjects.

2. **Some American Horticultural Periodicals.**

Amateur Gardening. Springfield, Mass. Monthly. 50 cents.
American Horticulturist. F. A. Waugh, editor. Topeka, Kan. Monthly. 50 cents. (Formerly Smith's Small Fruit Farmer.'

LITERATURE. 237

American Florist (trade). Chicago and New York. Weekly. $1.
American Gardening. New York, Rhinelander Building. Twice monthly. $1.
Baltimore Cactus Journal. A. M. Cordray, editor. Baltimore, Md. Monthly. 50 cents.
California Fruit Grower. W. C. Fitzsimmons, editor. San Francisco. Weekly. $3.
Canadian Horticulturist. L. Woolverton, editor. Toronto and Grimsby, Ont. Monthly. $1.
Florist's Exchange (trade). New York, Rhinelander Building. Weekly. $1.
Fruit Growers' Journal. A. M. DuBois, editor. Cobden, Ill. Twice monthly. 50 cents.
Fruit Trade Journal. New York. Weekly. $3.
Garden and Forest. E. S. Sargent, conductor. New York, Tribune Building. Weekly. $4.
Gardening. Wm. Falconer, editor. Chicago. Twice monthly. $2.
Grape Belt. Dunkirk, N.Y. National edition, monthly. $1. (Also a weekly local edition.)
Horticultural Trade Journal. Floral Park, N.Y. Monthly. 50 cents.
Landscape Architect. F. Tracy Nelson, managing editor. Rochester, N.Y. Monthly. $1.50.
Market Garden. Minneapolis. Monthly. 50 cents.
Mayflower. Floral Park, N.Y. Monthly. 50 cents.
Meehan's Monthly. Germantown, Pa. Monthly. $2.
National Nurseryman. Ralph T. Olcott, editor. Rochester, N.Y. Monthly. $1.
Park's Floral Magazine. George W. Park, editor. Libonia, Pa. Monthly. 50 cents.
Southern Florist and Gardener. Elizabeth Fry, editress. Louisville, Ky. Monthly. $1.
Success with Flowers. West Grove, Pa. Monthly. 25 cents.
Western Garden and Poultry Journal. Chas. N. Page, editor. Des Moines, Iowa. Monthly. 50 cents.

3. Experiment Station Literature.

The bulletins of the various Agricultural Experiment Stations can be obtained by addressing the directors or officers in charge of the stations, as follows:

ALABAMA — *Auburn:* College Station; W. L. Broun. *Uniontown:* Canebrake Station; H. Benton.
ARIZONA — *Tucson:* T. B. Comstock.
ARKANSAS — *Fayetteville:* R. L. Bennett.
CALIFORNIA — *Berkeley:* E. W. Hilgard.
COLORADO — *Fort Collins:* Alston Ellis.
CONNECTICUT — *New Haven:* State Station; S. W. Johnson. *Storrs:* Storrs Station; W. O. Atwater.
DELAWARE — *Newark:* A. T. Neale.
FLORIDA — *Lake City:* O. Clute.
GEORGIA — *Experiment:* R. J. Redding.
IDAHO — *Moscow:* C. P. Fox.
ILLINOIS — *Champaign:* Eugene Davenport.
INDIANA — *Lafayette:* C. S. Plumb.
IOWA — *Ames:* James Wilson.
KANSAS — *Manhattan:* G. T. Fairchild.
KENTUCKY — *Lexington:* M. A. Scovell.
LOUISIANA — *Audubon Park, New Orleans:* Sugar Station. *Baton Rouge:* State Station. *Calhoun:* North Louisiana Station. W. C. Stubbs.
MAINE — *Orono:* W. H. Jordan.
MARYLAND — *College Park:* R. H. Miller.
MASSACHUSETTS — *Amherst:* State Station; C. A. Goessmann. *Amherst:* Hatch Station; H. H. Goodell.
MICHIGAN — *Agricultural College:* C. D. Smith.
MINNESOTA — *St. Anthony Park:* W. M. Liggett.
MISSISSIPPI — *Agricultural College:* S. M. Tracy.
MISSOURI — *Columbia:* P. Schweitzer.
MONTANA — *Bozeman:* S. M. Emery.
NEBRASKA — *Lincoln:* C. L. Ingersoll.
NEVADA — *Reno:* J. E. Stubbs.
NEW HAMPSHIRE — *Durham:* G. H. Whitcher.

NEW JERSEY — *New Brunswick:* State Station; E. B. Voorhees. *New Brunswick:* College Station; A. Scott.
NEW MEXICO — *Las Cruces:* S. P. McCrea.
NEW YORK — *Geneva:* State Station; P. Collier. *Ithaca:* Cornell University Station; I. P. Roberts.
NORTH CAROLINA — *Raleigh:* H. B. Battle.
NORTH DAKOTA — *Fargo:* J. B. Power.
OHIO — *Wooster:* C. E. Thorne.
OKLAHOMA — *Stillwater:* James C. Neal.
OREGON — *Corvallis:* J. M. Bloss.
PENNSYLVANIA — *State College:* H. P. Armsby.
RHODE ISLAND — *Kingston:* C. O. Flagg.
SOUTH CAROLINA — *Clemson College:* E. B. Craighead.
SOUTH DAKOTA — *Brookings:* L. McLouth.
TENNESSEE — *Knoxville:* C. F. Vanderford.
TEXAS — *College Station:* J. H. Connell.
UTAH — *Logan:* J. H. Paul.
VERMONT — *Burlington:* J. L. Hills.
VIRGINIA — *Blacksburg:* J. M. McBryde.
WASHINGTON — *Pullman:* E. A. Bryan.
WEST VIRGINIA — *Morgantown:* J. A. Myers.
WISCONSIN — *Madison:* W. A. Henry.
WYOMING — *Laramie:* A. A. Johnson.

The Scientific Bureaus and Divisions of the Department of Agriculture, Washington, are as follows:

WEATHER BUREAU — M. W. Harrington, *Chief.*
BUREAU OF ANIMAL INDUSTRY — D. E. Salmon, *Chief.*
DIVISION OF STATISTICS — H. A. Robinson, *Statistician.*
DIVISION OF ENTOMOLOGY — L. O. Howard, *Entomologist.*
DIVISION OF CHEMISTRY — H. W. Wiley, *Chemist.*
DIVISION OF BOTANY — F. V. Coville, *Botanist.*
DIVISION OF FORESTRY — B. E. Fernow, *Chief.*
DIVISION OF ORNITHOLOGY AND MAMMALOGY — C. Hart Merriam, *Ornithologist.*
DIVISION OF POMOLOGY — S. B. Heiges, *Pomologist.*
DIVISION OF VEGETABLE PATHOLOGY — B. T. Galloway, *Chief.*

DIVISION OF MICROSCOPY — T. Taylor, *Microscopist*.
OFFICE OF EXPERIMENT STATIONS — A. C. True, *Director*.

Abstracts of all experiment station and scientific agricultural literature are published monthly in the *Experiment Station Record*, issued by the Office of Experiment Stations, Department of Agriculture.

CHAPTER XX.

NAMES, HISTORIES, AND CLASSIFICATION.

1. Vegetables which have Different Names in England and America.

In America.	In England.
Artichoke (*Helianthus tuberosus*)	Jerusalem artichoke. (The true artichoke is a very different plant, grown for its edible flower-heads.)
Bean	Kidney-bean, or French bean. (To distinguish it from the broad bean, *Vicia Faba*, which is the chief bean of history.)
Beet	Beet-root.
Lima bean	Lima kidney-bean.
Muskmelon	Melon.
Parsnip	Parsnep in many old books.
Pepper	Capsicum. ("Pepper" is properly applied to the black and white pepper of commerce.)
Pumpkin	Vegetable marrow. Gourd.
Rutabaga	Turnip-rooted cabbage, Swedish turnip.
Salsify	Salsafy.
Squash	Pumpkin. Gourd.
" Scallop	Custard-marrow.
" Winter Crookneck (*Cucurbita moschata*)	Muskmelon, rarely.
Swiss chard	Leaf-beet.
Turnip	Turnep in many old books.

2. Names of Fruits and Vege-

English.	French.	German.
Almond	Amandier	Mandel
Apple	Pommier	Apfel
Apricot	Abricotier	Aprikose
Artichoke	Artichaut	Artischoke
Asparagus	Asperge	Spargel
Banana	Banane	Pisang
Bean, Broad	Fève de Marais	Grosse Bohne and Garten Bohne
Bean, Kidney	Haricot	Türcksche Bohne
Beet	Betterave	Rothe Rübe
Berberry	Épine vinette	Berberitzenstrauch
Black Currant	Cassis and Groseille noir	Schwartze Johannisbeere
Borecole	Chou vert, or Non pommé	Grüner Kohl
Broccoli	Broccoli and Chau brocolis	Italienischer Kohl
Brussels Sprouts	Chou de Bruxelles or à jets	Sprossen Kohl
Cabbage	Chou pommé or Cabus	Kopfkohl
Cardoon	Cardon	Kardon
Carrot	Carotte	Möhre or Gelbe Rübe
Cauliflower	Chou-fleur	Blumen Kohl
Celery	Céleri	Sellerie
Cherry	Cerisier	Kirsche
Chicory or Succory	Chicorée Sauvage	Gemeine Cichorie
Cress, Garden	Cresson	Gemeine Garten Kresse
" Water	Cresson de Fontaine	Brünnen Kresse
" Winter	Cresson de Terre	Winter Kresse
Cucumber	Concombre	Gurke
Egg-plant	Melongène, Aubergine	Tollapfel and Eierpflanze
Endive	Chicorée des Jardins, Endive	Endivie
Fig	Figuier	Feige
Filbert	Noisette	Nussbaum
Garlic	Ail	Knoblauch
Gooseberry	Groseiller à Maquereau	Stachelbeere
Grape	Vigne	Traube and Weintrauben
Horseradish	Cranson or le Grand Raifort	Meerrettig
Kohlrabi or Turnip-cabbage	Chou-rave	Kohl Rabi
Leek	Poireau	Gemeiner Lauch or Porro Zwiebe
Lemon	Limonier	Limonie

NAMES, HISTORIES, AND CLASSIFICATION. 243

tables in Various Languages.

Dutch.	Italian.*	Spanish.
Amandelboom	Mandorlo	Almendro.
Appelboom	Melo or Pomo	Manzana.
Abrikozenboom	Albicocco	Albaricoque.
Artisjok	Carciofo	Cinauco.
Aspergie	Asparago or Sparagio	Esparrago.
Bananeboom	Banana	
Boon	Fava	Haba.
Turksche Boon	Fagiuolo	Judias and Fasoles.
Beetwortel or Karoot	Barba bietola	Betarraga.
Barbarisse	Berberi or Crespino	Berberis.
Aalbessenboom	Ribes nero	Grosella negro.
Gröne Kool	Cavolo verzotto or Verza	Col.
Scotsche Kool	Broccoli	Broculi.
Spruit Kool	Cavolo di Bruxelles	
Kool	Cavolo	Berza.
Spaansche Artisjok	Cardo	Cardo.
Gerle Wortel	Carota	Chirivia.
Bloem Kool	Cavoli fiori	Berza florida.
Selderij	Sedano	Appio hortense.
Keresenboom	Ciriegia	Cerezo.
Suikerei	Cicoria	Achicoria.
Tuinkers	Crescione	Mastuerzo.
Waterkers	Crescione di Sorgenti	Berro.
Winterkers	Erba di Santa Barbarea	Hierba de Santa Barbbara.
Komkommer	Citriuolo	Pepino or Cohombro.
Dolappel	Melanzana	Berengena.
Andijvie	Indivia	Endivia.
Vijgenboom	Fico	Higuera.
Hazelnotenboom	Avellano or Noccinolo	Avellano.
Knoflook	Aglio	Ajo.
Kruisbessenboom	Uva-spina	Uva-crespas.
Druif	Vite	Vina.
Rammenas	Ramolaccio	Rabano picante.
Look or Prei	Porro	Puerro.
Limoenboom	Limone	Limon.

*The Italian names have been revised for the third edition by Dr. Aser Poli, of the Instituto Tecnico, Piacenza, Italy.

Names of Fruits and Vegetables in

English.	French.	German.
Lettuce	Laitue	Gartensalat and Lattich
Melon, Musk	Melon	Melone
Mint, Common	Menthe des jardins	Munze
Mulberry	Mûrier	Maulbeere
Mushroom	Champignon comestible	Essbare Blätterschwamme
Mustard	Moutarde	Senf
Nectarine	Pêche lisse	Nectarpfirsch
Olive	Olivier	Oelbaum and Olive
Onion	Oignon	Zwiebel
Orange	Oranger	Pomeranze
Orach	Arroche	Meldekraut
Parsley	Persil	Petersilie
Parsnip	Panais	Pastinake
Pea	Pois	Erbse
Peach	Pêcher	Pfirsiche
Pear	Poirier	Birne
Pepper, Red or Chile	Piment	Spanischer Pfeffer
Pine-apple	Ananas	Ananas
Plum	Prunier	Pflaume
Pomegranate	Grenadier	Granatenbaum
Potato	Pomme de Terre	Kartoffel
Pumpkin or Gourd	Courge	Kürbis
Quince	Coignassier	Quitte
Radish	Radis and Rave	Rettig and Radies
Rape	Navette	Repskohl
Red Currant	Groseiller commun	Gemeine Johannisbeere
Rhubarb	Rhubarbe	Rhabarber
Sage	Sauge	Salbey
Salsify	Salsifis	Haferwurzel and Bocksbart
Savoy	Chou de Milan or pommé fraisé	Wirsing or Herzkohl
Sea-kale	Chou marin and Crambé	Meerkohl
Spinach	Épinard	Spinat
Strawberry	Fraisier	Erdbeer
Sweet Chestnut	Châtaignier and Marronier	Castanien
Thyme	Thym	Thimian
Tomato	Tomate	Liebesapfel
Turnip	Navet	Rübe
Walnut	Noyer	Wallnuss
White Currant	Groseiller commun	Gemeine Johannisbeere
Watermelon	Melon d'Eau	Wassermelone

NAMES, HISTORIES, AND CLASSIFICATION. 245

Various Languages. — *Continued.*

Dutch.	*Italian.*	*Spanish.*
Latouw	Lattuga	Lechuga.
Meloen	Mellone and Popone	Melon.
Munt	Menta	Menta.
Moerbezieboom	Moro or Gelso	Moral.
Kampernoelio	Pratajuolo bianco	Seta.
Mosterd	Senapa	Mostaza.
Kale Perzik	Pesche noci or Nettarine	Especie de Durazno.
Olijfboom	Ulivo	Olivo.
Uijen	Cipolla	Cebolla.
Oranjeboom	Arancio	Naranja.
Melde	Atreplice	Armuelle.
Pieterselie	Prezzemolo	Perejil.
Pinksternakel	Pastinaca	Chirivia and Pastinaca
Erwt	Pisello	Guisante.
Perzikboom	Pesco	Alberchigo.
Perenboom	Pero	Pera.
Spaansche Peper	Peperone	Pimiento.
Ananas	Ananasso	Pina.
Prufnboom	Susino	Ciruelo.
Grannatboom	Melagrano	Granada.
Aardappel	Patata	Batatas Inglezas.
Kauwörde	Zucca	Calabaza.
Kweeboom	Cotogno	Membrillo.
Radijs	Ravanello or Radice	Rabano.
Rapskool	Rapa selvatica	Naba silvestre.
Aalbessenboom	Ribes rosso	Grosella.
Rabarber	Rabarbaro	Ruibarbo.
Salie	Salvia	Salvia.
Boksbaard	Sassifica	Barba Cabruna.
Savojie Kool	Cappuccio	Berza de Saboya.
Zeekool	Crambe marina	Col marina.
Spinazie	Spinacio	Espinaca.
Aardbeziënplant	Fragola	Fresa.
Kastanjeboom	Castagno	Castano.
Gemeene Thyne	Timo	Tomillo.
Appeltjes der liefde and Tomaat	Pomodoro	Tomate.
Raap	Rapa	Nabo.
Walnotenboom	Noce	Noguera.
Aalbessenboom	Ribes rosso	Gresella.
	Cocomero or Anguria	Sandia.

3. Emblematic Flowers.

NATIONAL FLOWERS.

Canada . . . . Sugar maple.
China . . . . Narcissus.
Egypt . . . . Lotus (*Nymphæa Lotus*).
England . . . . Rose.
France . . . . Fleur-de-lis (*Iris*).
Germany . . . . Corn-flower (*Centaurea Cyanus*).
Greece (*Athens*) . . . . Violet.
Ireland . . . . Shamrock (*Trifolium*, usually *T. repens*).
Italy . . . . Lily.
Japan . . . . Chrysanthemum.
Prussia . . . . Linden.
Saxony . . . . Mignonette.
Scotland . . . . Thistle.
Spain . . . . Pomegranate.
Wales . . . . Leek.

PARTY FLOWERS.

Beaconsfield's followers . . . . Primrose.
Bonapartists . . . . Violet.
Ghibellines . . . . White lily.
Guelphs . . . . Red lily.
Prince of Orange . . . . The orange.

STATE FLOWERS.

(*Adopted by Legislatures and State Horticultural Societies.*)

Alabama . . . . . . Goldenrod.
California . . . . . California poppy, or Eschscholtzia.
Minnesota . . . . . Moccasin-flower, or Cypripedium.
Oregon . . . . . . Oregon grape (*Berberis Aquifolium*).
Washington . . . . Rhododendron (*R. Californicum*).

NAMES, HISTORIES, AND CLASSIFICATION. 247

4. Derivation of the Names of Various Fruits and Vegetables

A. FRUITS.

Apple. — Anglo-Saxon, *æppel.*
Apricot. — Indirectly from Latin *præcoquum*, early-ripe.
Blackberry. — From the color of the fruit.
Cherry. — Anglo-Saxon, *cirse.*
Cranberry. — Crane-berry, from the slender pedicel of the European species.
Currant. — Corruption of *Corinth*, Greece, whence came the "dried currants" (grapes), which were once called Corinths.
Gooseberry. — Probably from *groseberry* or *groiseberry*, from Old French *groisele*, the currant and gooseberry.
Grape. — French, *grappe;* allied to the word *grapple.*
Lemon. — French, *limon*, indirectly from the Arabic.
Mulberry. — German, *mulber*, indirectly from Latin *morus*, a mulberry tree.
Nectarine. — Nectar-like.
Orange. — From the Arabic, through the French.
Peach. — Corruption of *Persia*, whence the fruit was early obtained.
Pear. — *Pirum*, the Latin name.
Plum. — Anglo-Saxon, *plume;* indirectly from Latin *prunum*, a plum.
Quince. — Corruption of *Cydonia*, the Latin name, from *Cydon.*
Raspberry. — From *rasp*, referring to the prickles.
Strawberry. — In early times the berries were strung on straws when sold. This is a folk-explanation, but is erroneous. Evidently associated with Latin *fragum*, fragrant.

B. VEGETABLES.

Artichoke. — Italian, *articiocco;* indirectly from the Arabic.
Asparagus. — The Latin name, from the Greek.
Bean. — The Anglo-Saxon name.

Beet. — Latin, *beta*, the beet-plant.
Cabbage. — French, *cabus*, from the Latin *caput*, a head.
Carrot. — French, *carotte*, from Latin *carota*, the carrot.
Brussels sprouts. — From *Brussels*, Belgium.
Cauliflower. — Latin, *caulis*, stem, and *flower*.
Celery. — Latin, *selinon*, parsley.
Chervil. — Anglo-Saxon, *cerfille*, indirectly from a Greek combination signifying "pleasant leaf."
Chives or **Cives.** — Latin, *cepa*, onion.
Corn. — Anglo-Saxon, *corn*.
Cress. — Old German, *kresan*, to creep.
Cucumber. — Latin, *cucumis*.
Egg-plant. — From the egg-shaped fruit of some varieties.
Endive. — French, *endive*, indirectly from the Latin *intubus*, the endive or chicory.
Garlic. — Anglo-Saxon, *gar* and *leak*, spear-leaf, referring to the shape and position of the leaves.
Gumbo. — Portuguese, *quingombo*, from *quillobo*, an African name.
Horseradish. — Refers, evidently, to the strong and pungent character of the roots by reference to the strength of the horse.
Kohlrabi. — Corruption of the Latin *caulo-rapa*, stem-turnip.
Leek. — Anglo-Saxon, *leac* or *leak*.
Lettuce. — Latin, *lactuca*, the lettuce; from *lac*, milk, referring to the milky juice of the plant.
Melon. — Latin, *melo*, a certain small melon.
Mushroom. — French, *mousseron*, alluding to *mousse*, or moss, in which some mushrooms grow.
Mustard. — French, *mustarde*, from Latin *mustum*, the must, with which mustard was mixed.
Onion. — French, *oignon*; indirectly from Latin *unus*, one, *unis*, oneness, in allusion to a plant of which the bulb was formed in one piece.
Parsley. — From a Greek combination meaning "rock-parsley," a parsley-like plant.
Parsnip. — Latin, *pastinaca*.

NAMES, HISTORIES, AND CLASSIFICATION. 249

Pea. — French, *pois*, from Latin *pisum*, the pea.
Pepper, Red. — Latin, *piper*, the true pepper or black pepper, with which the present plant is compared in pungency.
Potato. — Spanish and Portuguese, *batata*, an aboriginal American name. First applied to the sweet-potato.
Pumpkin. — French, *pompion*, from Latin *pepo*, a pumpkin-like fruit.
Radish. — Latin, *radix*, root.
Rhubarb. — French, *rhubarbe;* probably indirectly from Latin *barbarus*, foreign.
Sage. — Latin, *salvus*, saved, evidently in allusion to medicinal properties of the plant.
Salsify. — French, *salsifis*.
Spinach or **Spinage.** — Latin, *spinacia*, spinach, from *spina*, a thorn, in reference to the prickly character of the plant.
Squash. — American Indian, *asquash*, a raw or green fruit.
Tomato. — *Tomate*, of South American origin.
Turnip. — Probably Welsh *turn*, round, and *maip*, turnip.

5. Periods of Cultivation and Native Countries of Cultivated Plants.

(Adapted from researches of De Candolle, and Gray and Trumbull.)

Almond. — Over 4000 years; Mediterranean basin, western temperate Asia.
Apple. — Over 4000 years; Europe, Anatolia, south of the Caucasus.
Apricot. — Over 4000 years; China.
Artichoke. — Less than 2000 years; Europe, Africa, Canaries, and Madeira.
Asparagus. — Over 2000 years; Europe, western temperate Asia.
Banana. — Over 4000 years; southern Asia.
Barley, Common. — (?); western temperate Africa.
Bean. — Over 4000 years; unknown wild. Probably North America.
Bean, Broad. — Over 4000 years; south of the Caspian (?).

Bean, Lima. — About 500 years; South America.
Blackberry. — About 40 years; North America.
Buckwheat. — Less than 2000 years; Mandschuria, central Siberia.
Buckwheat, Tartarian. — Less than 2000 years; Tartary, Siberia to Dahuria.
Cabbage. — Over 4000 years; Europe.
Carrot. — Over 2000 years; Europe, western temperate Asia (?).
Celery. — Over 2000 years; Europe, Asia, and Africa.
Cherry. — More than 2000 years; temperate Europe and Asia.
Chestnut. — (?); from Portugal to Caspian Sea, eastern Algeria.
Chives. — Less than 2000 years; temperate and northern Europe.
Citron. — Over 2000 years; India.
Corn-salad. — Less than 2000 years; Sardinia, Sicily.
Cotton, Herbaceous. — Over 2000 years; India.
Cranberry. — About 50 years; North America.
Cress. — Over 2000 years; Persia (?).
Cucumber. — Over 4000 years; India.
Currant, Black. — Less than 2000 years; Europe, western Himalayas.
Currant, Red. — Less than 2000 years; Europe to Himalayas.
Date-palm. — Over 4000 years; western Asia and Africa.
Egg-plant. — Over 4000 years; India.
Endive. — Less than 2000 years; Mediterranean basin.
Fig. — Over 4000 years; south of Mediterranean basin.
Garlic. — Over 2000 years; desert of the Kirghis.
Gooseberry. — Less than 2000 years; temperate Europe, western Himalayas. Houghton and Downing are from a native species.
Grape. — European or wine grape (the grape of history), over 4000 years; western Asia and Mediterranean basin. American grapes are natives, and have come into cultivation within this century.
Hop. — Less than 2000 years; Europe, Asia, United States.

Horseradish. — Less than 2000 years; eastern temperate Europe.
Jerusalem Artichoke. — Probably ancient; United States.
Kaki. — Ancient; Japan and China.
Leek. — Over 2000 years; Mediterranean basin.
Lemon. — More than 2000 years; India or China.
Lettuce. — Over 2000 years; Europe, Asia, and Africa.
Maize. — Very ancient; New Granada (?).
Melon, Musk. — Less than 2000 years; India, Beluchistan, Guinea.
Mushroom. — Less than 2000 years; Northern hemisphere.
Oats. — Over 2000 years; temperate Europe.
Okra. — Less than 2000 years; tropical Africa.
Olive. — More than 4000 years; Syria, etc.
Onion. — Over 4000 years; Persia, Afghanistan, Beluchistan, Palestine (?).
Onion, Welsh. — Less than 2000 years; Siberia.
Orach. — Less than 2000 years; northern Europe and Siberia.
Orange. — Less than 2000 years in Europe; probably ancient far East; China.
Parsley. — Less than 2000 years; Europe, Algeria, and Lebanon.
Parsnip. — Less than 2000 years; central and southern Europe.
Pea. — Over 2000 years; Caucasus to Persia (?), India (?).
Peach. — Over 4000 years; China.
Pear. — Over 4000 years; temperate Europe and Asia.
Pepper. — Over 500 years; Brazil (?).
Pineapple. — Over 500 years; Mexico, Central America.
Plum. — Over 2000 years; Anatolia, north of Persia. There are also many varieties of native species.
Pomegranate. — More than 4000 years; Persia, etc.
Potato. — Over 500 years; Chile, Peru.
Pumpkin and Squash. — Over 500 years; temperate North America.
Quince. — Over 4000 years; north of Persia, south of the Caucasus, Anatolia.
Radish. — Over 2000 years; temperate Asia.

Rampion. — Less than 2000 years; temperate and southern Europe.
Rape. — Over 4000 years; Europe, western Siberia (?).
Raspberry. — The European raspberry (represented by the Antwerp and Fontenay), less than 2000 years; Europe and Asia. Our common red and black raspberries are natives, and have come into cultivation within the last 40 years.
Rice. — Over 4000 years; India, southern China.
Rye. — Over 2000 years; eastern temperate Europe (?), southeast of Europe, Algeria.
Salsify. — Less than 2000 years (?); southeastern Europe, Algeria.
Scorzonera. — Less than 2000 years; southwestern Europe.
Sea-kale. — Less than 2000 years; western temperate Europe.
Shaddock. — Over 2000 years; Pacific Islands.
Shallot. — Less than 2000 years; unknown, wild.
Sorghum. — Over 4000 years; tropical Africa (?).
Spinach. — Less than 2000 years; Persia (?).
Strawberry. — Less than 300 years; Chile.
Sunflower. — Very ancient; United States.
Sweet Potato. — Very ancient; tropical America.
Tobacco. — Ancient; South America.
Tomato. — Over 500 years; Peru.
Turnip. — Over 4000 years; Europe, western Siberia (?)
Watermelon. — Over 4000 years; tropical Africa.
Wheat. — Over 4000 years; region of the Euphrates.

6. Statistics of the Vegetable Kingdom.

There are 200 natural families or orders of flowering plants, about 7600 genera, and over 100,000 species are known and described. The flowerless plants are much more numerous than the flowering plants, both in individuals and species. Ferns, mosses, mushrooms, and many smaller or even microscopic fungi, lichens, and seaweeds are flowerless plants.

The Ranunculaceæ or Crowfoot family includes over 1200

species of plants, inhabiting all parts of the world. The clematis, marsh-marigold or so-called cowslip, columbine, adonis, buttercup, Christmas rose, love-in-a-mist, larkspur, aconite, and peony are members of the Crowfoot family. The family comprises 30 genera.

There are about 100 species of clematis known.

About 40 distinct species of delphinium or larkspur are described, few of which are cultivated.

It is thought that there are about a half-dozen true species of peonies known, although many supposed species have been described.

The Magnolia family comprises about 70 species of trees and shrubs. Of these, 14 are magnolias proper, of which 6 or 7 are native of Japan, China, or the Himalaya region, and the remainder are North American. The tulip tree, of which but a single species is known, belongs to this order.

The Nymphæaceæ or Water-lily family contains 8 genera and about 35 species, all aquatic. The largest genus is nymphæa — by some called castalia — comprising some 20 species.

The Mustard family, Cruciferæ, comprises probably about 2000 species, many of which are grown for food and ornament. The cabbage, cauliflower, turnip, kohlrabi, radish, horseradish, sea-kale, cresses, and mustards are the leading edible species, while the stocks, alyssum, wallflower, honesty or lunaria are among the ornamental species. There are over 175 genera in the order.

The Violet family comprises about 250 species, generally distributed over the world. Of these, about 200 are violets. The order includes 21 genera. Some of the species, outside of viola proper, are shrubs or small trees.

The Caryophyllaceæ or Pink family has about 1000 species and 35 genera. The ornamental genera are dianthus, including the pinks and carnation, saponaria, silene, lychnis, and a few others of less importance. Dianthus, literally "Jove's flower," numbers some 200 species. The corn-cockle and catchflies belong to this family.

The Mallow family, Malvaceæ, has about 60 genera and 700 species. The best-known genera are althæa, the hollyhock; malva, the mallows; hibiscus; abutilon; and gossypium, the cotton.

The Basswoods or Lindens are 8 in number, growing in northern temperate climates. Three are natives of North America. Tiliaceæ, the Basswood family, comprises 40 genera and about 330 species.

Some 50 species of maples are known, inhabiting Europe, Asia, and America. Nine or 10 grow naturally in North America. The Sapindaceæ, to which family the maple belongs, is largely tropical. It comprises over 70 genera, and 600 or 700 species. Æsculus, the horse-chestnuts, belong here, and are about 14 in number.

The Leguminosæ or Pulse family is one of the most important orders of plants. It furnishes many foods, fine woods, dyes, medicines, and ornamental plants. Many of the species are extremely important in agriculture because of the great amount of nitrogen they contain. Peas, beans, clover, locusts, acacias, sensitive plant, belong to this family. It comprises about 400 genera and 6500 species.

The Rosaceæ or Rose family may be called the fruit family of the north temperate zone. Apples, pears, quinces, June-berries, strawberries, blackberries, raspberries, peaches, plums, apricots, almonds, cherries, all belong here. Prunus, which includes the stone fruits, has about 100 species in various parts of the world, and 25 are North American. Pyrus, including apple, pear, quince, and mountain-ash, has about 40 species, of which 9 are in North America. Of roses, over 250 have been described, but late authorities consider that there are only about 30 good species. Of strawberries, there are 3 or 4 species and of spireas about 50. The whole family has about 1000 species and 70 genera.

Vitis, the grape and its allies, has some 230 species. There are two or three other genera, and about a score of other species in the family, Vitaceæ or Ampelideæ, to which it belongs.

The Cucurbitaceæ includes the squashes, pumpkins, cucum-

NAMES, HISTORIES, AND CLASSIFICATION. 255

bers, melons, and gourds. The species are about 500 in number, and are mostly tropical or subtropical. Some 25 species are described as cucumis, to which the cucumber and muskmelon belong, and 2 as citrullus or watermelon. The pumpkins and squashes belong to cucurbita, of which about 10 species are known, several of them perennials. The family comprises about 70 genera.

About 350 species of begonia are known.

Of cacti, there are about 1000 species and 13 genera, all but one species native of the New World.

Umbelliferæ, comprising over 150 genera and about 1300 species, includes the parsnip, parsley, carrot, celery, caraway, anise, dill, and others. In Africa some of the species attain to the size of trees.

About one-ninth of all flowering plants are comprised in the Compositæ or Sunflower family. It is by far the largest order, containing nearly 800 genera and about 10,000 species. Very few of the species furnish esculent parts; the leading ones are lettuce, endive, chicory, artichoke, cardoon, and salsify. But the family comprises great numbers of ornamental plants, of which the leading one at the present time is the chrysanthemum. A very few of the species become small shrubs.

The Heath family, Ericaceæ, includes the heaths, heather of Europe, wintergreen, whortleberries or huckleberries, cranberries, azaleas, rhododendrons, and laurels. Certain white and flesh-colored parasitic plants also belong to it, as the Indian-pipe and the snow plant of the Rocky Mountains. About 80 genera and over 1300 species are known.

The Primulas belong to the Primulaceæ or Primrose family, and they number some 80 or more species, many of which are cultivated. The genus primula is commonly divided by florists into auriculas, polyanthuses, and primroses. One of the primulas is the true cowslip. Primulaceæ has about 20 genera and 250 species.

Oleaceæ, a family of 18 genera and nearly 300 species, includes the jasmine, forsythias, lilacs, ashes, privet, and olive. A dozen species of fraxinus, or ash, are native of North America.

There are about 120 species of jasminum or jasmine, 2 of forsythia, 6 or more of syringa or lilac, over 30 of fraxinus, about 25 of ligustrum or privet, and 35 of olea or olive.

The Convolvulus or Morning-glory family, Convolvulaceæ, has some 800 species, some of which are trees, and 32 genera. The dodders, peculiar parasitic plants, of which several are natives of the United States, belong here, as does also the sweet potato.

There are about 30 species of Phlox described, nearly all natives of North America. The common *Phlox Drummondii* is a native of Texas. These plants, with cobæa, polemonium, gilia, and some other genera, belong to the family Polemoniaceæ.

Solanaceæ is a large and important order, containing many esculent plants and many poisons. Here belong the potato, tomato, egg-plant, red pepper, and strawberry or husk tomato; also tobacco, belladonna, and nightshade. There are 66 genera and from 1200 to 1500 species. The genus solanum alone, to which the potato and egg-plant belong, contains from 700 to 900 species. Lycopersicum, the tomato genus, has about a half dozen species.

There are about 140 genera and 2600 species in the Labiatæ or Mint family. The order comprises a few tree-like and a few climbing plants. The species are aromatic, and most of our cultivated sweet herbs, and all the mints, belong to the family. It comprises many ornamental species, among the most prominent being species of coleus, of which about 50 species are described.

The Nettle family or Urticaceæ comprises many dissimilar plants. Here belong the nettles, mulberry, fig, bread-fruit, hackberry, osage-orange, elm, hemp, and hop. The family has in the neighborhood of 1500 species, and the accepted genera are 108. Five elms and 2 mulberries are native to North America, and 3 wild figs grow in southern Florida.

Five genera and about 30 species belong to the Juglandaceæ or Walnut family. All the hickories, 8 or 10, are natives of North America. There are 2 walnuts and 1 butternut in the United States.

Cupuliferæ, the Oak family, numbers 400 species and 10 genera. It gives us the oaks, about 300 in the world and 44 in the United States; chestnuts, beeches, hazels, and filberts, birches, alder, hornbeam, and ironwood. The United States has 2 chestnuts, 1 beech, about 8 birches, and 6 alders.

Orchidaceæ, the Orchid family, includes some 5000 singular herbs, distributed through 334 genera. Many of the species are epiphytes, that is, growing above ground on other plants. The species are the most specialized, perhaps, of any order, and they are usually uncommon or rare. A number of showy species grow in the United States, the best known of which are the lady-slippers. Our species usually inhabit bogs or deep woods.

Iridaceæ, the Iris family, comprises many showy garden plants; as, iris, gladiolus, sparaxis, tritonia or montbretia, babiana, ixia, crocus, tigridia, and the like. The family includes about 60 genera and 700 species.

The Amaryllis family, Amaryllidaceæ, includes many lily-like plants, such as nerine or guernsey lily, vallota, narcissus, galanthus, leucoium, hippeastrum, crinum, agave, polianthes or tuberose, eucharis, etc. About 700 species and 64 genera are included in the family.

Over 2000 species, in 187 genera, comprise Liliaceæ, or the Lily family. Some of the species are tree-like. Here belong the onion, asparagus, tulip, aloes, yuccas, hellebore, and many choice ornamental plants. Of lilies, there are about 50 species, tulips in the neighborhood of 50, and of hyacinths about 30.

The Palm family, Palmæ, includes 1100 or more species and 132 genera. Many species produce edible fruits, the best known in our markets being the date and the cocoanut.

The Gramineæ or Grass family is the most important order of plants to the agriculturist. Besides all the grasses, it furnishes all the cereal grains, including Indian corn and the sugar-cane. Genera about 300; species more than 3000.

The Pine or Spruce family is known as the Coniferæ, or cone-bearing family. It includes plants of very dissimilar kinds. Most of the species have needle-like and evergreen leaves, but some are deciduous, and the gingko has broad and flat leaves.

There are more than 30 genera and about 300 species in the family. Of pines there are about 70, and 35 of them are native to the United States.

There are about 74 genera of ferns or Filices, and in the neighborhood of 2400 species. Some of the species attain to the size of small trees.

7. Classification of Horticulture.

(*Bailey, Annals of Horticulture, 1891.*)

I. POMOLOGY, the art and science of growing fruit.
  1. *Viticulture*, or *Grape-Growing*.
  2. *Orchard Culture*, comprising:
      Pomaceous fruits; Drupaceous or Stone fruits; Citrous fruits; Nut fruits (Nuciculture); Palmaceous fruits; and others.
  3. *Small-Fruit Culture*, comprising:
      Bush fruits (raspberry, blackberry, dewberry, currant, gooseberry, juneberry, and others); Strawberries.
  4. *Cranberry Culture*.

II. CLERICULTURE, the art and science of growing kitchen-garden vegetables. Comprises the following groups or esculents:
  Radicaceous (potatoes and root crops); Brassicaceous (cabbage-like plants); Alliaceous (onion-like plants); Spinaceous and Acetariaceous (salad and salad-like plants); Asparagaceous (asparagus, chicory, sea-kale and the like); Leguminaceous (peas and beans); Cucurbitaceous (melons, cucumbers, squashes); Solanaceous (red peppers, tomatoes, egg-plants); Aromatic esculents and sweet herbs; Cryptogamic esculents (mushrooms).

III. FLORICULTURE, the art and science of cultivating ornamental plants for their individual uses.

IV. LANDSCAPE-HORTICULTURE, the art and science of growing ornamental plants, especially trees and shrubs, for their uses in the landscape. Generally confounded with landscape-gardening.

CHAPTER XXI.

ELEMENTS, SYMBOLS, AND ANALYSES.

1. The Elements and their Symbols, and the Composition of Various Substances.

Aluminium	Al.		Mercury	Hg.
Antimony	Sb.		Molybdenum	Mo.
Arsenic	As.		Nickel	Ni.
Barium	Ba.		Nitrogen	N.
Bismuth	Bi.		Osmium	Os.
Boron	B.		Oxygen	O.
Bromine	Br.		Palladium	Pd.
Cadmium	Cd.		Phosphorus	P.
Cæsium	Cs.		Platinum	Pt.
Calcium	Ca.		Potassium	K.
Carbon	C.		Rhodium	Rh.
Cerium	Ce.		Rubidium	Rb.
Chlorine	Cl.		Ruthenium	Ru.
Chromium	Cr.		Scandium	Sc.
Cobalt	Co.		Selenium	Se.
Columbium	Cb.		Silicon	Si.
Copper	Cu.		Silver	Ag.
Didymium	D.		Sodium	Na.
Erbium	Er.		Strontium	Sr.
Fluorine	F.		Sulphur	S.
Gallium	Ga.		Tantalum	Ta.
Glucinum	Gl.		Tellurium	Te.
Gold	Au.		Thallium	Tl.
Hydrogen	H.		Thorium	Th.
Indium	In.		Tin	Sn.
Iodine	I.		Titanium	Ti.
Iridium	Ir.		Tungsten	W.
Iron	Fe.		Uranium	U.
Lanthanum	La.		Vanadium	V.
Lead	Pb.		Yttrium	Y.
Lithium	Li.		Zinc	Zn.
Magnesium	Mg.		Zirconium	Zr.
Manganese	Mn.			

The Composition of Various Substances.

Acetic acid	$C_2H_4O_2$	Mercuric oxide	HgO
Ammonia	NH_3	Nitric acid	HNO_3
Aniline	$NH_2(C_6H_5)$	Nitric oxide	NO
Arsenious oxide	As_4O_6	Nitrous oxide	N_2O
Carbonic oxide	CO	Nitric peroxide	NO_2
Carbonic dioxide	CO_2	Sulphuretted hydrogen	H_2S
Chloroform	$CHCl_3$	Sulphurous oxide	SO_2
Ferric oxide	Fe_2O_3	Sulphuric oxide	SO_3
Ferrous oxide	FeO	Sulphuric acid	H_2SO_4
Hydrochloric acid	HCl	Water	H_2O

2. Analyses.

Compiled from many reliable sources, largely from the labors of Drs. Goessmann and S. W. Johnson.

(a) GENERAL ANALYSES OF FRUITS AND FRUIT-PLANTS.

1. *Various Fruits.* (*Fresenius.*)

	Sugar.	Free acid.	Albuminous substance.	Pectous substance.	Soluble matter.	Water.
Apples	6.83	.85	.45	.47	14.96	82.04
Apricots	1.531	.706	.389	9.283	12.723	82.115
Austrian Grapes	13.78	1.020	.832	.498	16.40	79.007
Cultivated Strawberries	7.575	1.133	.359	.119	9.066	87.474
Cultivated Raspberries	4.708	1.356	.544	1.746	8.835	86.557
Green Grapes	2.96	.96	.477	10.475	15.19	80.841
Heart-Cherries	13.11	.351	.903	2.286	17.25	75.37
Mulberries	9.193	1.86	.304	2.031	14.043	84.707
Peaches	1.580	.612	.463	6.313	9.39	84.99
Pears	7.00	.074	.26	3.281	10.90	83.95
Red Currants	4.78	2.31	.45	.28	8.36	85.84
Red Gooseberries	8.063	1.358	.441	9.69	11.148	85.565
Wild Raspberries	3.599	1.980	.546	1.107	7.500	83.86
Wild Strawberries	3.247	1.650	.019	.145	6.308	87.271

ELEMENTS, SYMBOLS, AND ANALYSES. 261

2. *Subtropical Fruits.* (*Parsons.*)

	Water.	Crude protein.	Free acids.	Glucose sugar.	Cane-sugar.	Ether extract.	Crude fiber.	Ash.	Albuminoid nitrogen.	Nitrogen-free extract.
Sweet Pomegranates	78.27	1.33	0.368	11.61	1.04	1.24	2.63	.761	.177	15.77
Sour "	75.41	1.60	1.85	10.40	0.26	2.05	2.83	.544	.203	17.57
Persimmons	66.12	0.827	0.000	13.54	1.03	0.701	1.78	.861		29.71
Florida Oranges —										
Bitter-sweet	86.86	0.615	0.417	5.71	0.84	0.243				
Tangerine	83.56	0.792	0.477	6.00	3.41	2.50				
Mandarin	79.95	0.834	0.855	4.77	8.07	0.146				
Bloods	85.57	0.700	0.670	5.70	3.94	0.100				
Navels	83.70	1.12	0.662	6.03						
Russets	83.18	0.905	0.817	7.29	4.51					
Common	86.58	0.862	0.756	4.60	4.38	0.076				
Sour	86.76	1.03	2.55	3.36	0.97	0.125				
Messina Oranges —										
Guy Pope	86.22	0.980	1.18	5.95	1.82	0.166				

3. *Strawberries, Average of 20 Varieties.* (*Stone.*)

Water 90.52
Solids 9.48
Free acid. 1.37
Glucose 4.78
Glucose after inversion 5.46
Difference calculated as cane-sugar 0.58

COMPOSITION OF DRY MATTER.

Ash 6.53
Crude fiber 16.35
Ether extract 6.75
Crude protein 10.51
Non-nitrogenous extract. 60.79

4. *Raspberries.* (*Weber.*)

	Reliance.	Gregg.
Sugar	1.78	2.82
Acid	0.92	0.64
Seed	3.5	5.612

	Reliance.	Gregg.
Pectose, protein, combined acids, etc.	3.02	5.01
Ash	0.43	0.42
Fiber	0.32	0.48
Water	89.13	84.12

5. Peach, Branches. (*Kedzie.*)

Ash constituents.	Healthy.	Diseased by yellows.
Silica, SiO_2	1.21	1.40
Oxide of iron, Fe_2O_3	0.92	0.84
Lime, CaO	43.67	45.02
Magnesia, MgO	2.53	2.40
Potash, K_2O	7.07	4.93
Soda, Na_2O	1.88	2.33
Phosphoric acid, P_2O_5	7.20	6.03
Sulphuric oxide, SO_3	0.54	0.83
Carbon dioxide, CO_2	34.71	35.85
Chlorine	0.07	0.11
Moisture and loss	0.30	0.26
Total	100.00	100.00

6. Peach, Fruit and Branches. (*Goessmann.*)

Ash Constituents.	Fruit — Crawford's Early peach, healthy.	Fruit — Crawford's Early peach, diseased with yellows.	Branch — Crawford's Early peach, restored.	Branch — Crawford's Early peach, diseased with yellows.
	Per cent.	Per cent.	Per cent.	Per cent.
Ferric oxide, Fe_2O_3	0.58	0.46	0.52	1.45
Calcium oxide, CaO	2.64	4.68	54.52	64.23
Magnesium oxide, MgO	6.29	5.49	7.58	10.28
Phosphoric acid, P_2O_5	16.02	18.07	11.37	8.37
Potassium oxide, K_2O	74.46	71.30	26.01	15.67
Total	100.00	100.00	100.00	100.00

ELEMENTS, SYMBOLS, AND ANALYSES. 263

7. *Fertilizing Constituents in Various Products.*

In Roots, Tubers, etc.

Name.	Ash.	Nitrogen.	Phosphoric acid.	Potash.
Potatoes	0.99	0.21	0.07	0.29
Red Beets	1.13	0.24	0.09	0.44
Sugar Beets	1.04	0.22	0.10	0.48
Mangels	1.22	0.19	0.09	0.38
Turnips	1.01	0.18	0.10	0.39
Ruta-bagas	1.06	0.19	0.12	0.49
Carrots	9.22	0.15	0.09	0.51

In Grains and Seeds.

Corn Kernels	1.53	1.82	0.70	0.40
Sorghum Seed	...	1.48	0.81	0.42
Barley	2.48	1.51	0.79	0.48
Oats	2.98	2.06	0.82	0.62
Winter Wheat	...	2.36	0.89	0.61
Rye	...	1.76	0.82	0.54
Rice	0.82	1.08	0.18	0.09
Buckwheat	...	1.44	0.44	0.21
Soja Beans	4.99	5.30	1.87	1.99

In the Ash of Fruits (Goessmann).

Name.	Potash.	Soda.	Lime.	Magn.	Phosphoric acid.
Lombard Plums	76.59	...	13.26	2.17	7.44
Peaches	74.46	...	2.64	6.29	16.03
Baldwin Apples	63.54	1.71	7.28	5.52	20.87
Asparagus, stem	42.94	3.58	27.18	12.77	12.31
roots	56.43	5.42	15.48	7.57	15.09
Clinton Grapes	57.40	3.51	13.10	7.24	17.87
Concord Grapes	62.29	...	15.50	1.76	18.49
Cranberries	47.96	6.58	18.58	6.78	14.27
White Currants	53.81	...	17.46	4.72	22.54
Black Raspberries	50.00	...	19.44	9.00	20.47
Blackberries	51.42	...	17.22	5.30	24.13
Blueberries	31.36	...	28.02	9.25	29.05

(b) ANALYSES OF FRUIT AND GARDEN PRODUCTS

8. Analysis of Garden Crops and Fertiliz-

ONE THOUSAND PARTS

Name.	Water.	Nitrogen.	Ash.	Potash.	Soda.
Corn, kernels	144.	16.0	12.4	3.7	0.1
stalk and leaves	150.	4.8	45.3	16.4	0.5
Potato, tubers	750.	3.4	9.5	5.8	0.3
vines	770.	4.9	19.7	4.3	0.4
Peas, seed	143.	35.8	23.4	10.1	0.2
vines	160.	10.4	43.1	9.9	1.8
Beans, seed	150.	39.0	27.4	12.0	0.4
vines	160.	....	40.2	12.8	3.2
Carrots, roots	850.	2.2	8.2	3.0	1.7
leaves	822.	5.1	23.9	2.9	4.7
Sugar Beet, roots	815.	1.6	7.1	3.8	0.6
leaves	897.	3.0	15.3	4.0	2.0
White Turnip, roots	920.	1.8	6.4	2.9	0.6
leaves	898.	3.0	11.9	2.8	1.1
Swedish Turnip, roots	870.	2.1	7.5	3.5	0.4
leaves	884.	3.4	19.5	2.8	0.8
White Cabbage, head	900.	3.0	9.6	4.3	0.8
roots	890.	2.4	15.6	5.8	1.5
Savoy Cabbage, head	871.	5.3	14.0	3.9	1.4
Cauliflower	904.	4.0	8.0	3.6	0.5
Horseradish, roots	767.	4.3	19.7	7.7	0.4
Spanish Radish, roots	933.	1.9	4.9	1.6	1.0
Parsnip, roots	793.	5.4	10.0	5.4	0.2
Artichoke, roots	811.	....	10.1	2.4	0.7
Asparagus, sprouts	933.	3.2	5.0	1.2	0.9
Common Onion, bulb	860.	2.7	7.4	2.5	0.2
Celery	841.	2.4	17.6	7.6	....
Spinage	923.	4.9	16.0	2.5	5.7
Common Lettuce	940.	....	8.1	3.7	0.8
Head Lettuce	943.	2.2	10.1	3.9	0.8
Roman Lettuce	925.	2.0	9.8	2.5	3.5
Cucumber	956.	1.6	5.8	2.4	0.6
Pumpkin	900.	1.1	4.4	0.9	0.9
Rhubarb, roots	743.5	5.5	23.8	5.3	....
stem and leaves	916.7	1.3	17.2	3.6	0.3
Apples	831.	0.6	2.2	0.3	0.6
Pears	831.	0.6	3.3	1.8	0.3
Cherries	825.	....	3.9	2.0	0.1
Plums	838.	....	2.9	1.7	....
Gooseberries	903.	....	3.3	1.3	0.3
Strawberries	902.	....	3.3	0.7	0.9
Grapes	830.	1.7	8.8	5.0	0.1
seeds	110.	19.0	22.7	6.9	0.5

ELEMENTS, SYMBOLS, AND ANALYSES.

WITH REFERENCE TO THEIR FERTILIZING CONSTITUENTS.
ing Constituents. (*Wolff and Goessmann.*)
OF THE PLANTS CONTAIN:

NAME.	Lime.	Magnesia.	Phosphoric acid.	Sulphuric acid.	Chlorine.	Silicic acid.
Corn, kernels	0.3	1.9	5.7	0.1	0.2	0.3
stalk and leaves	4.9	2.6	3.8	2.4	0.6	13.1
Potato, tubers	0.3	0.5	1.6	0.6	0.3	0.2
vines	6.4	3.3	1.6	1.3	1.1	0.9
Peas, seed	1.1	1.9	8.4	0.8	0.4	0.2
vines	15.9	3.5	3.5	2.7	2.3	2.9
Beans, seed	1.5	2.1	9.7	1.1	0.3	0.2
vines	11.1	2.5	3.9	1.7	3.1	1.9
Carrots, roots	0.9	0.4	1.1	0.5	0.4	0.2
leaves	7.9	0.8	1.0	1.8	2.4	2.4
Sugar Beet, roots	0.4	0.6	0.9	0.3	0.3	0.2
leaves	3.1	1.7	0.7	0.8	1.3	1.6
White Turnip, roots	0.7	0.2	0.8	0.7	0.3	0.1
leaves	3.9	0.5	0.9	1.1	1.2	0.5
Swedish Turnip, roots	0.9	0.3	1.1	0.7	0.5	0.1
leaves	6.5	0.8	2.0	2.3	1.5	2.1
White Cabbage, head	1.2	0.4	1.1	1.3	0.5	0.1
roots	2.8	0.6	1.4	2.4	1.3	0.1
Savoy Cabbage, head	3.0	0.5	2.1	1.2	1.1	0.7
Cauliflower	0.5	0.3	1.6	1.0	0.8	0.3
Horseradish, roots	2.0	0.4	2.0	4.9	0.3	1.5
Spanish Radish, roots	0.7	0.2	0.5	0.3	0.5	...
Parsnip, roots	1.1	0.6	1.9	0.5	0.4	0.2
Artichoke, roots	1.0	0.4	1.1	1.3	0.5	0.1
Asparagus, sprout	0.6	0.2	0.9	0.3	0.3	0.5
Common Onion, bulb	1.6	0.3	1.3	0.4	0.2	0.7
Celery	2.3	1.0	2.2	1.0	2.8	0.7
Spinach	1.9	1.0	1.6	1.1	1.0	0.7
Common Lettuce	0.5	0.2	0.7	0.3	0.4	1.3
Head Lettuce	1.5	0.6	1.0	0.4	0.8	0.8
Roman Lettuce	1.2	0.4	1.1	0.4	0.4	0.3
Cucumber	0.4	0.2	1.2	0.4	0.4	0.5
Pumpkin	0.3	0.2	1.6	0.1	...	0.3
Rhubarb, roots	5.0	1.6	0.6	...	...	...
stem and leaves	3.4	1.3	0.2	...	...	...
Apples	0.1	0.2	0.3	0.1	...	0.1
Pears	0.3	0.2	0.5	0.2	...	0.1
Cherries	0.3	0.2	0.6	0.2	0.1	0.4
Plums	0.3	0.2	0.4	0.1	...	0.1
Gooseberries	0.4	0.2	0.7	0.2	...	0.1
Strawberries	0.5	...	0.5	0.1	0.1	0.4
Grapes	1.0	0.4	1.4	0.5	0.1	0.3
seeds	5.6	1.4	7.0	0.8	0.1	0.2

9. *Apple-Pomace.*

Water	69.90
Ash	0.71
Albuminoids	1.58
Fiber	4.87
Nitrogen-free extract	21.24
Fat	1.71
	100.00

10. *Cranberry-Vines.*

Moisture at 100° C.	13.07	Phosphoric acid	0.268
Nitrogen	0.77	Magnesium oxide	0.253
Ash constituents	2.45	Sodium oxide	0.080
Ferric oxide	0.087	Potassium oxide	0.329
Calcium oxide	0.404	Insoluble matter	0.834

11. *Corn-Fodder.*

Moisture at 100° C.	24.87	Potassium oxide	1.465
Nitrogen	0.995	Sodium oxide	0.794
Phosphoric acid	0.201	Ferric oxide	0.026
Calcium oxide	0.310	Insoluble matter	1.318
Magnesium oxide	0.093		

12. *Corn Kernels, New.*

Water	20.00
Ash	1.25
Albuminoids	8.06
Fiber	1.54
Nitrogen-free extract	65.38
Fat	3.77
	100.00

13. *Pea-Straw.*

Potash	4.73
Lime	54.91
Magnesia	6.88

ELEMENTS, SYMBOLS, AND ANALYSES. 267

Oxide of iron 0.40
Oxide of Manganese 0.15
Phosphoric acid 4.83
Sulphuric acid 6.77
Chlorine 0.09
Alumina 1.21
Silica 20.03
                                        ——
                                        100.00

14. Peas.

Potash 36.05
Soda 7.42
Lime 5.29
Magnesia 18.46
Oxide of iron 0.99
Phosphoric acid 33.29
Sulphuric acid 4.36
Chloride of sodium 3.13
Silica 0.51
                                        ——
                                        100.00

15. Beet, Egyptian Turnip.

Moisture at 100° C. .	85.800	Magnesium oxide . .	0.035
Nitrogen	0.177	Sodium oxide . . .	0.061
Phosphoric acid . .	0.070	Ferric oxide	0.002
Potassium oxide . .	0.303	Insoluble matter . .	0.018
Calcium oxide . .	0.049		

16. Carrots.

Moisture at 100° C. .	90.02	Potassium oxide . . .	0.54
Ferric oxide	0.01	Sodium oxide	0.11
Phosphoric acid . . .	0.10	Nitrogen	0.14
Magnesium oxide . .	0.02	Insoluble matter . . .	0.01
Calcium oxide . . .	0.07		

17. Turnip, Ruta-baga.

Moisture at 100° C. .	87.230	Magnesium oxide . .	0.030
Nitrogen	0.211	Sodium oxide . . .	0.051

Phosphoric acid . . 0.136 Ferric oxide 0.002
Potassium oxide . . 0.546 Insoluble matter . . 0.001
Calcium oxide . . 0.106

(c) ANALYSES OF ANIMAL EXCREMENTS.

18. Common Barnyard Manure, Fresh.

Water . . . . . . 710.0 Lime 5.7
Organic substance . . 246.0 Magnesia 1.4
Ash . . . . 44.1 Phosphoric acid . . . 2.1
Nitrogen . . . . . 4.5 Sulphuric acid 1.2
Potash . . . . . . 5.2 Silica and sand . . . 12.5
Soda . . . . . . 1.5 Chlorine and fluorine . 1.5

19. Common Barnyard Manure, Moderately Rotted.

Water . . . . . . 750.0 Lime 7.0
Organic substance . . 192.0 Magnesia 1.8
Ash . . . . 58.0 Phosphoric acid . . . 2.6
Nitrogen . . . . . 5.0 Sulphuric acid 1.6
Potash . . . . . . 6.3 Silica and sand . . . 16.8
Soda . . . . 1.9 Chlorine and fluorine . 1.9

20. Common Barnyard Manure, Thoroughly Rotted.

Water . . . . . . 790.0 Lime 8.8
Organic substance . . 145.0 Magnesia 1.8
Ash . . . . 65.0 Phosphoric acid . . . 3.0
Nitrogen . . . . 5.8 Sulphuric acid . . . 1.3
Potash . . . . . . 5.0 Silica and sand . . . 17.0
Soda . . . . . . 1.3 Chlorine and fluorine . 1.6

21. Cattle-Feces, Fresh.

Water . . . . 838.0 Lime 3.4
Organic substance . . 145.0 Magnesia 1.3
Ash . . . . 17.3 Phosphoric acid . . . 1.7
Nitrogen . . . . . 2.0 Sulphuric acid 0.4
Potash . . . . . . 1.0 Silica and sand . . . 7.2
Soda . . . . 0.2 Chlorine and fluorine . 0.2

ELEMENTS, SYMBOLS, AND ANALYSES. 269

22. Cattle-Urine, Fresh.

Water	938.0	Lime	0.1
Organic substance	35.0	Magnesia	0.4
Ash	27.4	Sulphuric acid	1.3
Nitrogen	5.8	Silica and sand	0.3
Potash	4.9	Chlorine and fluorine	3.8
Soda	6.4		

23. Horse-Feces, Fresh.

Water	757.0	Lime	1.5
Organic substance	211.0	Magnesia	1.2
Ash	31.6	Phosphoric acid	3.5
Nitrogen	4.4	Sulphuric acid	0.6
Potash	3.5	Silica and sand	19.6
Soda	0.6	Chlorine and fluorine	0.2

24. Horse-Urine, Fresh.

Water	901.0	Lime	4.5
Organic substance	71.0	Magnesia	2.4
Ash	28.0	Sulphuric acid	0.6
Nitrogen	15.5	Silica and sand	0.8
Potash	15.0	Chlorine and fluorine	1.5
Soda	2.5		

25. Sheep-Feces, Fresh.

Water	655.0	Lime	4.6
Organic substance	314.0	Magnesia	1.5
Ash	31.1	Phosphoric acid	3.1
Nitrogen	5.5	Sulphuric acid	1.4
Potash	1.5	Silica and sand	17.5
Soda	1.0	Chlorine and fluorine	0.3

26. Sheep-Urine, Fresh.

Water	872.0	Lime	1.6
Organic substance	83.0	Magnesia	3.4

Ash	45.2	Phosphoric acid	0.1
Nitrogen	19.5	Sulphuric acid	3.0
Potash	22.6	Silica and sand	0.1
Soda	5.4	Chlorine and fluorine	5.5

27. Swine-Feces, Fresh.

Water	820.0	Lime	0.9
Organic substance	150.0	Magnesia	1.0
Ash	30.0	Phosphoric acid	4.1
Nitrogen	6.0	Sulphuric acid	0.4
Potash	2.6	Silica and sand	15.0
Soda	2.5	Chlorine and fluorine	0.3

28. Swine-Urine, Fresh.

Water	967.0	Soda	2.1
Organic substance	28.0	Magnesia	0.8
Ash	15.0	Phosphoric acid	0.7
Nitrogen	4.3	Sulphuric acid	0.8
Potash	8.3	Chlorine and fluorine	2.3

29. Human Feces, Fresh.

Water	772.0	Lime	6.2
Organic substance	198.0	Magnesia	3.6
Ash	29.9	Phosphoric acid	10.9
Nitrogen	10.0	Sulphuric acid	0.8
Potash	2.5	Silica and sand	1.9
Soda	1.6	Chlorine and fluorine	0.4

30. Human Urine, Fresh.

Water	963.0	Lime	0.2
Organic substance	24.0	Magnesia	0.2
Ash	13.5	Phosphoric acid	1.7
Nitrogen	6.0	Sulphuric acid	0.4
Potash	2.0	Chlorine and fluorine	5.0
Soda	4.6		

ELEMENTS, SYMBOLS, AND ANALYSES. 271

31. Hen-Manure, Fresh.

Water	560.0	Lime	24.0
Organic substance	255.0	Magnesia	7.4
Ash	185.0	Phosphoric acid	15.4
Nitrogen	16.3	Sulphuric acid	4.5
Potash	8.5	Silica and sand	35.2
Soda	1.0		

32. Goose-Manure, Fresh.

Water	771.0	Lime	8.4
Organic substance	134.0	Magnesia	2.0
Ash	95.0	Phosphoric acid	5.4
Nitrogen	5.5	Sulphuric acid	1.4
Potash	9.5	Silica and Sand	14.0
Soda	1.3		

33. Duck-Manure, Fresh.

Water	566.0	Lime	17.0
Organic substance	262.0	Magnesia	3.5
Ash	172.0	Phosphoric acid	14.0
Nitrogen	10.0	Sulphuric acid	3.5
Potash	6.2	Silica and sand	28.0
Soda	0.5		

34. Dove-Manure, Fresh.

Water	519.0	Lime	16.0
Organic substance	308.0	Magnesia	5.0
Ash	173.0	Phosphoric acid	17.8
Nitrogen	17.6	Sulphuric acid	3.3
Potash	10.0	Silica and sand	20.2
Soda	0.7		

(d) ANALYSES OF VARIOUS MATERIALS WHICH ARE USED FOR FERTILIZERS.

35. Peruvian Guano.

Moisture at 100° C.	12.17	Total nitrogen	5.13
Total phosphoric acid	18.45	Actual ammonia	3.94

Soluble phosphoric acid 1.54 Organic nitrogen . . 0.86
Reverted phosphoric acid 5.92 Nitrogen as nitric acid 0.33
Insoluble phosphoric acid 10.99 Insoluble matter . . 13.64
Potassium oxide . . . 3.46

36. Oak-Leaves.

Moisture at 100° C. . 9.601   Potassium oxide . . . 0.549
Organic matter . . . 83.360   Phosphoric acid . . . 0.058
Mineral matter . . . 6.840   Nitrogen . . . . . *. 0.930
Ferric oxide . . . . 0.027   Soluble silica 0.018
Calcium oxide . . . 0.548   Insoluble silica . . . 4.333
Magnesium oxide . . 0.267

37. Seaweed. (Two samples.)

	I.	II.
Moisture at 100° C.	12.05	14.96
Nitrogen	1.66	1.28
Phosphoric acid	0.44	0.17
Potassium oxide	3.81	0.36
Calcium oxide	2.73	3.86
Magnesium oxide	1.48	1.30
Sodium oxide	11.75	8.40
Chlorine	6.40	5.28
Insoluble matter	7.73	0.78

38. Tobacco-Stems.

Water 13.47
Organic and volatile matters (containing nitrogen 1.93) . 70.85
Ash (containing phosphoric acid .53) 15.68
                                                   ──────
                                                   100.00

39. Dissolved Bone-Black.

This material is a superphosphate prepared by treating refuse bone-black from sugar refineries with oil of vitriol, which renders nearly all the phosphoric acid soluble in water.

Soluble phosphoric acid 14.55
Reverted phosphoric acid 2.39
Insoluble phosphoric acid 0.20

ELEMENTS, SYMBOLS, AND ANALYSES. 273

40. Bone-Black.

Moisture at 100° C.	5.04	Phosphoric acid	16.56
Ash	67.43	Insoluble matter	0.37

41. Bone Charcoal.

Moisture at 100° C.	18.16	Reverted phosphoric acid	5.18
Ash	72.24		
Total phosphoric acid	25.58	Insoluble phosphoric acid	20.02
Soluble phosphoric acid	0.38		
		Insoluble matter	0.69

42. Ground Bones. (Two samples.)

	I.	II.
Moisture at 100° C.	3.97	12.43
Ash	49.35	64.21
Total phosphoric acid	19.49	25.67
Reverted phosphoric acid	3.80	6.20
Insoluble phosphoric acid	15.69	19.34
Nitrogen	4.04	2.68
Insoluble matter	0.78	0.42

43. Dried Blood.

Moisture . . . . . 15.02   Nitrogen 8.24

44. Dry Ground Fish.

Moisture at 100° C.	8.34
Ash	37.76
Total phosphoric acid	8.23
Soluble phosphoric acid	0.10
Reverted phosphoric acid	3.81
Insoluble phosphoric acid	4.32
Nitrogen	6.81
Insoluble matter	0.82

45. Sulphate of Ammonia.

This article, now manufactured on a large scale as a by-product of gas-works, usually contains over 20 per cent of nitrogen,

T

the equivalent of from 94 to 97 per cent of sulphate of ammonia. The rest is chiefly moisture.

Nitrogen . . . . . . 20.02   Equivalent ammonia . . 24.30

46. Sulphate of Potash. (Two samples.)

The double sulphate of potash and magnesia is usually sold as "sulphate of potash."

	I.	II.
Actual potash	27.76	51.28
Equivalent sulphate of potash	51.3	94.80

47. Sulphate of Magnesia.

Moisture at 100° C. . . 29.01   Sulphuric acid 30.35
Magnesium oxide . . . 15.87   Insoluble matter . . . 6.29

48. Nitrate of Soda.

Nitrate of soda is mined in Chile and purified there before shipment. It usually contains about 16 per cent of nitrogen, equivalent to 97 per cent of pure nitrate of soda. It contains, besides, a little salt and some moisture.

Moisture 35   Sulphate of soda . . . 0.21
Salt (sodium chloride) . . .23   Pure nitrate of soda . . 99.21

49. Muriate of Potash. (Two samples.)

Commercial muriate of potash consists of about 80 per cent of muriate of potash (potassium chloride); 15 per cent or more of common salt (sodium chloride), and 4 per cent or more of water.

	I.	II.
Actual potash	50.0	52.82
Equivalent muriate	79.2	83.70

50. German Potash Salts—Average of 11 Analyses.

Moisture at 100° C. . . 13.14   Magnesium oxide. . . 9.25
Potassium oxide . . . 21.63   Sulphuric acid 10.85
Sodium oxide . . . . 13.76   Chlorine 35.63
Calcium oxide . . . . 0.85   Insoluble matter . . . 2.08

ELEMENTS, SYMBOLS, AND ANALYSES. 275

51. *Kainit — Average of 3 Analyses.*

Moisture at 100° C.	9.26	Magnesium oxide	8.97
Potassium oxide	14.04	Sulphuric acid	21.05
Sodium oxide	21.38	Chlorine	32.38
Calcium oxide	1.12	Insoluble matter	0.89

52. *Land-Plaster or Gypsum.*

Hydrated sulphate of lime 74.88
Matters insoluble in acid 1.23
Moisture 1.18
Other matters chiefly carbonate of lime 22.66

53. *Ashes (Wood), Unleached.*

Moisture at 100° C. 15.72
Calcium oxide 28.61
Magnesium oxide 3.00
Ferric oxide 1.03
Potassium oxide 8.72
Phosphoric acid 0.32
Insoluble matter, before calcination 18.49
     " after " 12.12

54. *Ashes (Wood), Leached.*

Moisture at 100° C. 13.72
Calcium oxide 48.07
Magnesium oxide 6.06
Ferric oxide 0.08
Potassium oxide 1.92
Phosphoric acid 1.79
Insoluble matter, before calcination 5.49
     " after " 2.57

55. *Coal Ashes, Bituminous.*

Water	5.0	Soda	0.4
Organic substance	5.0	Magnesia	3.2
Ash	95.0	Phosphoric acid	0.2
Potash	0.4	Sulphuric acid	8.5

56. Coal Ashes, Anthracite.

Water	5.0	Soda	0.1
Organic substance	5.0	Magnesia	3.0
Ash	90.0	Phosphoric acid	0.1
Potash	0.1	Sulphuric acid	5.0

57. Gas-Lime—*Average of* 4 *Analyses.*

Moisture at 100° C.	22.28	Sulphur	20.73
Calcium oxide	42.66	Insoluble matter	6.05

(e) TRADE VALUES FOR 1895 OF FERTILIZING INGREDIENTS IN RAW MATERIALS AND CHEMICALS. ADOPTED BY EXPERIMENT STATIONS OF MASS., N. J., PENN., AND CONN.

Cts. per lb.

Nitrogen in ammoniates 18½
" nitrates 15
Organic nitrogen in dry and fine ground fish, meat and blood 16½
" " cotton-seed meal 12
" " fine bone and tankage 16
" " fine medium bone and tankage . . . 14
" " medium bone and tankage 11
" " coarser bone and tankage 5
" " hair, horn-shavings, and coarse fish-scrap 5
Phosphoric acid, soluble in water 6
" " ammonium citrate 5½
" dry ground fish, fine bone and tankage . . 5½
" fine-medium bone, and tankage 4½
" medium bone and tankage 3
" coarser bone and tankage 2
" fine ground fish, cotton-seed meal, and wood ashes 5
" mixed fertilizers insoluble in ammonium citrate 2
Potash as high-grade sulphate and in forms free from muriate (or chlorides) 5¼
" muriate 4½

CHAPTER XXII.

GLOSSARY.

Acclimation. The spontaneous or natural process of becoming, or the state or condition of being, inured or habituated to a climate at first injurious.

Acclimatization. The act of man in inuring or habituating to a climate at first injurious, or the state or condition of being thus inured or habituated by man.

Adventive. Said of foreign plants which grow spontaneously, but which are not thoroughly established.

Agriculture. The art and science of cultivating land and of raising plants and animals for economic purposes. The term is often restricted to include only the cultivation of grains and forage-plants and the rearing of domestic animals, with the operations and studies incident thereto.

Alburnum. Sap-wood.

Ammonia. A pungent gas, composed of 1 atom of nitrogen to 3 of hydrogen. In the commercial form, it is dissolved in water.

Annual. Living for one year only.

Arm. In grape-culture, a vine-branch more than a year old.

Assimilation. In botany, the production of organic matter from inorganic matter.

Bacterium (pl. *bacteria*). As popularly used, the term is applied to an extensive class of microscopic organisms, usually classed with plants. The term *microbe* is used in the same sense.

Basin. In descriptions of apples and related fruits, the depression at the apex of the fruit. The calyx sits in the basin.

Berry. In botany, and properly, a separate fruit which is pulpy and juicy throughout, as the grape, currant, tomato. The word is commonly employed to denote any soft fruit or fruit-like part which is borne upon a woody or perennial plant. The raspberry and blackberry are collections of little fruits.

Biennial. Persisting two years. As a rule, biennial plants do not blossom until the second year.

Bigeneric half-breed. The product of a cross between varieties of species belonging to different genera.

Bigeneric hybrid. A hybrid between species of different genera; bigener.

Blight. The dying without apparent cause of the tenderer parts of plants, especially of the leaves, flowers, and young fruit; as pear-blight.

Botany. The science of plants.

Bottle-grafting. A modification of whip-grafting, by which a heel of the scion is conducted into a bottle of water to supply temporary nourishment.

Bottom heat. Heat applied underneath plants by artificial means.

Bract. A much-reduced leaf. Bracts are usually present about the inflorescence.

Break. A radical departure from the type. Ordinarily used in the sense of *sport*, but in its larger meaning it refers to the permanent appearance of apparently new or very pronounced characters in a species.

Bud. A bud which is inserted in a plant with the intention that it shall grow.

Budding. The operation and practice of inserting a bud in a plant with the intention that it shall grow.

Bud-variety. A strange variety or form appearing, without obvious cause, upon a plant or in cuttings or layers; a sport. A bud-variety springs from a bud, in distinction to those which spring from a seed.

Bulb. A large, more or less permanent leaf-bud, usually occupying the base of the stem, and emitting roots from its lower portion. Bulbs are of two leading sorts: scaly, when composed of narrow and mostly loose scales, as in the lily; laminated or tunicated, when composed of more continuous and closer-fitting layers, as in the onion.

Bulbel. A small bulb borne about a mother-bulb, as in some bulbous irises and some onions; bulbule.

Bulblet. A small bulb borne entirely above ground, as in the axils of leaves, in the inflorescence, etc.

Bulbo-tuber. A corm.

Bulbule. A bulbel.

Bush. A small woody plant having no central trunk or stem; shrub.

Bush-fruit. Small fruits, as the currant, gooseberry, raspberry, and the like.

Callus. The new and protruding tissue which forms over a wound, as over the end of a cutting.

Calyx. The outer envelope of the flower. The parts, when distinct, are called sepals. In apples, pears, etc., part of the calyx persists on top of the fruit.

Cambium. The layer of new tissue which lies underneath the bark. It is usually thin and more or less mucilaginous in spring and early summer.

Cane. A young growth of hard-wooded plants. Usually applied to ripened or hardened shoots a year or less old.

Cantaloupe. A class of muskmelons characterized by firm and warty or scaly rinds.

Capsule. A dry seed-vessel which splits open at maturity; pod.

Carbon dioxide. A gas composed of 1 atom of carbon to 2 of oxygen. Carbonic acid gas; it is heavier than air.

Carbonic acid. Carbon dioxide.

Carpel. A simple pistil, or one of the divisions of a compound pistil.

Cavity. In descriptions of apples and similar fruits, the depression about the stalk or stem.

Chlorophyl. The green coloring matter of plants.

Cion. See SCION.

Cleft-graft. A sort of grafting in which the scion is cut wedge-shape at the lower extremity, and is then inserted in a cleft in the end of a trunk or branch which has been severed.

Close-fertilization. The action of pollen upon the pistil of the same flower; self-fertilization.

Coldframe. A frame covered with glass, cloth, or paper, without bottom heat, used for starting plants early in spring, for receiving plants transplanted from a hotbed or forcing-house, or for protecting plants during the winter.

Conservatory. A glass house for preserving or growing tender plants. Popularly, the term is applied to houses in which plants are grown for display of flowers.

Corm. A solid bulb-like tuber, as in the gladiolus and crocus; bulbo-tuber.

Corolla. The inner envelope of the flower. The parts, when distinct, are called petals.

Corymb. A flower-cluster which is flat or convex on top, and in which the outer flower blooms first.

Cotyledon. A small leaf borne in the seed; seed-leaf. In many plants the cotyledons rise to the surface when the seed germinates, and increase in size.

Cross. The offspring of any two flowers which have been cross-fertilized.

Cross-breed. A cross between varieties of the same species; half-breed, mongrel, variety-hybrid.

Cross-fertilization. The action of pollen upon the pistil of another flower of the same species. Cross-fertilization is commonly used to denote the mere conveyance of pollen — pollination — but better usage confines the term to the action of pollen upon the pistil.

Cross-pollination. The conveyance of the pollen to the stigma of another flower.

Crossing. The operation or practice of cross-pollination.

Crown-grafting. Grafting at or near the surface of the ground.

Cryptogam. One of the class of flowerless plants. These

plants propagate by spores instead of seeds. Ferns, fungi, mosses, and seaweeds are examples.

Cucurbit. A plant of the family Cucurbitaceæ, as pumpkin, squash, gourd, melon, cucumber, gherkin, wild balsam-apple, etc.

Cuttage. The practice or process of multiplying plants by means of cuttings, or the state or condition of being so propagated.

Cutting. A portion of a plant which is inserted in soil or water with the intention that it shall grow ; slip.

Cyme. A flower-cluster, flat or convex on top, and in which the central flowers open first.

Deciduous. Said of plants whose leaves fall in autumn.

Derivative hybrid. A hybrid between hybrids, or between a hybrid and one of its parents; derivation-hybrid; secondary hybrid.

Dibber. See DIBBLE.

Dibble. A pointed instrument used for making holes in the ground for the planting of seeds and roots ; dibber.

Diœcious. Said of species in which the stamens and pistils are borne on different plants.

Disbudding. The practice or operation of removing buds.

Double-graft. A plant twice grafted for the purpose of overcoming the lack of affinity between stock and scion.

Double-grafting. The practice and process of twice grafting or budding a plant so that the root, the stem or a part of it, and the top, shall each represent a different variety. It is used when a certain variety will not grow upon a given root, but which will grow on some variety that unites with that root ; double-working.

Double-working. See DOUBLE-GRAFTING.

Drupe. A fleshy or soft fruit formed entirely from the ovary, and containing a hard pit ; stone-fruit. The peach and cherry are examples.

Embryo. The rudimentary plant contained in the seed ; seed-germ.

Entomology. The science of insects.

Evergreen. Said of plants which hold their leaves during winter.

Eye. A cutting composed of a single bud. A bud upon a tuber, as a potato eye.

Family. A group of genera and species, as *Cruciferæ*, mustard family; *Gramineæ*, grass family. In botany, *order* is the same.

Fecundation. The action of the pollen upon the pistil; fertilization; impregnation.

Female. Used to designate flowers or plants which bear only pistils.

Fertilization. The action of the pollen upon the pistil; fecundation; impregnation.

Fertilizer. 1. Any substance which promotes plant-growth. 2. Plant-food.

Fertilizing. The act or process of applying fertilizers to plants. The word "fertilization" should be restricted to designate the action of pollen.

Flagging. Wilting of newly set plants or herbaceous cuttings.

Flat. A shallow box used by gardeners in which to sow seeds or handle plants.

Floriculture. The cultivation of flowers.

Florist. One who practices floriculture.

Flower. An organ which contains a stamen or pistil, or both. It is usually provided with some kind of an envelope, as calyx and corolla.

Forcing-house. A structure in which plants are grown or forced out of their season.

Frame. The structure forming the sides and ends of coldframes or hotbeds. A *frame* is usually understood to be the area covered by a single sash, when areas are to be designated.

Fruit. 1. Botanically, a ripened ovary containing the seeds. 2. Popularly, any edible or ornamental organ or collection of organs which are closely associated in their origin with the flower.

Fungicide. A substance employed to destroy fungi.

Fungoid (*adj.*). Fungus-like in general appearance or characteristics. A *fungoid* disease is one which appears to be due to a fungus, but whose character is not understood.

Fungous (*adj.*). Pertaining or due to a fungus or to fungi; as, a *fungous* disease.

Fungus (pl. *fungi*). A flowerless plant, devoid of chlorophyl, drawing its nourishment from living plants or animals, or from decaying matter.

Gardener. One who practices horticulture on a small or on an intensive scale.

Gardening. The art and science of raising kitchen-garden vegetables, fruits, and ornamental plants; horticulture. The term is commonly restricted, however, to the operations of growing kitchen-garden vegetables and flowers.

Genus (pl. *genera*). A group or kind containing a greater or less number of closely related species; as *Rosa*, the rose genus, *Tilia*, the linden genus.

Germination. The act or process by which a seed or spore gives rise to a new and independent plant.

Gourd. An ambiguous term, used in America to designate various small fruits of the pumpkin and squash genus which are grown for ornament and curiosity. In other countries the term is generic for most pumpkins and squashes.

Graft. Scion, which see.

Graftage. The process of grafting, or the condition or state of being grafted.

Grafting. The operation of inserting a bud or scion upon a stock. It is commonly restricted to the operation of inserting scions of dormant wood, or to those operations in which wax or mastic is used to dress the wounds.

Greenhouse. A glass house in which plants are grown. Originally and properly, however, it was applied to houses in which plants were simply preserved green during the winter.

Ha-ha. A sunken fence.

Half-breed. A cross between varieties of the same species; cross-breed, mongrel, variety-hybrid.

Half-hardy (*adj.*). A term applied to plants which need protection during winter, but which can endure some frost.

Half-hybrid. The product of a cross between a species and a variety of another species.

Hand-box. A box of size sufficient to cover a hill of plants, provided with a cover of glass, cloth, or paper, used to force plants in the hill.

Hardiness. Capability to endure a given climate.

Hardy (*adj.*). Able to withstand a given climate.

Heart-wood. The inner and colored wood of trees. The deeper color and greater hardness of heart-wood are due chiefly to the deposition of mineral matter in the cells.

Heeling-in. The process and operation of temporarily covering the roots of plants to preserve them until wanted for permanent planting.

Herb. A plant possessing but a small amount of hard, woody fiber, the stem of which dies at the approach of winter.

Herbarium. A collection of preserved plants. The plants are usually dried and glued on sheets of paper.

Horticulture. The art and science of raising fruits, kitchen-garden vegetables, flowers, and ornamental trees and shrubs.

Horticulturist. One who practices horticulture.

Hotbed. A frame covered with glass, cloth, or paper, provided with bottom heat, and used for forcing plants.

Hothouse. A glass house, artificially warmed, in which plants are grown.

Humus. Vegetable mold. Black or brown earth-like material formed of decayed vegetable and other organic matter.

Hy'brid or **hyb'rid.** The offspring of plants of different species.

Hy'bridism or **hyb'ridism.** The state, quality, or condition of being a hybrid; hybridity.

Hy'bridist. One who practices hybridizing.

Hy'bridity or **hyb'ridity.** Hybridism.

Hy'bridization or **hyb'ridization.** 1. The state or condition of being hybridized; or the process or act of hybridizing.

GLOSSARY. 285

2. The action of the pollen of one species upon the pistil of another species.

Hy'bridizing or **hyb'ridizing.** The operation or practice of crossing species.

Impregnation. The action of the pollen upon the pistil; fertilization; fecundation.

Inarching. The process of grafting contiguous plants or branches while the parts are both attached to their own roots. When the parts unite, one is severed from its own support.

Individual fertilization. Fertilization between flowers upon the same plant.

Inorganic. Pertaining to unorganized substances, as minerals, rocks, chemicals, etc.

Insect. An articulate animal which in the mature state has three distinct divisions and six legs.

Insecticide. A substance employed to destroy insects.

Kitchen-garden. An area devoted to the cultivation of "vegetables," or annual plants which yield edible parts.

Kitchen-garden vegetable. An edible portion of an annual plant. A loose term, commonly shortened to *vegetable*.

Landscape-gardening. The art of embellishing grounds in such manner that they shall have nature-like or landscape effects. It demands a high appreciation of natural scenery, and an ability to represent it in grounds.

Landscape-horticulture. The operations and manual appliances employed in embellishing grounds; the industrial phase of landscape-gardening.

Larva (pl. *larvæ*). The worm-like stage of insects. A larva is commonly called a worm.

Lawn. An area of greensward used for ornamental purposes.

Layer. A shoot of a plant bent down and partly or wholly covered with earth with the intention that it shall take root, when it can be severed from and become independent of the parent plant.

Layerage. The state or condition of being layered, or the operation or practice of layering plants.

Legume. A simple pod composed of two valves or parts, as pea and bean pods.

Leguminous. Of or pertaining to legumes. Used to designate plants of the pea and bean family.

Loam. Friable, mellow, rich soil which contains humus, and does not bake or leach. Clay loam has a basis of clay. Hard clay soil becomes clay loam by careful and thorough tillage and the addition of humus. Sandy loam has a basis of sand, and is formed from sandy soils by the addition of humus.

Maiden (*adj.*). Applied to young plants which have not borne.

Male. Used to designate flowers or plants which bear only stamens.

Manure. 1. Any substance which promotes plant-growth. 2. Plant-food.

Microbe. A term applied to various microscopic organisms usually classed with plants, which play an important rôle in disease, chemical decomposition, and decay.

Mildew. A powdery or mold-like growth attached lightly to the surface of the plant, particularly when it is white or nearly so, as gooseberry-mildew.

Mongrel. A cross between varieties of the same species; half-breed; cross-breed; variety-hybrid.

Monœcious. Said of plants in which the stamens and pistils are borne in different flowers on the same plant.

Mother-bulb. The large bulb about which bulbels are formed.

Mycology. The science of fungi.

Nursery. An establishment for the rearing of plants. In America the word is generally used in connection with woody plants only.

Offscape. The landscape which lies adjacent to one's grounds.

Olericulture. The cultivation of kitchen-garden vegetables; vegetable-gardening.

Open. An unplanted portion of grounds; an open lawn or field.

Order. Family, in botany.

Organic. Pertaining to organized or living bodies or their remains.

Ovary. The lower extremity of the pistil, which, when mature, becomes the fruit. It contains the ovules.

Ovule. A body borne in the ovary, the result of sexual union, which, when mature, becomes the seed.

Panicle. An open and more or less compound flower-cluster.

Papilionaceous. Butterfly-like; said of flowers of the pea and bean family, from their fancied resemblance to butterflies.

Parasite. A plant or animal which lives upon living plants or animals.

Pedicel. The stalk of a particular flower in a cluster. A flower which is borne singly has a peduncle.

Peduncle. A stalk of a flower which is borne singly, or of a cluster of flowers.

Pepo. A berry-like fruit in which the rind is hardened, and which belongs to the gourd family, as the pumpkin, melon, cucumber, etc.

Perfect. Said of flowers which bear both stamens and pistils.

Perennial. Persisting from year to year. The term "perennial" is commonly understood to designate herbaceous plants which live for many years.

Perianth. The leaves of a flower. Usually applied to those flowers in which the calyx and corolla are nearly alike, as the lily.

Pet'al, or **Pe'tal.** One of the separate parts of the corolla; an inner leaf of a flower.

Petiole. The stem of a leaf.

Phenogam. One of the class of flowering plants. These plants propagate by seed.

Pip. A term applied to certain small seeds or seed-like fruits of berries and other fruits.

Pip'ing. A cutting.

Pistil. That portion of the flower which receives the pollen and bears the seeds. It always has two parts, the stigma and the ovary, and these are usually connected by a style. It is the female organ of the plant.

Pistillate. Bearing pistils alone; female.
Plantlet. The little plant just emerged from the seed. It becomes a plant when it is able to assimilate and lead an independent existence.
Pod. A dry seed-vessel which splits open at maturity; capsule.
Pollen. A product of the anthers, which is capable of fertilizing the stigma. It is usually granular and powdery.
Pollination. The conveyance of pollen from the anther to the stigma.
Polygamous. Said of plants or species which bear both perfect and imperfect flowers.
Pome. A fleshy fruit with a papery core surrounded by a greatly thickened calyx, as the apple, quince, etc.
Race. A fixed variety; that is, a variety which reproduces itself more or less uniformly from seeds.
Raceme. A more or less elongated and simple flower-cluster with one-flowered pedicels.
Regermination. Second germination. Seeds which have been checked after germination has begun may resume the process under favorable conditions.
Root. A part of the plant which bears neither leaves nor buds, and which absorbs nourishment for the plant, or serves as a support for it. It may be subterranean or aërial.
Root-cap. The covering upon the end of a growing root. The elongation of the root takes place just behind the root-cap.
Root-grafting. Grafting upon the root.
Root-hair. A very delicate prolongation of a cell of a young root. Root-hairs are active agents in absorbing plant-food.
Rot. The decay of the thicker part of plants, however brought about; the amount of moisture present determines whether it shall be called wet or dry rot.
Runner. A procumbent or creeping herbaceous shoot which takes root at the joints.
Rust. Any plant-disease in which the surface of the plant is apparently converted into a powder or scurf, particularly when of a ferruginous or blackish color, as wheat-rust.
Saddle-graft. A sort of grafting in which the scion is split

GLOSSARY. 289

below and inserted over the end of the stock, which is cut wedge-shape.

Salad. A dish of uncooked herbs, or chopped meat combined with uncooked herbs.

Sap. A term designating loosely the liquid contents of plants.

Saprophyte. A plant which lives upon dead or decaying matter, as a mushroom or toadstool.

Scion, or Cion. A portion of a plant which is mechanically inserted upon the same or another plant with the intention that it shall grow; a graft. As commonly used, a scion, in distinction from a bud, bears two or more buds.

Secondary hybrid. A hybrid between hybrids, or between a hybrid and one of its parents; derivative hybrid; derivation-hybrid.

Seed. The reproductive organ of flowering plants; a ripened ovule. Its essential part is the embryo, or rudimentary plantlet.

Seedage. The process of propagation by seeds, or the state or condition of being propagated by seeds.

Seed-germ. The rudimentary plant contained in the seed; embryo.

Seedling. A plant growing directly from the seed, without the intervention of grafts or cuttings.

Self-fertilization. The action of pollen upon a pistil of the same flower; close-fertilization.

Self-pollination. The transfer of pollen to a pistil of the same flower.

Se'pal, or Sep'al. One of the separate parts of the calyx; an outer leaf of a flower.

Separation. The act or process of multiplying plants by means of naturally detachable asexual organs, or the state or condition of being so multiplied.

Shoot. A soft and growing branch.

Shrub. A small and bushy woody plant, with no central stem or trunk; a bush.

Side-graft. A sort of grafting in which the scion is inserted in a slit or oblique cleft in the side of the stock.

U

Slip. A cutting.

Small-fruit. Low and bush-like fruit-plants, and the fruits they produce, as the currant, gooseberry, blackberry, strawberry, and the like.

Splice-graft. A sort of grafting in which both the scion and stock are cut off obliquely and the cut surfaces applied to each other, the two scions being held secure by bands of string.

Spore. The reproductive body of a flowerless plant, answering to the seed of a flowering plant. It contains no embryo.

Sport. A marked new variety or form, coming from either a seed or a bud without any apparent reason. Commonly and properly restricted to forms originating from buds; a bud-variety.

Spur. A very short and small branch bearing leaves or flowers.

Stalk. In descriptions of apples and similar fruits, the stem or pedicel.

Stamen. That portion of the flower which bears the pollen. It consists of the anther and filament. It is the male organ of the plant.

Staminate. Bearing stamens alone; male.

Stem. That portion of the plant which bears leaves or buds, or both. It may be aërial or subterranean.

Stigma. The upper extremity of the pistil upon which the pollen is received. It is usually more or less papillose and glutinous.

Stipule. A more or less leaf-like and usually small appendage at the base of a petiole. Stipules are borne in pairs, but they are not always present.

Stock. 1. The parentage of a particular strain or variety. 2. A plant or part of a plant upon which a bud or graft is set.

Stolon. A decumbent shoot which roots at or near the tip, as the shoots of black raspberries.

Stove. A very warm glass house, used for growing tropical plants.

GLOSSARY. 291

Strain. A sub-variety, or individuals of a variety, which has been improved and bred under known conditions.
Stub. A portion of a trunk or branch which has been recently grafted. Usually applied to top-grafting.
Style. The more or less slender portion of the pistil connecting the stigma and ovary.
Tongue-graft. Whip-graft.
Top-grafting. Grafting upon the top of a plant.
Tree. A woody plant attaining the height of a man or more, and having a definite central stem or trunk.
Truss. Loosely applied to clusters of flowers or fruits.
Tuber. A prominently thickened root or stem, usually subterranean.
Umbel. A flower-cluster which is flat or flattish on top, and whose pedicels start from a common point, or nearly so.
Variety-hybrid. A cross between varieties of the same species; half-breed; cross-breed; mongrel.
Vegetable. 1. A plant. 2. In horticulture, an edible portion of an annual plant; kitchen-garden vegetable. In the latter sense a loose term.
Vegetable-gardening. The cultivation of kitchen-garden vegetables; olericulture.
Vegetation. 1. Vegetable or plant life. 2. The process or act of vegetating or growing.
Veneer-graft. A sort of grafting in which the scion is applied to the side of the stock, only the bark being removed between them.
Viticulture. Grape-culture.
Weed. A plant which grows where it is not wanted and which becomes troublesome.
Whip-graft. A species of grafting in which the scion is secured to the stock by means of a tongue which is inserted in a cleft in the stock; tongue-graft.
Wilding. A wild or uncultivated plant. Commonly used to designate the wild individuals of a cultivated species.
Wind-shake. An injury to the trunk of a tree, consisting of the more or less complete separation of the concentric

annual layers or of the separation of the bark from the wood. The injury is commonly ascribed to the wind, but it is oftener due to frost and other causes.

Winter-killing. The process or act by which a plant is killed by the climate of winter.

Worm. A term properly applied to a large class of legless articulated animals of which the angleworm, or earthworm, and trichina, are examples. The term is commonly, but improperly, applied to the larvæ of insects.

INDEX.

Abies pectinata, seeds of, 103.
Abraxis ribearia, 27.
Abutilon, classification, 254.
Acacias, classification, 254.
Acanthacara similis, 38.
Acer dascycarpum, seeds of, 103.
Acer platanoides, seeds of, 103.
Acer rubrum, seeds of, 103.
Acer saccharinum, seeds of, 103.
Aconite, classification, 253.
Acorus gramineus, 165.
Acre, number of plants on, 115.
Acre, quantity of seed for, 98.
Acrobasis Vaccinni, 25.
Acrocystis Batatas, 74.
Actinomena Rosæ, 71.
Adiantum cuneatum, 164.
Adiantum gracillimum, 164.
Adonis, classification, 253.
Æsculus, classification, 254.
Æsculus glabra, seeds of, 103.
Agave, classification, 257.
Agriculture, department of, 239.
Agrotis, 27.
Ailanthus glandulosus, seeds of, 103.
Ailanthus, weight of seeds, 103.
Alcohol for preserving, 188.
Alcoholic waxes, 86.
Alder, classification, 257.
Alkali and oil, wash, 9.
Allen, Charles L., book by, 230.
Almond, disease of, 52.
Almond, stocks for, 127.
Almonds, classification, 254.
Aloes and soda, 14.
Aloes, classification, 257.
Aloysia citriodora, 164.
Althæa, classification, 254.
Alyssum, classification, 253.

Amaryllis family, 257.
Ambergris, in perfumery, 190.
American Blight, 20.
American Carnation Soc., 208.
American Chrysanthemum Soc., 208
American Florists, rules, 195.
American Pom. Soc., rules, 193, 201.
American Rose Soc., 208.
Ammonia, sulphate of, 273.
Ammoniacal carbonate of copper, 46.
Ampelideœ, classification, 254.
Ampelophaga Myron, 30.
Amphicerus bicaudatus, 21.
Analyses, 260–276.
Anarsia lineatella, 36, 44.
Angles of roofs, 159.
Angleworm, 17.
Angoumois Grain-Moth, 25.
Anise, classification, 255.
Anthomyia Raphani, 40.
Anthonomus quadrigibbus, 18.
Anthonomus suturalis, 25.
Anthonomus signatus, 44.
Ants, 32.
Aphides, 17.
Aphids, fumigating, 6.
Aphis, 17.
Aphis Forbesii, 44.
Aphis, on house plants, 164.
Aphis Persicæ-niger, 35.
Aphodius granarius, 24.
Aponogetons, 165.
Apothecaries' measure, 131.
Apothecaries' weight, 129.
Apple boxes, 144.
Apple, diseases of, 53.
Apple, how multiplied, 127.
Apple, insects of, 17.
Apple-Maggot, 18.

Apple, stocks for, 127.
Apples, analyses of, 260, 263, 264, 266.
Apples, classification, 254.
Apples, contents of bins, 150.
Apples, measures, 140, 142, 143.
Apples, pollination of, 122.
Apples, storing, 168.
Apples, to measure in bins, 150.
Apples, weights of, 149.
Apples, wholesale quantities, 148.
Apples, yield of, 124.
Apricot boxes, 146.
Apricot, disease of, 54.
Apricot, insects of, 21.
Apricot, stocks for, 128.
Apricots, analysis of, 260.
Apricots, classification, 254.
Aquatic plants, 164, 165.
Arkansas, weight in, 140.
Arsenate of lead, 2.
Arsenate of soda, 2.
Arsenate of soda, on walks, 84.
Arsenic, 1.
Arsenic acid, for herbaria, 181.
Arsenite of soda on walks, 84.
Arsenites, 2.
Arsenites and glue, wash, 6.
Arsenites and soap, 13.
Artichoke, analysis of, 264.
Artichoke, classification, 255.
Artichoke, yield of, 125.
Artificial flowers, 186.
Artificial stone, to make, 94.
Artipus Floridanus, 34.
Artotrogus DeBaryanus, 58.
Asafœtida for rabbits, 80.
Ascochyta Ellisii, 60.
Ascomyces deformans, 64.
Ash, classification, 255.
Ash, seeds of, 103, 104.
Ashes, analyses of, 275, 276.
Asparagus, analyses of, 263, 264.
Asparagus, classification, 257.
Asparagus, insects of, 21.
Asparagus medeoloides, 166.
Aspidiotus perniciosus, 42.
Aster, disease of, 54.
Aster-Worm, 22.
Attar of roses, 190.
Audoynaud process, 48.
Auriculas, classification, 255.

Austrian money, 138.
Avoirdupois pound, in various states, 143.
Avoirdupois weight, 129.
Awards, rules for, 201.
Azaleas, classification, 255.
Azolla Caroliniana, 165.

Babiana, classification, 257.
Bacillus Cloacæ, 57.
Baedeker, money table, 139.
Bag-Worm, 22.
Bailey, L. H., books by, 229, 234.
Bailey, tomato score, 209.
Bait, 4.
Balaninus, 24.
Balm of Gilead, disease of, 54.
Balsam of fir, 7.
Bananas, wholesale quantities, 148.
Bandage, waxed, 88.
Barberry, how multiplied, 127.
Barberry, seeds of, 103.
Barker, Michael, book by, 230.
Bark-Lice, 17.
Bark-Louse, Apple, 18.
Barley, analysis of, 263.
Barnard, Charles, book by, 229.
Barnyard manure, analyses, 268.
Barometer indications, 220.
Barrels, mending, 91.
Barry, P., book by, 234.
Baryta, carbonate of, for mice, 78.
Basket plants, 164.
Basket-Worm, 22.
Basswood family, 254.
Basswood, seeds of, 103.
Battles' scale of points, 214.
Bean-Bug, 22.
Bean, disease of, 54.
Beans, analyses of, 264.
Beans, bushel of, 140.
Beans, classification, 254.
Beans, Green or Snap, yield of, 125.
Beans, Lima, yield of, 125.
Bean-Weevil, 22.
Bearing age of plants, 123.
Beeches, classification, 257.
Beefsteak geranium, 164.
Bees, number in a pound, 150.
Beeswax grafting-wax, 86.
Beet, diseases of, 54.

INDEX.

Beets, analyses of, 263, 264, 267.
Beets, weight of, 141.
Beets, yield of, 125.
Begonias, 164, 165.
Belladonna, classification, 256.
Bellis perennis, 166.
Bembecia marginata, 40.
Benzine, 4.
Berberis Aquifolium, 246.
Berberis vulgaris, seeds of, 103.
Berries, weight of, 141.
Berries, wholesale quantities, 149.
Betula alba, seeds of, 104.
Bichloride of mercury, 48.
Biggle, Jacob, book by, 234.
Bins, contents of, 150.
Birch-bark, 77.
Birch, seeds of, 104.
Birches, classification, 257.
Bird-poisons, 80.
Bisulphide of carbon, 4.
Bisulphide of carbon and kerosene, 5.
Blackberries, analysis of, 263.
Blackberries, classification, 254.
Blackberries, weight of, 141, 150.
Blackberry, diseases of, 55.
Blackberry, how multiplied, 127.
Blackberry, insects of, 22.
Blackberry, yield of, 125.
Black-Knot, 68.
Black, J. J., book by, 234.
Black Locust, seeds of, 104.
Black-Rot of grapes, 59.
Bleeding, to prevent, 89.
Blepharida Rhois, 44.
Blight, of pear, 66.
Blister-Beetle, 22.
Blood, analysis, 273.
Blood, for rabbits, 79.
Blood, in cement, 91.
Blueberries, analysis of, 263.
Blue-grass, 83.
Blue-grass seed, bushel of, 140.
Blue vitriol, 49.
Bog plants, 165.
Boiler cements, 90.
Boiler estimates, 156.
Boilers, mending, 90, 91.
Boilers, to protect, 160.
Bone-black, analyses, 272, 273.
Bone charcoal, analysis, 273.

Bones, analyses of, 273.
Books, list of, 229.
Borax, in glue, 96.
Bordeaux mixture, 47.
Borders, concrete for, 92, 93.
Borer, Currant, 26.
Borer, Flat-headed, 19.
Borer, Pin-hole, 36.
Borer, Round-headed, 20.
Boric acid preservative, 187.
Boston, dates for sowing at, 109.
Bostrichus bicaudatus, 21.
Botanical Club rules, 200.
Botrytis vulgaris, 62.
Bottles, preparing old, 189.
Bottom onion sets, weight of, 141.
Box elder, seeds of, 103.
Boxes for fruits, 142–147.
Bran, in bait, 4.
Bread-fruit, classification, 256.
Brickwork, 92.
Brill, Francis, books by, 232.
Bruchus obtectus, 22.
Bruchus Pisi, 35.
Brunswick green, in cement, 92.
Bucculatrix, 17.
Buckwheat, analysis of, 263.
Buckwheat, bushel of, 140.
Budding, 126.
Bud-Moth, 18.
Buhach, 10.
Bulletins, 238.
Bunch, 148.
Bundle, 148.
Burning insects, 5.
Burpee, W. Atlee, books by, 232.
Bush & Son & Meissner, book by, 234
Bushel, standards, 140.
Buttercup, classification, 253.
Butternut, classification, 256.
Butternut, seeds of, 103.
Buttonwood, disease of, 55.

Cabbage, analyses of, 264.
Cabbage, classification, 253.
Cabbage, Club-root, 55.
Cabbage, insects of, 22.
Cabbage, keeping, 168.
Cæoma luminatum, 71.
California fruit packages, 144–147.
California, rabbit poisons, 79, 80.

INDEX.

California scores, 209.
California, weights in, 140.
Caltha palustris, 165.
Campbell, Ella Grant, book by, 230.
Camphor for mice, 78.
Canada thistle, 83.
Canadian score cards, 209.
Cane-Borer, 40.
Canker-Worm, 19.
Capacities of pipes and tanks, 151, 152.
Caraway, classification, 255.
Carbolic acid, 48.
Carbolic acid and soap mixtures, 5.
Carbolic acid and water, 5.
Carbolic acid emulsion, 5.
Carbolic acid on walks, 85.
Carbolized plaster, 5.
Carbon, bisulphide of, 4.
Carbonate of baryta for mice, 78.
Carbonate of copper, ammoniacal, 46.
Carbonate of copper, cost, 46.
Carbonate of copper, precipitated, 48.
Cardoon, classification, 255.
Carex, 85.
Carman, E. S., book by, 232.
Carnation, classification, 253.
Carnation, diseases of, 55.
Carnation, Twitter, 23.
Carpenter, R. C., on heating, 154.
Carpocapsa pomonella, 19.
Carrot, classification, 255.
Carrot, insect of, 23.
Carrots, analyses of, 263, 264, 267.
Carrots, weight of, 141.
Carrots, yield of, 125.
Carya alba, seeds of, 103.
Caryophyllaceæ, 253.
Castalia, classification, 253.
Castanea vesca, var., seeds of, 103.
Catalpa speciosa, seeds of, 103.
Catchflies, classification, 253.
Cattle-feces, analyses, 268.
Cattle-urine, analyses, 269.
Cauliflower, analysis of, 264.
Cauliflower, classification, 253.
Cauliflower, insects of, 23.
Cedar apples, 53.
Cedar, seeds of, 103.
Celery, analysis of, 264.
Celery, classification, 255.
Celery, disease of, 56.

Celery, insects of, 23.
Celery, keeping, 169.
Celsius thermometer, 153.
Cements, 90.
Cement wash, 5.
Centigrade thermometer, 153.
Ceratocystis fimbriata, 73.
Cercospora angulata, 58.
Cercospora Apii, 56.
Cercospora beticola, 54.
Cercospora circumcissa, 52.
Cercospora rosæcola, 71.
Cercospora Violæ, 76.
Cereal grains, classification, 257.
Chain measure, 131.
Chalk, in cement, 90.
Chautauqua grape figures, 178.
Cheese, in cement, 91.
Cherries, analyses of, 260, 264.
Cherries, classification, 254.
Cherries, weight of, 141.
Cherry boxes, 145, 146.
Cherry, diseases of, 56.
Cherry, insects of, 23.
Cherry, seeds of, 103.
Cherry, stocks for, 128.
Chestnuts, classification, 257.
Chestnut, seeds of, 103.
Chestnut-Weevil, 24.
Chicory, classification, 255.
Chinese sacred lily, 164.
Chiswick flower-pots, 160.
Chorlton, William, book by, 234.
Christmas rose, classification, 253.
Chrysanthemum, classification, 255
Chrysanthemum, insects of, 24.
Chrysanthemum, leaf-spot, 57.
Chrysanthemum, scales of, 214.
Chrysanthemum, species, 166.
Chrysobothris femorata, 19.
Cider, 150.
Citrous fruits, scale of, 209.
Citrullus, classification, 255.
Citrus trifoliata, 128.
Cladosporium carpophilum, 64.
Cladosporium fulvum, 74.
Cladosporium on orange, 63.
Classification of horticulture, 258.
Clay, grafting, 87.
Clay, in cement, 90, 91.
Clematis, classification, 253.

INDEX. 297

Click-Beetles, 45.
Clisiocampa, 21.
Cloth, for sash, 160.
Cloth, paints for, 95.
Cloth, waxed, 88.
Clover, classification, 254.
Club-root, 55.
Coal ashes, analyses of, 275, 276.
Coal-tar, for wounds, 88.
Coal-tar fumes, 5.
Coal-tar on walks, 85.
Cobæa, classification, 256.
Coccotorus scutellaris, 28.
Cocoanut, classification, 257.
Cocoanuts, how shipped, 150.
Cocos Weddelliana, 164.
Codlin-Moth, 19.
Coleosporium Sonchi-arvensis, 54.
Coleus, 164.
Coleus, classification, 256.
Collecting specimens, 180.
Colletotrichum Lindemuthianum, 54.
Colletotrichum Spinaceæ, 72.
Collingwood, H. W., book by, 234.
Collodion for wounds, 89.
Colorado, weights in, 140.
Columbine, classification, 253.
Commercial weight, 129.
Compositæ, 255.
Compositions of various substances, 260.
Computation tables, 129.
Concrete, 92.
Coniferæ, 257.
Connecticut, weights in, 140, 141.
Conotrachelus nenuphar, 20, 38.
Convolvulaceæ, 256.
Cook's emulsion, 7.
Copper, ammoniacal carbonate of, 46.
Copper carbonate, cost of, 46.
Copper, cement for, 91.
Copper, precipitated carbonate, 48.
Copper, sulphate of, 49.
Copper sulphate, cost of, 46.
Copperas, 5.
Corn, analyses of, 263, 264, 266.
Corn, bushel of, 140.
Corn-cockle, classification, 253.
Corn, contents of bins, 150.
Corn, diseases of, 57.
Corn, insects of, 24.

Corn, sweet, weight, 150.
Corn, to measure in bins, 150.
Corn, yield of, 125.
Corrosive sublimate, 48.
Corrosive sublimate, for herbaria, 181.
Corrosive sublimate preservative, 187.
Corrosive sublimate wash, 6.
Cotton, classification, 254.
Cottonwood, disease of, 57.
Cottonwood Leaf-Beetle, 39.
Covent Garden measures, 147.
Cowslip, classification, 253.
Crambus, 24.
Cranberries, analyses, 263, 266.
Cranberries, classification, 255.
Cranberries, weight of, 141.
Cranberry box in New Jersey, 142.
Cranberry culture, 258.
Cranberry, diseases of, 57.
Cranberry, how multiplied, 127.
Cranberry, insects of, 25.
Cranberry, yield of, 125.
Craponius inæqualis, 29.
Cresses, classification, 253.
Cricket, 40.
Crinum, classification, 257.
Crioceris Asparagi, 21.
Crocus, classification, 257.
Crosses, naming, 196, 198.
Crowfoot family, 252.
Crown-Gall, 41.
Crows, 81.
Crozier, A. A., book by, 232.
Crozier, William, book by, 229.
Cruciferæ, 253.
Crystallized fruit, 170.
Cubic measure, 132.
Cucumber, analysis of, 264.
Cucumber, diseases of, 58.
Cucumber, insects of, 25.
Cucumber, yield of, 125.
Cucumbers, classification, 254.
Cucumis flexuosus, 101, 105.
Cucurbita moschata, 241.
Cucurbitaceæ, 254.
Cultivation, periods of, 249.
Cummins, D., book by, 232.
Cupric steatite, 49.
Cupuliferæ, 257.
Curculio, Apple, 18.
Curculio, Grape, 29.

298   INDEX.

Curculio, Plum, 20, 38.
Curl of peach leaves, 64.
Currant, diseases of, 58.
Currant, how multiplied, 127.
Currant, insects of, 26.
Currant, yield of, 125.
Currants, analyses of, 260, 263.
Currants, weight of, 141.
Customary weights, 140, 143.
Customs rates, 219.
Cut flowers, 166.
Cutting bottles, 189.
Cuttings, 126.
Cut-Worm, 27.
Cut-Worm, climbing, 27.
Cut-Worms, bait for, 4.
Cyanide bottle, 188.
Cylindrosporium Padi, 67.
Cyperus alternifolius, 164, 165.
Cyperus Papyrus, 165.
Cystopus IpomϾ-panduranæ, 74.

Dactylopius adonidum, 33.
Dahlia, insects of, 27.
Daisy, ox-eye, 83.
Dakotas, weight in, 141.
Dakruma convolutella, 29.
Dalmatian insect powder, 10.
Damping-off, 58.
Date, classification, 257.
Dates for seed-sowing, 108.
Dates of various fruits, 178.
Datura Stramonium, 185.
Day, J. W., books by, 232.
Definitions, 277.
Delaware, weights in, 140.
Delphinium, classification, 253.
Department of agriculture, 239.
Depressaria heracliana, 35.
Derivation of names, 247.
Destroying affected parts, 48.
Dewberry, how multiplied, 127.
Dew-point, 222.
Diabrotica, 26.
Dianthus, classification, 253.
Dill, classification, 255.
Diplosis pyrivora, 37.
Directory of Experiment Stations, 238.
Distances for planting, 112, 113.
Docks, 83.
Dodders, classification, 256.

Dolichos sesquipedalis, 100, 104.
Doryphora decemlineata, 39.
Dove-manure, analysis, 271.
Downing, A. J., book by, 234.
Downing, Charles, book by, 234.
Dried flowers, 181.
Dried fruit, 149.
Dried fruit boxes, 145.
Dried fruits, packages for, 145.
Dried peaches, weight of, 141.
Dried plums, weight of, 141.
Dropsy, 63.
Drying plants, 180.
Dry measure, 130.
Duck-manure, analysis, 271.
Dutch money, 138.
Dutch, names in, 243.
Dwarf Juneberry, how multiplied, 127

Earthenware cement, 91.
Earthworm, 17.
Eau céleste, 48.
Eau Grison, 49.
Egg-plant, classification, 256.
Egg-plant, insect of, 28.
Egg-plant, yield of, 125.
Eichhornia, 164, 165.
Eisen, Gustav, book by, 234.
Ekimis, 150.
Elaphidion, 21.
Eleme, 150.
Elements, 259.
Elliott, F. R., book by, 230.
Ellwanger, attar of roses, 190.
Ellwanger, H. B., book by, 230.
Elm, classification, 256.
Elm, insects of, 28.
Elm, seeds of, 103, 104.
Emblematic flowers, 246.
Emphytus maculatus, 44.
Empoa albopicta, 27.
Emulsion, kerosene, 7, 8.
Endive, classification, 255.
Endive, insect of, 28.
Engle, leaf-prints, 185.
English measures, 147.
English money, 137.
English sparrows, 81.
Entomosporium maculatum, 66, 70.
Entyloma Ellisii, 72.
Epiphyllum truncatum, 164.

INDEX. 299

Ericaceæ, 255.
Erysiphe Cichoracearum, 58, 75.
Erysiphe Martii, 64.
Erythroneura vitis, 31.
Esteve process, 50.
Eucharis, classification, 257.
Eudemis botrana, 29.
Eudioptis hyalinata, 33.
Eudioptis nitidalis, 25.
Eufitchia ribearia, 27.
Evaporated fruits, 149.
Excrements, analyses of, 268.
Exhibition, rules of, 201.
Exhibition, specimens for, 187.
Exoascus deformans, 64.
Exoascus Pruni, 68.
Experiment Station literature, 238.
Experiment Stations, directory, 238.

Fahrenheit thermometer, 153.
Fairchild, on pollination, 122.
Falconer, William, book by, 232.
Fall Web-Worm, 19.
Farmer, L. J., book by, 234.
Feces, analysis, 268-271.
Fences, wash for, 94.
Ferns, in houses, 165.
Ferns, statistics of, 258.
Ferry, D. M. & Co., model garden, 119.
Fertilization of fruits, 121.
Fertilizers, analyses of, 268, 271.
Fertilizers, values of, 276.
Fertilizing ingredients, values of, 276.
Ficus elastica, 164.
Fidia viticida, 30.
Fig boxes, 145.
Fig, classification, 256.
Figs, grades of, 150.
Figs, how multiplied, 127.
Figs, keeping, 170.
Filberts, classification, 257.
Filices, 258.
Fir, seeds of, 103.
Fire-proof cement, 91.
Fire-proof paint, 95.
Fire-Worm, 25.
Fish, analysis of, 273.
Fitz, James, books by, 232, 234.
Flag weather signs, 225.
Flat-headed Borer, 19.
Flea-Beetle, 18.

Flies, 11.
Floors, cements for, 92, 93.
Floral arrangements, 214.
Floriculture, classification, 258.
Florida fruit packages, 143.
Florists' plants, 166.
Flower gum, 97.
Flower-pots, sizes, 159.
Flower-pots, to clean, 161.
Flower scores, 214.
Flowers, artificial, 186.
Flowers, books on, 230.
Flowers, emblematic, 246.
Flowers, registration of, 208.
Flowers, to keep fresh, 186.
Fluid measure, 131.
Forcing, plants for, 165, 166, 167.
Forcing, temperatures for, 167.
Forest tree seeds, 103.
Formalin, 188.
Formica, 32.
Formic acid preservative, 188.
Forsythias, classification, 255.
Four-striped Plant-Bug, 28.
Fowler, A. B., book by, 229.
Fragaria Indica, 164.
Fraxinus Americana, seeds of, 103.
Fraxinus, classification, 255.
Fraxinus sambucifolia, seeds of, 103.
Fraxinus viridis, seeds of, 104.
Freesia refracta, 164.
French money, 188.
French, names in, 242.
French waxes, 87.
Fresenius, analyses by, 260.
Frosts, to predict, 222.
Fruit, measures, 140-147.
Fruit packages, 143.
Fruits, compositions of, 260.
Fruits, distances for planting, 112.
Fruits, keeping, 168.
Fruits, propagation of, 127.
Fruits, to preserve, 187.
Fuchsias, 164, 165.
Fuller, A. S., books by, 229, 234, 235.
Fulton, Alexander, book by, 235.
Fumigation, 6.
Fungicides, 46.
Fusarium niveum, 76.
Fusicladium dendriticum, 53.
Fusicladium pyrinum, 67.

INDEX.

Galanthus, classification, 257.
Galleruca xanthomelæna, 28.
Gallons, in tanks and pipes, 151, 152.
Galls, 41.
Garden borders, cement for, 93.
Gardeners, rules for, 193.
Gary, Thomas A., book by, 235.
Gas, for insects, 6.
Gas-lime, analyses of, 276.
Gelechia cerealiella, 25.
Georgia, dates for sowing in, 111.
Georgia fruit packages, 144.
Georgia, weights in, 140.
Geraniums, 164, 165.
German ivy, 164.
German money, 138.
German, names in, 243.
German potash salts, 274.
Germination of seeds, 99.
Gilia, classification, 256.
Gingko, classification, 257.
Gipsy-Moth, 29.
Girdling by mice, 77.
Gironde, copper mixture of, 47.
Glacé fruit, 170.
Gladiolus, classification, 257.
Glass, cement for, 91.
Glass, cooling of, by wind, 158.
Glass, light reflected from, 158.
Glazing, 161.
Gleditschia triacanthos, seeds of, 103.
Glœosporium fructigenum, 53, 62.
Glœosporium necator, 70.
Glœosporium nervisequum, 67.
Glœosporium Ribis, 58.
Glossary, 277.
Glue and arsenites wash, 6.
Glues, 96.
Goessmann, analyses by, 260, 262, 263, 265.
Goff, emulsion, 8.
Gooseberries, analyses of, 260, 264.
Gooseberries, keeping, 171.
Gooseberries, weight of, 141.
Gooseberry, how multiplied, 127.
Gooseberry, insects of, 29.
Gooseberry, mildew, 59.
Gooseberry, yield of, 125.
Goose-manure, analysis, 271.
Gopher remedies, 80.
Gossypium, classification, 254.

Gourds, classification, 255.
Grades of fruit, 143.
Grades of fruits, etc., 150.
Grading fruit, 176.
Grafting, 126, 127.
Grafting waxes, 86.
Grains, cereal, 257.
Gramineæ, 257.
Grape boxes, 145.
Grape, diseases of, 59.
Grape, how multiplied, 127.
Grape, insects of, 29.
Grape, yield of, 125.
Grapes, analyses of, 260, 263, 264.
Grapes, classification, 254.
Grapes, harvesting, etc., 178.
Grapes, keeping, 171.
Grapes, pollination of, 122.
Grapes, weight of, 141, 150.
Grapes, wholesale quantities, 149.
Graptodera chalybea, 30.
Grass family, 257.
Grass seed, bushel of, 140.
Grass seed, for lawns, 82, 83.
Grasses, as weeds, 83.
Grasshoppers, 31.
Grasshoppers, bait for, 4.
Grate surface, 154.
Gray, Asa, book by, 229.
Gray, Dr., herbarium poison, 181.
Green, S. B., book by, 235.
Green, W. J., dried berries, 150.
Green-Fly, 17, 32.
Greenhouse heating, 154.
Greenhouse heating, book on, 229.
Greenhouse work, etc., 154.
Gregory, J. J. H., books by, 233.
Greiner, T., books by, 233.
Grison liquid, 49.
Ground-Squirrel remedies, 80.
Grout, 92.
Gryllotalpa borealis, 39.
Guano, analysis, 271.
Guernsey lily, classification, 257.
Gum-ammoniac, 91.
Gum-galbanum, 91.
Gum-mastic, 91.
Gum or glue, 97.
Gurney, C. W., book by, 235.
Gymnosporangium, 53.
Gypsum, analysis of, 275.

Hackberry, classification, 256.
Hair, for plastering, 92.
Half-sieve, 147.
Halliday, Robert J., books by, 230.
Haltica rufipes, 36.
Haltica striolata, 28.
Hand, 148.
Hanging plants, 164.
Harcourt, Helen, book by, 235.
Hardy catalpa, seeds of, 103.
Hardy vegetables, 112.
Harlequin Cabbage-Bug, 23.
Harris, Joseph, book by, 233.
Hay, estimate of stacks, 151.
Hazels, classification, 257.
Healing-paint, 88.
Heath family, 255.
Heating greenhouses, 154.
Heinrich, Julius J., book by, 230.
Helianthus tuberosus, 241.
Heliothis armiger, 45.
Hellebore, classification, 257.
Hellebore, white, 16.
Heliotropha atra, 24.
Hemp, classification, 256.
Henderson, dates for sowing, 110.
Henderson, Peter, books by, 229, 230, 233.
Hen-manure, analysis, 271.
Herbarium, poisons for, 181.
Herbarium specimens, 180.
Heterodera radicicola, 41.
Heterosporium echinulatum, 56.
Hibiscus, classification, 254.
Hickories, classification, 256.
Hickory (Shellbark), seeds of, 103.
Hilgard's wash, 14, 50.
Hills, William H., book by, 235.
Hinges, to preserve, 96.
Hippeastrum, classification, 257.
Histories and names, 247, 249.
Hoffmann, on phenology, 227.
Hollyhock-Bug, 32.
Hollyhock, classification, 254.
Hollyhock disease, 62.
Honesty, classification, 253.
Honey-locust, seeds of, 103.
Hop, classification, 256.
Hornbeam, classification, 257.
Horse-chestnuts, classification, 254.
Horse-chestnut, seeds of, 103.

Horse-feces, analysis, 269.
Horseradish, analysis of, 264.
Horseradish, classification, 253.
Horseradish, yield of, 125.
Horse-urine, analysis, 269.
Horticulture, classification of, 258.
Hoskin's wax, 88.
Hotbed sash, 160.
Hot iron for bleeding vines, 89.
Hot water for insects, 7.
Household measures, 138.
House-plants, insects, 32.
Hubbard-Riley emulsion, 7.
Huckleberries, classification, 255.
Human feces, analysis, 270.
Human urine, analysis, 270.
Hunt, M. A., book by, 231.
Husk tomato, classification, 256.
Husmann, books by, 235.
Hutchins, Rev. W. T., book by, 231.
Hyacinths, 164.
Hyacinths, classification, 257.
Hybrids, naming, 196, 198.
Hydrocleys Commersonii, 165.
Hydrocyanic gas, 6.
Hyphantria cunea, 19.

Illinois, weights in, 140.
Impost rules, 215.
Inarching, 126.
Indiana, weights in, 140, 141.
Indian corn, classification, 257.
Ink for labels, 192.
Insecticides, 1.
Insects, 17–45.
Insects, collecting, 188.
Iowa, weights in, 140, 141.
Ipomœa pandurata, 74.
Iridaceæ, 257.
Iris, classification, 257.
Iris family, 257.
Iron, cement for, 90.
Iron-filings, in cement, 90, 91.
Iron, hot, for bleeding vines, 89.
Iron, sulphate of, 5, 50.
Ironwood, classification, 257.
Isosoma vitis, 29.
Italian money, 138.
Italian, names in, 243.
Ivory-black, in cement, 92.
Ixia, classification, 257.

Jasmine, classification, 255.
Jewelers' weight, 129.
Johnson, Rev. E. A., book by, 231.
Johnson, S. W., analyses by, 260.
Journals, list of, 236.
Judging fruits and flowers, 208.
Juglandaceæ, 256.
Juglans cinerea, seeds of, 103.
Juglans nigra, seeds of, 103.
Juncus effusus, variegated, 166.
Juneberries, classification, 254.
June-grass, 83.
Juniperus Virginiana, seeds of, 103.
Junk, 148.

Kainit, analysis of, 275.
Kainit for insects, 10.
Kansas, weights in, 140, 141.
Katydid, 34, 38.
Kedzie, analyses by, 262.
Kedzie, on frosts, 222.
Keeping fruits, 168.
Keeping-power of seeds, 104.
Kemp, Edward, book by, 231.
Kentucky, weights in, 140, 141.
Kerosene and bisulphide carbon, 5.
Kerosene and condensed milk emulsion, 8.
Kerosene and milk emulsion, 8.
Kerosene and water emulsion, 8.
Kerosene emulsion, 7.
Kerosene for insects, 7.
Kerosene to preserve fruits, 188.
Kettles, mending, 91.
Kitchen garden, model, 119.
Knitting cotton for grafting, 88.
Kohlrabi, classification, 253.
Kohlrabi, yield of, 125.

Labels, 191.
Labels, gum for, 97.
Labiatæ, 256.
Lachnosterna fusca, 32.
Lacy, T. Jay, book by, 235.
Lady-slippers, classification, 257.
Læstadia Bidwellii, 59.
Lamborn, L. L., book by, 231.
Lampblack, in cement, 92.
Land plaster, analysis, 275.
Landreth, Burnet, book by, 233.
Landscape gardening, books on, 229.

Landscape horticulture, 258.
Lansing, dates for sowing at, 108.
Larkspur, classification, 253.
Laurels, classification, 255.
Lavender bag, 190.
Lawns, ants in, 32.
Lawns, to make, 82, 83.
Layering, 126.
Lead, arsenate of, 2.
Lead, red, for cement, 90.
Leaf-Crumpler, 32.
Leaf-Curl, 64.
Leaf-Hopper 27.
Leaf-Prints, 185.
Leather, paints for, 95.
Lecanium, 39.
Lefort's wax, 86.
Legal weights, 140.
Leguminosæ, 254.
Lelong, B. M., book by, 235.
Lemon scores, 212.
Lemons, wholesale quantities, 149.
Lettuce, analyses of, 264.
Lettuce, classification, 255.
Lettuce, diseases of, 62.
Lettuce, insects of, 32.
Leuchars, on cooling glass, 158.
Leucoium, classification, 257.
Lice, 32.
Lichen on trees, 62, 85.
Light reflected from glass, 158.
Ligustrum, classification, 256.
Lilacs, classification, 255.
Lilium Harrisii, 166.
Lily family, 257.
Lily-of-the-valley, 85, 166, 167.
Lima bean, disease of, 54.
Lime and soap, 13.
Lime, in cement, 91.
Lime, on walks, 84.
Lime spray, 8.
Limnanthemum, 165.
Limnocharis Humboldtii, 165.
Lina scripta, 39.
Lindens, classification, 254.
Linear measure, 131.
Line measure, 131.
Linseed oil, in cement, 90.
Linseed oil, in washes, 94.
Linseed oil, in wax, 86.
Liquid manure, 163.

INDEX.

Liquid measure, 130.
Liquid putty, 161.
Literature, 229.
Litharge, in cement, 91.
Live-forever, 83.
Liver of sulphur, 50.
Livingston, A. W., book by, 233.
Lixus concavus, 41.
Locusts, classification, 254.
Lodeman, E. G., book by, 230.
London purple, 2.
Long, E. A., books by, 231.
Longevity of fruit-plants, 124.
Longevity of seeds, 104.
Loudon's rules, 193.
Louisiana, weights in, 140.
Love-in-a-mist, classification, 253.
Lunaria, classification, 253.
Lychnis, classification, 253.
Lycopersicum, classification, 256.
Lye and sulphur wash, 9.
Lye and whale-oil soap, 9.
Lye wash, 9.
Lysimachia nummularia, 85.
Lytta, 22.

Maceration, skeletonizing by, 185.
Maclura aurantiaca, seeds of, 103.
McMillan, William, book by, 231.
McNeil, J. W., book by, 235.
Macrodactylus subspinosus, 42.
Macrosila quinquemaculata, 45.
Macrosporium Solani, 69.
Macrosporium Tomato, 75.
Maggot, apple, 18.
Maggot, cabbage, 23.
Magnesia, sulphate of, 274.
Magnolia family, 253.
Mahernia odorata, 164.
Mail rates, 215.
Maine, weights in, 140, 141.
Maize, diseases of, 57.
Mallow family, 254.
Malva, classification, 254.
Malvaceæ, 254.
Mangels, analysis of, 263.
Mangels, weight of, 141.
Manure, liquid, 163.
Manures, analysis of, 263.
Manville, A. H., book by, 235.
Maple disease, 62.

Maple family, 254.
Maple, seeds of, 103.
Margaronia quadristigmalis, 39.
Marguerite, 166.
Market dates, 178.
Marsh-marigold, classification, 253.
Marvin, Arthur Tappan, book by, 235
Maryland, weights in, 140.
Mason-work, estimates, 92.
Massachusetts Hort. Soc. rules, 202.
Massachusetts, weights in, 140, 141.
Mastics, 86.
Mathews' scale of points, 214.
Mathews, F. Schuyler, book by, 231.
Maturities of various crops, 123.
May-Beetle, 32.
May-Bug, 32.
Maynard, lettuce mildew, 78.
Maynard, wash, 78.
Mealy Bug, 33, 164.
Measures, legal, 140.
Measures, miscellaneous, 132.
Measures, tables of, 130.
Medlar, stocks for, 128.
Meech, W. W., books by, 235.
Melampsora populina, 68.
Melittia Ceto, 43.
Melon boxes, 145.
Melon disease, 63.
Melon, insects of, 33.
Melons, classification, 255.
Melons, wholesale quantities, 149.
Mercuric bichloride, 48.
Metals, to prevent rusting, 96.
Methylated spirit, in cement, 91.
Metric tables, 134.
Mice, to protect from, 77, 78.
Michigan Hort. Soc. rules, 204.
Michigan, weights in, 140, 141.
Microcentrum retinervis, 34.
Micrococcus amylovorus, 66.
Middlings, in bait, 4.
Mineral pitch, 93.
Minnesota, weights in, 140.
Mint family, 256.
Mints, classification, 256.
Missouri, weights in, 140, 141.
Mite, 33, 34.
Mitzky, C., & Co., book by, 235.
Model kitchen garden, 119.
Mole-Cricket, 39.

Money tables, 137.
Moneywort, 85.
Monilia fructigena, 56, 64.
Monilochætes infuscans, 73.
Montana, weights in, 140, 141.
Montbretia, classification, 257.
Moore, Rev. T. W., book by, 235.
Morning-glory family, 256.
Mortars, 90.
Morthiera Mespili, 66.
Morton, James, books by, 231.
Mosquito-bar covering, 81.
Mosquitoes, 11.
Moss, on lawns, 85.
Moss, on trees, 62, 85.
Moulton, F. C., quoted, 2.
Mountain-ash, classification, 254.
Mountain-ash, seeds of, 104.
Mowing lawns, 83.
Mulberries, analyses of, 260.
Mulberry, classification, 256.
Mulberry, how multiplied, 127.
Mulberry, stocks for, 128.
Mules, naming, 198.
Multiplication of plants, 126, 127.
Murgantia histrionica, 23.
Muriate of potash, 274.
Mushroom-Fly, 34.
Muskmelon disease, 63.
Mustard family, 253.
Myriophyllum proserpinacoides, 165.
Myrtus communis, 164.
Mytilaspis Pomorum, 18.
Myzus Persicæ, 36.

Nails, to preserve, 96.
Names, derivations of, 247.
Names in various languages, 242.
Names of plants, 241.
Narcissus, 164.
Narcissus, classification, 257.
National flowers, 246.
Native countries of plants, 249.
Nebraska, weights in, 140.
Nectarine, stocks for, 128.
Negundo aceroides, seeds of, 103.
Nelumbium, kinds of, 165.
Nemaspora ampelicida, 60.
Nematus ventricosus, 26.
Nerine, classification, 257.
Netting, bird, 81.

Nettle family, 256.
Nettles, classification, 256.
Nevada, weights in, 140.
New Hampshire, weights in, 140.
New Jersey, weights in, 140.
New York, dates for sowing at, 110
New York, weights in, 140.
Nicotyl, 16.
Nightshade, classification, 256.
Nitrate of soda, 274.
Niven, Robert, book by, 233.
Nomenclature, rules of, 193–201.
Norfolk, dates for sowing at, 110.
North Carolina, weights in, 140.
Nuciculture, 258.
Number of plants on an acre, 115.
Nuphar advena, 165.
Nursery stock, diseases of, 63.
Nuts, dates of, 178.
Nymphæa Lotus, 246.
Nymphæa, species, 165.
Nymphæaceæ, 253.

Oak family, 257.
Oak-leaves, analysis of, 272.
Oats, analysis of, 263.
Oberea bimaculata, 40.
Ochre, in waxes, 87.
Ocneria dispar, 29.
Œcanthus niveus, 40.
Œdema, 63.
Oemler, A., book by, 233.
Oemler, dates for sowing, 111.
Ohio, weights in, 140, 141.
Oil and alkali wash, 9.
Oil of vitriol on walks, 84.
Olea, classification, 256.
Oleaceæ, 255.
Olericulture, classification, 258.
Olive, classification, 255.
Olive, how multiplied, 127.
Oncideres cingulatus, 38.
Onion, analysis of, 264.
Onion book, 233.
Onion, classification, 257.
Onion, diseases of, 63.
Onion-Maggot, 34.
Onion, yield of, 125.
Onions, bushel of, 140.
Onions, storing, 174.
Oospora scabies on beet, 55.

INDEX. 305

Oospora scabies on potatoes, 69.
Orange disease, 63.
Orange, how multiplied, 127.
Orange, insects of, 34.
Orange packages, 143, 145.
Orange scores, 209.
Orange, stocks for, 128.
Orange trees, distance for planting, 113.
Oranges, analyses of, 261.
Oranges, keeping, 174.
Oranges, wholesale quantities, 149.
Orchard culture, classification, 258.
Orchidaceæ, 257.
Orchid family, 257.
Oregon, weights in, 140.
Orgyia leucostigma, 21.
Orris-root, 190.
Orthotylus delicatus, 32.
Osage-orange, classification, 256.
Osage-orange, seeds of, 103.
Oscinis, 24.
Othonna crassifolia, 164.
Othonnopsis cheiritolia, 164.
Otto of roses, 190.
Out-buildings, wash for, 94.
Ouvirandra fenestralis, 165.
Ox-eye daisy, 83.

Packages for fruits, 142–147.
Packing fruit, 176.
Paint, estimates of, 96.
Paints, 94.
Paleacrita vernata, 19.
Palm family, 257.
Pansy rust, 63.
Paper-birch, 77.
Paper for artificial flowers, 186.
Paper, for sash, 160.
Paper, paint for, 96.
Papers, list of, 236.
Papilio Asterias, 34.
Papyrus, 165.
Paraffine oil, 7.
Paris code, 197.
Paris daisy, 166.
Paris green, 3.
Parsley, classification, 255.
Parsley-Worm, 34.
Parsnip, analysis of, 264.
Parsnip, classification, 255.
Parsnip, insects of, 35.

Parsnips, weight of, 141.
Parsnips, yield of, 125.
Parsons, analyses by, 261.
Parsons, Samuel, Jr., book by, 231.
Parsons, S. B., book by, 231.
Partrigeon Bordeaux mixture, 47.
Party flowers, 246.
Pattison, W. M., keeping grapes, 172.
Pea boxes, 144, 147.
Pea-Bug, 35.
Pea mildew, 64.
Pea-Weevil, 35.
Pea, yield of, 125.
Peach and other stone fruits, how multiplied, 127.
Peach boxes, 146.
Peach, diseases of, 64.
Peach, insects of, 35.
Peach, stocks for, 128.
Peach, yield of, 125.
Peaches, analyses of, 260, 262, 263.
Peaches, classification, 254.
Peaches, measures, 140, 142, 143.
Peaches, weight of, 141.
Peaches, wholesale quantities, 149.
Pear boxes, 144, 147.
Pear, diseases of, 66.
Pear, how multiplied, 127.
Pear, insects of, 37.
Pear, stocks for, 128.
Pear, yield of, 125.
Pears, analyses of, 260, 264.
Pears, barrel of, 142.
Pears, classification, 254.
Pears, pollination of, 121.
Pears, storing, 174.
Pears, wholesale quantities, 149.
Peas, analyses of, 264, 266, 267.
Peas, bushel of, 140.
Peas, classification, 254.
Pelargoniums, 164.
Pennsylvania, weights in, 140.
Peony, classification, 253.
Pepper, yield of, 125.
Perfumery, 190.
Periodicals, list of, 236.
Periwinkle, 85.
Peronospora effusa, 72.
Peronospora gangliformis, 62.
Peronospora Schleideniana, 63.
Peronospora Violæ, 63, 76.

x

INDEX.

Peronospora viticola, 61.
Persian insect powder, 10.
Persimmon, Japanese, stocks for, 128.
Persimmon Twig-Girdler, 38.
Persimmons, analysis, 261.
Peruvian guano, 271.
Phenic acid, 48.
Phenology, 226.
Phin, John, book by, 285.
Phlegethontius celeus, 45.
Phlox Drummondii, classification, 256.
Phlox family, 256.
Phoma Batatæ, 73.
Phoma ustulatum, 60.
Phoma Uvarum, 60.
Phoma uvicola, 59.
Phorbia Brassicæ, 28.
Phorbia Ceparum, 34.
Phosphorus for mice, 78.
Phoxopteris comptana, 44.
Phragmidium mucronatum, 72.
Phycis indigenella, 32.
Phyllosticta acericola, 62.
Phyllosticta ampelopsidis, 60.
Phyllosticta bataticola, 73.
Phyllosticta Chenopodii, 72.
Phyllosticta Labruscæ, 60.
Phyllosticta on beet, 54.
Phyllosticta viticola, 60.
Phyllotreta vittata, 28.
Phylloxera, 30.
Physalospora Bidwellii, 60.
Phytophthora Cactorum, 58.
Phytophthora infestans, 69.
Phytophthora Phaseoli, 54.
Phytoptus Pyri, 37.
Pickle-Worm, 25.
Pieris Rapæ, 22.
Pine family, 257.
Pine, seeds of, 103.
Pineapple, Katydid, 38.
Pineapples, wholesale quantities, 148.
Pin-hole Borer, 36.
Pink family, 253.
Pinks, classification, 253.
Pinus Strobus, seeds of, 103.
Pipe, dimensions of, 157.
Pipe, size of for heating, 156.
Pipes, capacities of, 151.
Pipes, mending, 91.
Piqueria trinervia, 166.

Pistia Stratiotes, 166.
Pitch, in washes, 94.
Pitch, mineral, 93.
Pitch waxes, 87.
Plane tree, diseases of, 67.
Plant diseases, 52.
Planting-tables, 108.
Plant-Lice, 17.
Plants, collecting, 180.
Plants for houses, 164.
Plants, number on an acre, 115.
Plasmidiophora Brassicæ, 55.
Plasmopara Cubensis, 63.
Plaster and kerosene, 10.
Plaster and turpentine, 10.
Plaster, carbolized, 5.
Plastering, estimates of, 92.
Plastics, for grafting, 86.
Plowrightia morbosa, 68.
Plum boxes, 146.
Plum, diseases of, 67.
Plum, insects of, 38.
Plum, stocks for, 128.
Plum, yield of, 125.
Plums, analyses of, 263, 264.
Plums, classification, 254.
Plums, pollination of, 122.
Plusia Brassicæ, 32.
Podeschard's powder, 49.
Podosphæra Oxyacanthæ, 53.
Pœcilocapsus lineatus, 28.
Points, scales of, 208.
Poisons, for herbarium, 181.
Poisons for mice, etc., 78-81.
Polemoniaceæ, 256.
Polemonium, classification, 256.
Poli, Dr. Aser, 243.
Polianthes, classification, 257.
Pollination of fruits, 121.
Polyanthuses, classification, 255.
Polyporus versicolor, 67.
Pomegranate, how multiplied, 127.
Pomegranates, analysis, 261.
Pomology, books on, 234.
Pomology, classification, 258.
Pomology, definition, 258.
Pontederia cordata, 166.
Poplar, disease of, 68.
Poplar, insects of, 39.
Portland cement, for concrete, 92-94.
Postage rules, 215.

INDEX. 307

Postal rates, 215.
Posts, to preserve, 192.
Potash for insects, 10.
Potash, muriate of, 274.
Potash, sulphate of, 274.
Potassium sulphide, 50.
Potato, classification, 256.
Potato, diseases, 69.
Potato, insects of, 39.
Potato, yield of, 125.
Potatoes, analyses of, 263, 264.
Potatoes, contents of bins, 150.
Potatoes, measures, 140, 142, 143.
Potatoes, to measure in bins, 150.
Pots, sizes, 159.
Pots, to keep clean, 161.
Potsherds, in cement, 90.
Potting earth, 162.
Potting plants, 162.
Pottle, 148.
Powell, E. C., books by, 231, 236.
Preserving fruits, 187.
Preserving posts, 192.
Pressing plants, 180.
Prim, insect of, 39.
Primrose, Chinese, 164.
Primrose family, 255.
Primulaceæ, 255.
Printing plants, 184.
Pristophora identidem, 25.
Privet, classification, 255.
Privet, insect of, 39.
Promoting growth, 10.
Propagation, methods of, 126, 127.
Propagation of plants, 126, 127.
Protective compounds, 94.
Prunes, grading, 147.
Prunus, classification, 254.
Prunus Pennsylvanica, 128.
Prunus serotina, seeds of, 103.
Psychrometer, 222.
Psylla pyricola, 37.
Pteris serrulata, 164.
Puccinia Malvacearum, 62.
Puccinia Peckiana, 71.
Puccinia Pruni-spinosæ, 67.
Pulse family, 254.
Pumpkin, analysis of, 264.
Pumpkin, disease of, 70.
Pumpkins, classification, 254.
Punnet, 147.

Putty, liquid, 161.
Pyrethro-kerosene emulsion, 7.
Pyrethrum, 10.
Pyrethrum cinerariæfolium, 10.
Pyrethrum roseum, 10.
Pyrus Americana, seeds of, 104.
Pyrus, classification, 254.
Pythium omnivorum, 58.

Quantity of seed for acre, 98.
Quassia, 11.
Quicklime, in cement, 91.
Quin, recipes by, 182, 183.
Quince, diseases of, 70.
Quince, how multiplied, 127.
Quince, insects of, 39.
Quince, pollination of, 122.
Quince, stocks for, 128.
Quince, yield of, 125.
Quinces, barrel of, 142.
Quinces, classification, 254.
Quinces, storing, 174.
Quinces, weight of, 141.
Quincunx planting, 119.
Quinn, P. T., books by, 233, 236.

Rabbits, to protect from, 78–80.
Radiating surface, 155, 156.
Radish, analysis of, 264.
Radish, classification, 253.
Radish-Maggot, 40.
Railroad-Worm, 18.
Raisin boxes, 146.
Raisins, grapes for, 150.
Ramularia, 72.
Rand, E. S., Jr., books by, 231, 232.
Ranunculaceæ, 252.
Raspberries, analyses of, 260, 261, 263.
Raspberries, black, how multiplied, 127.
Raspberries, classification, 254.
Raspberries, dried, 150.
Raspberries, red, how multiplied, 127
Raspberries, seeds in, 150.
Raspberries, weight of, 141.
Raspberry, diseases of, 70.
Raspberry, insects of, 40.
Raspberry, yield of, 125.
Rats, 78.
Rattles of grapes. 61.
Rawson, dates for sowing, 100.

Rawson, W. W., books by, 233.
Reaumur thermometer, 153.
Red lead, for cement, 90.
Red ochre, in waxes, 87.
Red pepper, classification, 256.
Red spider, 40.
Registration of flowers, 208.
Resin and fish oil, 12.
Resin and petroleum, 12.
Resin and soda wash, 14.
Resin soap, 12.
Resin, soda, and tallow, 12.
Resin wax, 86.
Rexford, Eben E., book by, 232.
Rhizopus nigricans, 73.
Rhode Island, weights in, 140, 141.
Rhodites radicum, 40.
Rhodium, oil of, 79.
Rhododendron Californicum, 246.
Rhododendrons, classification, 255.
Rhopobota vacciniana, 25.
Rhubarb, analysis of, 264.
Rhubarb-Curculio, 41.
Ribes Grossularia, 59.
Rice, analysis of, 263.
Rice corn, weight of, 141.
Robinia Pseudacacia, seeds of, 104.
Roe, E. P., books by, 230, 236.
Rœstelia, 53.
Roll, 148.
Roofs, angles of, 159.
Roofs, light reflected from, 158.
Roofs, shading, 161.
Root, A. I., books by, 232, 236.
Root crops, weight of, 141.
Root-Gall, 41.
Root Gall-Fly, 40.
Root-grafting, string for, 89.
Root-Knot, 41.
Root-Louse, 20.
Roots, measures of, 140-142.
Roots, storing, 174.
Rosaceæ, 254.
Rose-Beetle, 20, 42.
Rose diseases, 71.
Rose family, 254.
Rose, insects of, 42.
Roses, attar of, 190.
Roses, classification, 254.
Rosette, of peaches, 64.
Rotation of crops, 13, 49.

Round-headed Borers, 20.
Royal Hort. Soc. rules, 195.
Rubble-work, 92.
Rules of nomenclature, 193.
Rural Science Series, 236.
Russian money, 138.
Rusting of metals, 96.
Ruta-bagas, analyses of, 268, 267
Ruta-bagas, weight of, 141.
Rye, analysis of, 263.

Sacidium viticolum, 60.
Sagittaria Montevidensis, 166.
Sal ammoniac, in cement, 90.
Salicylic acid preservative, 187.
Salsify, classification, 255.
Salsify, yield of, 125.
Salt and lime wash, 13.
Salt, in cement, 90.
Salt on walks, 84.
Salvinia natans, 166.
Sand, drying plants in, 188.
Sand, in cement, 91.
Sanina exitiosa, 36.
San José scale, 42.
Saperda, 20.
Sapindaceæ, 254.
Saponaria, classification, 253.
Sarracenia purpurea, 166.
Sash, cloth and paper for, 160.
Sash, mending, 91.
Saunders, William, book by, 236.
Saxifraga sarmentosa, 164.
Scab of potatoes, 69.
Scale in boilers, 160.
Scales of points, 208.
Schæfell's healing-paint, 88.
Schizocerus ebenus, 44.
Schizoneura lanigera, 20.
Sciapteron polistiformis, 30.
Scirpus Tabernæmontani, 166.
Scolytus rugulosus, 36.
Score, 148.
Score cards, 209, 214.
Scott, F. J., book by, 232.
Scraping trees, 85.
Scribner, F. Lamson, book by, 236
Sea-kale, classification, 253.
Sealing cements, 92.
Seasons of various fruits, 178.
Seaweed, analysis, 272.

INDEX. 309

Sediment, to prevent, 160.
Sedum Sieboldii, 164.
Seed, quantity for an acre, 98.
Seedage, 126.
Seed-crops, yields of, 107.
Seeds, longevity of, 104.
Seeds, number in a pound, 103.
Seeds, time to germinate, 99.
Seeds, weight and size of, 99.
Seed-tables, 98.
Selandria Cerasi, 24.
Selandria Rubi, 40.
Selandria vitis, 30.
Self-fertile fruits, 121.
Self-sterile fruits, 121.
Sempers, F. W., book by, 230.
Senecio scandens, 164.
Sensitive plant, classification, 254.
Septoria cerasina, 67.
Septoria Dianthi, 56.
Septoria, on chrysanthemum, 57.
Septoria Ribis, 58.
Septoria viticola, 60.
Sesia Pyri, 37.
Sesia tipuliformis, 26.
Setting plants, dates of, 108.
Shading roofs, 161.
Sheehan, James, book by, 232.
Sheep-feces, analysis, 269.
Sheep, protecting trees from, 78.
Sheep-urine, analysis, 269.
Sieve, 147.
Signals of weather bureau, 225.
Signs of weather, 220.
Silene, classification, 253.
Silvanus Surinamensis, 24.
Size of seeds, 99.
Sizes, legal and society, 141, 143.
Skeletonizing plants, 185.
Skim-milk, in washes, 94, 95.
Slate flour, for cements, 91.
Small-fruit boxes, 145.
Small-fruit culture, 258.
Smoking, 6.
Smudging, 6.
Snails, 43.
Snapping-Beetles, 45.
Snow plant, classification, 255.
Snuff, 13.
Snuff and sulphur, 15.
Soap and arsenites, 13.

Soap and carbolic acid, 5.
Soap and lime, 13.
Soap and soda, 13.
Soap and tobacco, 14.
Soap, fish-oil, 14.
Society standards and sizes, 143.
Soda and aloes, 14.
Soda and resin wash, 14.
Soda and soap, 13.
Soda and whale-oil soap, 14.
Soda bisulphite preservative, 188.
Soda, nitrate of, 274.
Soda, resin, and tallow, 12.
Soda, sulphide, 14.
Soda wash, 14.
Soja beans, analysis of, 263.
Solanaceæ, 256.
Solid measure, 132.
Solly, George A. & Son, book by, 232
Sorghum seed, analysis, 263.
Sowing plants, dates of, 108.
Spalding, William A., book by, 236.
Spanish money, 138.
Spanish, names in, 243.
Sparaxis, classification, 257.
Sparrows, to destroy, 81.
Specimens, bottles for, 189.
Specimens, collecting, 180.
Specimens, gum for, 97.
Sphaceloma Ampelinum, 59.
Sphærella Fragariæ, 72.
Sphæria Bidwellii, 60.
Sphæria morbosa, 68.
Sphæropsis Malorum, 70.
Sphæropsis uvarum, 60.
Sphærotheca Castagnei, 73.
Sphærotheca Mors-uvæ, 59.
Sphærotheca pannosa, 71.
Spinage, analysis of, 264.
Spinage, diseases, 72.
Spinage, yield of, 125.
Spireas, classification, 254.
Spraying, defined, 14.
Spruce family, 257.
Square measure, 132.
Squash-Borer, 43.
Squash, mildew, 72.
Squashes, classification, 254.
Squashes, keeping, 174.
Squirrels, mischief by, 80.
Standard measures, 140.

310 INDEX.

State flowers, 246.
States, legal measures in, 140.
States, legal weights in, 140.
Statistics of vegetable kingdom, 252.
Stewart, Henry, book by, 230.
Stewart, H. L., book by, 233.
Stictocephala festina, 45.
Stocks, classification, 253.
Stocks for fruit plants, 127.
Stocks, to measure, 150.
Stone cement, 91.
Stone, to make artificial, 94.
Storing, 168.
Stoves, mending, 91.
Strawberries, analyses, 260, 261, 264.
Strawberries, classification, 254.
Strawberries, pollination of, 122.
Strawberries, weight of, 141.
Strawberries, wholesale quantities, 149.
Strawberry, diseases of, 72.
Strawberry, how multiplied, 127.
Strawberry, insects of, 43.
Strawberry, yield of, 125.
String, waxed, 88.
Strong, W. C., book by, 236.
Strychnine, 79.
Stucco, in plastering, 92.
Subtropical fruits, analyses, 261.
Suet, in waxes, 87.
Sugar-cane, classification, 257.
Sulfo-steatite, 49.
Sulphate of ammonia, 273.
Sulphate of copper, 49.
Sulphate of copper, cost, 46.
Sulphate of iron, 5, 50.
Sulphate of magnesia, 274.
Sulphate of potash, 274.
Sulphatine powder, 50.
Sulphide of potassium, 50.
Sulphide-of-soda wash, 14, 50.
Sulphur, 15, 50.
Sulphur and lime, 51.
Sulphur and snuff, 15.
Sulphur and whale-oil soap, 15.
Sulphur, for preserving flowers, 182.
Sulphur, for rabbits, 79.
Sulphur, on walks, 84.
Sulphur preservative, 187.
Sulphuret of potassium, 50.
Sulphuric acid, 51.
Sulphuric acid on walks, 84.

Sulphurous acid preservative, 187
Sumac, insects of, 44.
Sunburn of strawberries, 72.
Sunflower family, 255.
Surface measure, 132.
Surveyors' measure, 131, 132.
Sweet corn, weight of, 150.
Sweet herbs, classification, 256.
Sweet potato, classification, 256.
Sweet-potato diseases, 73.
Sweet-potato Saw-Fly, 44.
Sweet potatoes, storing, 175.
Swine-feces, analysis, 270.
Swine-urine, analysis, 270.
Symbols, chemical, 259.
Synchytrium Vaccinii, 57.
Syringa, classification, 256.
Syrup, in bait, 4.

Tables of weights, etc., 129.
Taft, L. R., book by, 230.
Taft, on greenhouse roofs, 159.
Tallies, 191.
Tallow, in waxes, 86.
Tallow, resin, and soda soap, 12.
Tally, 148.
Tanks, capacities of, 151, 152.
Taphrina deformans, 64.
Tar, 15.
Tariff rates, 219.
Tarred paper, 78.
Tartar emetic for mice, 78.
Temperatures for plants, 167.
Tender vegetables, 112.
Tennessee, weights in, 140.
Tent-Caterpillars, 21.
Teras vacciniivorana, 25
Termites, 45.
Terry, T. B., books by, 234, 236.
Tetranychus bimaculatus, 33.
Tetranychus 6-maculatus, 34.
Tetranychus telarius, 40.
Texas, weights in, 140.
Thermometer scales, 153.
Thermometer, wet and dry bulb, 222
Thomas, J. J., book by, 236.
Thompson, Fred S., book by, 234.
Thyridopteryx ephemeræformis, 22.
Tigridia, classification, 257.
Tilia Americana, seeds of, 103.
Tiliaceæ, 254.

INDEX. 311

Timber, to preserve, 192.
Tmetocera ocellana, 18.
Toad-flax, 83.
Tobacco, 16.
Tobacco and soap, 14.
Tobacco, classification, 256.
Tobacco-stems, analysis, 272.
Tomato, classification, 256.
Tomato diseases, 74.
Tomato, insects of, 45.
Tomato score, 209.
Tomato, yield of, 125.
Tomatoes, keeping, 176.
Tracy, W. W., model garden, 119.
Tradescantia zebrina, 164.
Trade values, fertilizers, 276.
Transplanting, dates for, 108.
Trapa natans, 166.
Treat, Mrs. Mary, book by, 230.
Tree-Cricket, 40.
Trees, seeds of, 103.
Trichobaris trinotata, 39.
Trifolium repens, 246.
Tritonia, classification, 257.
Troy weight, 129.
True cowslip, classification, 255.
Tryon, J. H., book by, 236.
Trypeta pomonella, 18.
Tuberose, classification, 257.
Tuberous begonias, book on, 232.
Tulip, classification, 257.
Tulip tree, classification, 253.
Turnip, classification, 253.
Turnip-Maggot, 45.
Turnip, yield of, 125.
Turnips, analyses of, 263, 264, 267.
Turnips, bushel of, 140.
Turpentine, in emulsion, 7.
Turpentine, in waxes, 87.
Tussock-Moth, 21.
Twig-Borer, 21.
Twig-Pruners, 21.
Twitter, of carnations, 23.
Tyloderma Fragariæ, 43.
Typha latifolia, 166.
Typhlocyba Rosæ, 42.

Ulmus Americana, seeds of, 104.
Ulmus fulva, seeds of, 104.
Ulmus racemosa, seeds of, 103.
Umbelliferæ, 255.

Uncinula spiralis, 61.
United States weather signs, 225.
Urine, analysis, 269–271.
Urocystis Cepulæ, 63.
Uromyces Betæ, 55.
Uromyces caryophyllinus, 56.
Urticaceæ, 256.
Ustilago Maydis, 57.

Vallota, classification, 257.
Vallota purpurea, 164.
Values of fertilizing materials, 276.
Van Bochove, G., book by, 234.
Vanessa antiopa, 45.
Vaughan, J. C., book by, 234.
Vegetables, books on, 232.
Vegetables, compositions of, 266.
Vegetables, date of sowing, 108.
Vegetables, distances for planting, 113.
Vegetables for forcing, 165.
Vegetables, keeping, 168.
Vegetables, names of, 241.
Vegetables, naming, 194.
Vegetables, tender and hardy, 112.
Venetian red, in waxes, 88.
Verbena mite, 33.
Verbena rust, 75.
Vermont, weights in, 140, 141.
Veratrum album, 16.
Vicia Faba, 241.
Victoria regia, 166.
Vilmorin, seed-tables, 99, 104.
Vinca minor, 85.
Vinca variegata, 164.
Vines, to prevent bleeding, 89.
Violet, disease of, 76.
Violet family, 253.
Virginia, weights in, 140.
Vitaceæ, 254.
Viticulture, classification, 253.
Vocabulary, 277.
Volutella, on carnation, 55.

Waite, on pollination, 121, 122.
Walks, concrete for, 92, 93.
Walks, to make, 84, 92.
Wallflower, classification, 253.
Walls, washes for, 95.
Walnut family, 256.
Walnut, seeds of, 103.
Wandering Jew, 164, 165.

INDEX.

Washes, for fences, etc., 94.
Washes, for trees, 12–16, 50.
Washington, weights in, 140, 141.
Washington, wholesale quantities in, 148.
Water, in pipes and tanks, 151, 152.
Water-lily family, 253.
Watering plants, 163.
Watering-pots, mending, 91.
Watermelon, classification, 255.
Watermelon, diseases of, 76.
Watermelons, how shipped, 150.
Watermelons, wholesale quantities, 149.
Waterproof cloth, 160.
Water-proofing paints, 95.
Waterproof paper, 160, 186.
Watson, B. M., Jr., quoted, 126.
Waxes, for grafting, 86.
Weather, 220.
Weather bureau signals, 225.
Webb, James, book by, 236.
Weber, analyses by, 261.
Web-Worm, 19.
Weed, C. M., books by, 230.
Weeds, 82–84.
Weidenmann, J., book by, 232.
Weight of seeds, 99.
Weights, legal, 140.
Weights of apples, 149.
Weights, tables of, 129.
Wells, capacities of, 151.
West Virginia, weights in, 140.
Whale oil and soda, 14.
Whale oil and sulphur, 15.
Whale-oil soap, 16.
Wheat, analysis of, 263.
Wheat, bushel of, 140.
Whistle weather signs, 226.

White ants, 45.
White hellebore, 16.
White, J. J., book by, 236.
White, William N., book by, 234.
Whiting, in cement, 92.
Whitner, J. N., book by, 234.
Wholesale quantities, 148.
Whortleberries, classification, 255.
Wickson, E. J., book by, 236.
Wickson, fruit packages, 144.
Wild peaches, weight of, 141.
Willow-Worm, 45.
Wind, cooling glass, 158.
Window-garden plants, 164.
Window-garden work, 154.
Window-screen protector, 78.
Wintergreen, classification, 255.
Wire-Worm, 45.
Wisconsin, weights in, 140, 141.
Wolff, analyses by, 264.
Wood alcohol, in cement, 91.
Wood, to preserve, 192.
Woodward, F. W., book by, 236.
Woodward, George E., book by, 236.
Woolverton, score cards, 209.
Wounds, waxes for, 38.

Xyleborus Pyri, 37.

Yellow ochre, in waxes, 87.
Yellows, in peaches, 65.
Yields, 124.
Yields of seed-crops, 107.
Yuccas, classification, 257.

Zebrina pendula, 164.
Zinc chloride preservative, 187.
Zizania aquatica, 166.

THE RURAL SCIENCE SERIES.

NOW READY.

The Soil. By FRANKLIN H. KING, Professor of Agricultural Physics, University of Wisconsin. 16mo. Cloth. pp. 303. 75 cents.

The Spraying of Plants. By ERNEST G. LODEMAN, Cornell University pp. 399. $1.00.

IN PREPARATION.

The Apple in North America. By L. H. BAILEY, Editor of the Series
The Fertility of the Land. By I. P. ROBERTS, Cornell University.
Milk and its Products. By H. H. WING, Cornell University.
Bush Fruits. By FRED W. CARD, University of Nebraska.
The Grass. By W. H. BREWER, Yale College.
The Feeding of Animals. By W. H. JORDAN, Experiment Station of Maine.
Leguminous Plants and Nitrogen-Gathering. By E. W. HILGARD, University of California.
Irrigation. By F. H. KING, author of "The Soil."
Seeds and Seed-Growing. By GILBERT H. HICKS, Curator of Seeds, Division of Botany, Department of Agriculture.
Physiology of Plants. By J. C. ARTHUR, Purdue University.
Pathology of Plants. By B. T. GALLOWAY, Chief of the Division of Vegetable Pathology, Department of Agriculture, assisted by ERWIN F. SMITH and ALBERT F. WOODS.

UNDER the editorship of Professor L. H. BAILEY of Cornell University, MACMILLAN & CO. purpose issuing a series of books upon agricultural subjects to be known as the **Rural Science Series.** These volumes are designed to treat rural subjects fundamentally, setting forth in readable form the latest and best science and opinion as applied to agriculture in its broadest sense. Whilst it is expected that the books shall describe the current practices of rural occupations, it is nevertheless their chief mission to expound the principles which underlie these practices, and thereby to lead, by true educational methods, to the betterment of every rural pursuit. These monographs are to be written by men of recognized attainments, in various parts of the country; and it is expected that the series will be continued from year to year until it eventually covers the whole field of agriculture.

The Spraying of Plants.

A SUCCINCT ACCOUNT OF THE HISTORY, PRINCIPLES, AND PRACTICE OF THE APPLICATION OF LIQUIDS AND POWDERS TO PLANTS FOR THE PURPOSE OF DESTROYING INSECTS AND FUNGI.

By E. G. LODEMAN,

Instructor in Horticulture in the Cornell University.

With Preface by B. T. GALLOWAY.

Uniform with "The Soil." 399 pages. Very thoroughly illustrated. $1.00.

It is a remarkable confirmation of the common saying that this is a time of progress, that the subject of the spraying of plants has developed so rapidly within the last ten years as to have outrun the opportunities of even most experimenters to keep pace with it. The literature of the subject is so scattered and in so many languages that students and readers have little exact knowledge of what has really been accomplished. The first historian of the subject has now appeared, with a volume of four hundred pages crammed full of the records and results of this latest great contribution of science to agriculture. The book traces the complete evolution of the idea of the spraying of plants, discusses all the mixtures and materials, the pumps and nozzles, and the most approved methods. Specific instructions are given for the treatment of every important insect and fungus of the farm, orchard, garden, and greenhouse, arranged in such a way as to be available for instant reference. The book is indispensable and valuable alike to the experimenter and the practical horticulturist.

THE MACMILLAN COMPANY,
66 FIFTH AVENUE, NEW YORK.

THE GARDEN-CRAFT SERIES.

By L. H. BAILEY.

UNDER this title, MACMILLAN & Co. are issuing a series of handbooks upon horticultural practices. The books expound the accepted methods of performing the various operations of the garden, orchard, and glass-house, in simple and direct language. They are bound in flexible cloth, and are designed to be carried in the pocket, and to be used by busy men. Various subjects are now in preparation. **The Horticulturist's Rule-Book** and the following have been already issued : —

PLANT-BREEDING.

BY

L. H. BAILEY,

PROFESSOR OF HORTICULTURE IN THE CORNELL UNIVERSITY; EDITOR OF "THE RURAL SCIENCE SERIES," ETC.

12mo.   293 pages.   Cloth.   Price $1.00.

CONTENTS.

LECTURE   I. The Fact and Philosophy of Variation.
"   II. The Philosophy of the Crossing of Plants.
"   III. Specific Means by which Garden Varieties originate.
"   IV. Borrowed Opinions, of B. Verlot, E. A. Carrière, and W. O. Focke, on Plant-Breeding.
"   V. Detailed Directions for the Crossing of Plants.
GLOSSARY.

THE MACMILLAN COMPANY,
66 FIFTH AVENUE, NEW YORK.

The Horticulturist's Rule-Book.

A COMPENDIUM. OF USEFUL INFORMATION FOR FRUIT-GROWERS
TRUCK-GARDENERS, FLORISTS, AND OTHERS.

By L. H. BAILEY,

Professor of Horticulture in the Cornell University.

Fourth Edition, with Many Additions.

12mo. 312 pages. Limp Cloth, 75 Cents.

This volume is the only attempt ever made in this country to codify and condense all the scattered rules, practices, recipes. figures, and histories relating to horticultural practice, in its broadest sense. It is much condensed, so that its three hundred pages comprise several thousand facts, the greater part of which the busy man would never possess if he were obliged to search them out in the voluminous literature of recent years. **All the approved methods of fighting insects and plant diseases used and discovered by all the experiment stations are set forth in shape for instant reference. This feature alone is worth the making of the book.**

Amongst the additions to the volume, in the present edition, are the following: A chapter upon "Greenhouse and Window-garden Work and Estimates," comprising full estimates and tables of heating glass-houses, list of plants for forcing, for cut flowers, for window-gardens, aquaria, and the like, with temperatures at which many plants are grown, directions for making potting-earth and of caring for plants, etc.; a chapter on "Literature," giving classified lists of the leading current writings on American horticulture, with publisher's addresses and prices, and a list of periodicals, and directories of officers of whom the bulletins of the various experiment stations may be obtained; lists of self-fertile and self-sterile fruits; a full account of the method of predicting frosts and of averting their injuries; a discussion of the aims and methods of phenology, or the record of climate in the blooming and leafing of trees; the rules of nomenclature adopted by botanists and by various horticultural societies; score-cards and scales of points for judging various fruits, vegetables, and flowers; a full statement of the metric system, and tables of foreign money.

THE MACMILLAN COMPANY,
66 FIFTH AVENUE, NEW YORK.

WORKS BY L. H. BAILEY.

PROFESSOR OF HORTICULTURE IN CORNELL UNIVERSITY.

Talks Afield: About Plants and the Science of Plants. pp. 173. Illustrated.

Field Notes on Apple Culture. pp. 90. Illustrated.

The Horticulturist's Rule-Book: A Compendium of Useful Information for Fruit-Growers, Truck-Gardeners, Florists, and Others. Fourth edition. pp. 312.

The Nursery-Book: A Complete Guide to the Multiplication and Pollination of Plants. pp. 304. Illustrated.

American Grape Training. pp. 95. Illustrated.

Annals of Horticulture in North America for the Year 1889: A Witness of Passing Events and a Record of Progress. pp. 249. Illustrated.

Annals of Horticulture for 1890. pp. 312. Illustrated.

Annals of Horticulture for 1891. pp. 415. Illustrated.

Annals of Horticulture for 1892. pp. 387. Illustrated.

Annals of Horticulture for 1893: Comprising an Account of the Horticulture of the Columbian Exposition. pp. 179. Illustrated.

Gray's Field, Forest, and Garden Botany: A Simple Introduction to the Common Plants of the United States East of the 100th Meridian, Both Wild and Cultivated. Revised and extended by L. H. BAILEY, Editor of *The Rural Science Series* of agricultural and horticultural books.

Plant-Breeding: Being Five Lectures upon the Amelioration of Domestic Plants. pp. 293. Illustrated.

THE MACMILLAN COMPANY,
66 FIFTH AVENUE, NEW YORK.

www.ingramcontent.com/pod-product-compliance
Lightning Source LLC
Chambersburg PA
CBHW030738230426
43667CB00007B/757